D1528755

THE REFORMATION AND THE
VISUAL ARTS

CHRISTIANITY AND SOCIETY IN THE MODERN WORLD
General editors: Hugh McLeod and Bob Scribner

Already available:
A SOCIAL HISTORY OF RELIGION IN SCOTLAND
Callum Brown
THE JEWS IN CHRISTIAN EUROPE
John Edwards
A SOCIAL HISTORY OF FRENCH CATHOLICISM
Ralph Gibson
SOCIAL DISCIPLINE IN THE REFORMATION
R. Po-Chia Hsia

Forthcoming titles:
WOMEN AND RELIGION IN ENGLAND 1500–1720
Patricia Crawford
CALVINISM AND SOCIETY
Philip Benedict
POPULAR EVANGELICALISM 1730–1870
Louis Billington
THE CLERGY IN MODERN EUROPE
Gregory Freeze
RELIGION AND SOCIAL CHANGE IN INDUSTRIAL BRITAIN
David Hempton
RELIGION AND REVOLUTION 1400–1650
Michael Baylor
THE BRITISH MISSIONARY MOVEMENT 1700–1950
Jeff Cox
THE ANABAPTISTS
H.-J. Goertz
REPRESENTING WITCHCRAFT
Charles Zika
RELIGION AND URBAN LIFE IN NINETEENTH-CENTURY
EUROPE
Hugh McLeod (ed.)

THE REFORMATION AND THE VISUAL ARTS

The Protestant image question in Western and Eastern Europe

Sergiusz Michalski

London and New York

First English edition published 1993
by Routledge
11 New Fetter Lane, London EC4P 4EE

Simultaneously published in the USA and Canada
by Routledge
29 West 35th Street, New York, NY 10001

Originally published in Polish as *Protestanci a Sztuka*
© by Państwowe Wydawnictwo Naukowe, Warsaw 1989

English edition © 1993 Sergiusz Michalski

Typeset in 10 on 12 point Garamond by
Intype, London
Printed in Great Britain by
T J Press (Padstow) Ltd, Padstow, Cornwall

British Library Cataloguing in Publication Data
Michalski, Sergiusz
The Reformation and the visual arts: the
Protestant image question in Western and
Eastern Europe. – (Christianity &
Society in the Modern World Series)
I. Title II. Series
246

Library of Congress Cataloging in Publication Data
Michalski, Sergiusz.
[Protestanci a sztuka. English]
The Reformation and the visual arts: the Protestant image
question in Western and Eastern Europe/Sergiusz Michalski. – 1st
English ed.
p. cm.
Translation of: Protestanci a sztuka.
Includes bibliographical references and index.
1. Reformation in art.   2. Christian art and symbolism–Modern
period. 1500–   I. Title.
N7862.M5313   1993
704.9'482'0940903–dc20   92–13311

ISBN 0–415–06512–7

To my parents

Contents

Plates

Acknowledgements

The author and publishers would like to thank the following for permission to use illustrations:

The Kunsthistorisches Museum, Vienna for plate 11.
The Deutscher Kunstverlag, Munich, and the Schnütgen-Museum, Cologne for plate 2.
The Kunstsammlungen der Veste Coburg for plate 3.
The Staats- und Stadtbibliothek Augsburg for plate 5.
The Hamburger Kunsthalle for plate 7.
The British Library for plate 10.

Introduction

The problem of the legitimacy of religious images has confronted the great monotheist religions since time immemorial. Judaism and Muhammadanism have solved it with a strict prohibition: the consequences for Jewish and Muslim art have been fateful and are still widely felt. Less well-known is the fact that in the two millennia of Christianity there have been few periods of unquestioning acceptance of religious imagery. Even in periods of an almost exuberant flowering of religious art – as in the late Gothic or the Baroque period – the feeling persisted in quite a few theological and intellectual circles that the religious image as a medium for transmitting religious truth was replete with inner contradictions. Following periods of exuberance, an austere reaction tended to set in – the question of the legitimacy and adequacy of religious imagery then came automatically to the fore. Not only fear of a recurrence of the heathen idol cults of the Old Testament (an improbable scenario, but one which often served as a convenient battle-cry) but also the striving for an 'enlightened' form of church and religion tended to put religious art on the defensive. Although its critics initially focused their attention on the manifold abuses connected with the cult of images as part of popular piety, the logical next step was to question the ontological status of the religious work of art.

The great Byzantine conflict over the legitimacy of religious art (726–843) had a profound influence on the political, religious and cultural history of the Eastern empire. References to the history of that 'battle over icons' were to play an important part in later debates, both in the historically conscious sixteenth century and in the endeavours of the Eastern Orthodox Churches to counter Protestant iconoclastic propaganda. A whole string of lesser-known medieval heresies had as their most common trait the rejection of religious imagery. Whether they paved the way for Reformation iconoclasm – as might be the case in England (later Lollards) or in Russia – is still debated, as it is in this book. The temptation to construct such causal chains over the *longue durée* has to be restrained by the need for scientific verification of such hypotheses. After all, iconophobia makes for strange bedfellows.

This does not mean that the Bogomils, Hussites, Waldensians, Cathars and Lollards or various 'Judaizers' did not expound other – and from a theological standpoint maybe more important – grievances against established religion and its practices. However, iconophobia has always had a very emotive character arousing through its demonstrative vividness – to use a somewhat tautological analogy – disproportionately great public interest. The same applies to the Reformation image controversy which will be discussed in this book.

The Protestant image controversy has had a rather contradictory reception historically. On the one hand even those who neither know nor care to know much about religion and art are aware of the fundamental difference between the interior decoration and outfitting of a Calvinist and a Catholic church; this disparity has even found its way into popular proverbs – a fact that attests its continuing relevance. On the other hand the question of images proper, the underlying theological debate and the rites and modes of iconoclasm did not attract much academic interest before the last two decades.

An older generation of art historians, educated in the aesthetic temple of classic and Italian art, had little interest in either the Protestant art of Northern Europe and its roots in the new doctrines or in iconoclastic actions. These scholars refused to see in iconoclasm any psychologically authentic expression of religious anguish, and reduced it to mere vandalism. In the 1950s, Hermann Heimpel's 1954 adage 'The image-breakers were the image-makers', a saying whose wordplay can be summarized as 'the iconoclast cares', was one of the first signs of impending change. But little was done in the way of scholarly investigation until the 1970s. The change thereafter was all the more dramatic.

An important external stimulus to the subsequent boom in studies on art and the Reformation was provided by the great Dürer, Cranach and Luther anniversaries, of 1971, 1972 and 1983 respectively. There must have been other reasons, however, besides the habitual academic activism connected with anniversaries or even the careerist imperative to explore hitherto 'neglected' fields that generated here an imposing growth of scholarly work (even in strictly bibliographical terms).

One reason, of course, is the demise of religious art in the traditional sense, another the startling fact that the profound, though from a conservative viewpoint very debatable, changes instituted by Vatican II in the liturgical structure of church buildings exhibit a strong 'Protestantizing' flavour. Conservative critics of those reforms spoke of a new 'iconoclasm from above' and of a posthumous triumph not so much perhaps of the iconophobic Calvin as of the reductionist Luther. All this imbued the question of images with a new relevance. Moreover, a new current emerged in the historical interpretation of abstract art which tended to stress the role and importance of Calvinist aniconism for the doctrinaire abstractionism of Mondrian and Malevich. An important manifestation of this kind which tried to historicize and connect the image debate of the sixteenth century with later phenomena was the brilliant 1983 exhibition in Hamburg prepared by Werner Hofmann, 'Luther und die Folgen für die Kunst' ('Luther and the consequences for art'). Despite inevitable simplifications, a genealogy connecting the Reformation with Northern Romanticism (C. D. Friedrich, Runge) and various forms of twentieth-century art has found and continues to find many adherents.

In recent years the appearance of important studies by Hans Belting (*Bild und Kult*, 1990), David Freedberg (*The Power of Images*, 1989) and Margaret Aston (*England's Iconoclasts*, 1988) testifies to continuing interest in the problems of the cult of images in general and the Reformation image question in particular. Needless to say, each of these books has a different focus of interest, and the convergences of method with my more modest undertaking are not that great.

It is the premise of this book – originating in studies conceived in the mid-1970s and thus not unquestioningly following current general trends – that the study of the image question can provide us with many convenient starting-points for the study of art-historical, historical, anthropological and, last but not least, theological problems. The image problem may have a narrowly defined theological point of departure, based on scriptural exegesis, but its wide cultural and social ramifications are relevant to central problems in cultural history. The symbolics of iconoclastic destruction and rites of degradation, the many facets of the concept of image, the meeting of Western iconophobia with an often extreme Eastern iconodulism (image-friendliness) – these problems, or rather configurations of problems, promise much in the heuristic field. They seem to concur with the evolution of modern anthropology and cultural studies towards an ever more encompassing mode of cross-cultural comparison.

A comprehensive history of the Protestant image problem cannot be attempted here. If carried out in full breadth, it would make rather tedious reading struggling through often uninspired and very repetitive debates. What I attempt here is to provide as broad a presentation as possible of the *problems and modes of interpretation* pertaining to the image question.

The English edition of a book conceived for a different public usually presents something of a challenge, since the habitual Anglo-Saxon style of academic discourse differs so much from that on the European continent. However, by forcing me to think about necessary clarity and stringency, it rewards both myself and the reader in the long run. Many parts of the original Polish edition have been deleted, over-long notes mercilessly pruned; conversely, however, some smaller fragments have been added, primarily in response to recent research, and the notes and bibliography have been brought up to date. My debt to many colleagues has been expressed in the original edition; here I should like additionally to mention the three important colloquies on iconoclasm held in Wolfenbüttel in 1986 (organized by Bob Scribner and Martin Warnke), in Istanbul in 1987 (organized by Professor Walter Brandmüller) and in Strasburg in 1989 (Section IV of the CIHA Congress).

My thanks go to Mr Chester Kisiel, who translated the greater part of the book – smaller fragments, additions, notes and a general revision being undertaken by the author, who feels himself fully responsible for its stylistic shape. My wife allowed me the luxury of a separate study-room; our friends Elisabeth and Christian Pfaud in Augsburg provided one. Mrs Stoller-Hofmann typed the difficult text admirably.

Bob Scribner I should like to thank for his help and inspiration during the whole of the past decade. The book is dedicated to my parents, who taught me cultural tolerance.

1

Martin Luther: cultic abuse, religious art and Christian freedom

In an irate moment, the great German Expressionist poet Gottfried Benn, musing on the aesthetic decline of German culture, singled out the culprit – none other than Martin Luther. According to Benn, this 'dirty Saxon' had, by turning to secondary problems of conscience, destroyed the great artistic forms of the Middle Ages, the symbiosis between art and Church. Worse still, Luther himself had not even the least inkling of 'problems of Form'.[1]

Since Catholicism is generally perceived as the aesthetic religion *per se*, such criticisms were not confined to angry poets. Lesser spirits have vented their anger at the 'iconoclast Protestants', the destroyers and enemies of visual and sensual culture, and in this context pointed the accusing finger at Luther as the founder and shaper of the Reformation. A chain of 'aesthetically motivated' conversions to Catholicism, started by Winckelmann and continued by the St Lucas Brotherhood at the beginning of the nineteenth century brought this problem to popular attention. The response of Protestant German leaders in projecting an image of Lutheranism as an enlightened 'high religion' implied some oversensitivity on the subject, but it was unable to create a new aesthetic approach.

It must be said, however, that most of the anti-Luther critiques were manifestly misdirected. As the imagery of his writings attests, Luther was a man of strong visual and sensual impulses. He would also be the last to claim to have devised a new order of culture or civilization or what his compatriots (almost untranslatably) call *Weltentwurf* (a universal paradigm). His ambitions certainly did not go that far.

Despite the fact that history ranks him alongside the great founders of new faiths, such as Muhammad or Buddha, Luther

1

himself always repudiated states of ecstatic communion with God or open aspirations to spiritual leadership. He regarded himself only as a humble exegete of the Scriptures and, more importantly, wished to be regarded as no more than that – as one of those who by their actions and their example lead the Christian community back to its sources. In his own mind he was only trying to rectify a rampant evil in the universal Church.

In one sense the post-biblical and medieval tradition in the Church, which Luther denounced as illegitimate, had some natural basis, for it had grown up as a result of centuries of intermingled religious experiences, both good and bad, and was unquestionably a hallowed tradition in the eyes of individual believers. Although Luther did not advocate a concept of Christian life as all-embracing or – to use a somewhat discredited word – as holistic as that of the Catholic Church (most of the disputes and controversies in the Reformation camp would hinge on the pivotal point of the highly ambiguous notion 'freedom of the Christian man', which was formulated by none other than Luther himself), nevertheless he had in a brief period of time to define his position on the whole life of the Christian world. In a longer perspective his solution would expand the limits of Christian freedom; in the short term it had to be normative and arbitrary. The changes initiated by Luther involved a dialectic of continual conflict, a constant oscillation between liberty (*libertas*) and law (*lex*) – to use his own terms. This dialectic can be perceived in the problem that interests us here: namely, that of art and its place in the Protestant world.

Art obviously belonged to the second, non-canonical part of ecclesiastical and public life; it had grown up and assumed certain forms in the millennium and a half of Christian history. Up to Luther's time art had been almost exclusively religious. In Northern Europe the division into secular and religious art had not yet crystallized and impinged on the consciousness of wider circles of artists and viewers of art; moreover, the notion of 'secular things' often had a pejorative sense.[2] Despite this, art had no direct canonical sanction, no biblical legitimation. Quite the contrary: many passages from the Bible seemed to deny its validity. Art was only part of the sanctioned practice of Christian life, part of what Luther called the visible Church.

When Luther and his followers launched a large-scale attack on the structure of this Church, the problem of art was only marginal

2

to their interests. It so happened, however, that the question of art confronted Luther in dramatic form, in the shape of the Wittenberg iconoclastic riots, and forced him to take an unequivocal and, what is worse, an instant stance. Luther was not a man who radically changed a position once it had been taken, so that his decisions were not always based on adequate reflection. Many of his pronouncements on less important matters – and this was how he regarded the dispute over art – were instrumental, calculated for immediate effect. Except for a few shorter passages and two longer sections in his tract *Against the Heavenly Prophets* and in the so-called *Lenten Sermons*, his views are scattered throughout his vast writings of more than a hundred volumes, in brief remarks in letters, and in the less reliable source of his *Table Talk*.[3]

During his youth, which was spent in Eisleben, in Eisenach, and then as a student and monk in Erfurt, Luther did not have many opportunities to encounter the problem of art. It did not play a very important role in the social life of Germany, with the possible exception of Nuremberg. It was not only that the social sphere to which Luther belonged, the traditional lower middle class, was indifferent to art, for even the humanists of Northern Europe, including the great Erasmus, showed little understanding of its problems, while the patriciate was only just preparing itself for its new role as patrons of art.

In the theologians' camp there were also numerous signs of a negative approach to the various manifestations of the cult of images,[4] although this was an entirely marginal problem in the general consciousness of the age. Luther accepted wholly uncritically the forms of religious art which he encountered in his own environment, just as he zealously accepted all manifestations of late medieval devotion. To him the visible Church was an intermediary and not an obstacle to attaining the majesty and grace of God. A dozen years or so after the watershed of 1517, when, according to his *Table Talk*, he harked back to the years of his youth, he rarely made any mention of his attitude towards what were often extreme manifestations of image worship. To some extent this shows that it was not a problem that initially concerned him.

The appearance of a new theological consciousness in Luther, at odds with existing doctrine, was a subcutaneous process of which he himself was hardly aware. Luther did not want to create a new doctrine: he only sought to answer several questions on the salvation of man that were troubling him, and he certainly did not want to bring about a schism in the Church. The role of leader of a new faith was largely imposed on him by his opponents and a set of infelicitous circumstances. Personal and historical coincidences confronted the young lecturer (and, from 1512, Doctor of Theology) at the newly founded University of Wittenberg with theological and social problems of such magnitude and in such a context that their solution became a logical stage in the birth-process of Reformation theology. Luther instinctively found his theological starting-points and just as instinctively moved away from them, indeed from entire theological positions, when they no longer satisfied him.

Luther started from nominalism. This fact is particularly emphasized by Catholic scholars, for it enables them to find 'Catholic features' even in Luther's later Reformation views. His nominalist formation contributed to the fact that he conceived of the image as a conventional, relative sign: this was later to weigh heavily in his stance on images. From nominalism also came his characteristic awareness of the immeasurable distance between God and humanity. Luther, however, immediately asked himself the next, famous question: 'How can I gain the grace of God?'. This was a key question, for it played the main role in deliberations on human salvation. The nominalists, who emphasized the omnipotence of God, pushed Christ into the background: what is more, they did not perceive the role of grace in the process of salvation. For them God was the foundation of faith, but he could not be grasped through reason. With the nominalists, however, to give up asking questions about God did not lead to questions about the human condition. And this was what chiefly interested Luther.

Not until 1516, in his *Lectures on the Epistle to the Romans*, did he find a formula with which to characterize the human condition. Man is 'simul iustus et simul peccator' (simultaneously a sinner and simultaneously just), thanks to faith in justice and above all in the grace of God. Luther put the main emphasis on faith in God's grace, without which there can be no salvation. Thirty years later, when the Lutheran theologian Osiander wanted to return to the conception of God's justice as the main element in the work of salvation, he met with a violent reaction from other Lutherans. This was justified by the circumstances: the notion of

4

grace was to be the key element of the future Lutheran doctrine. Here the influence of St Augustine was most strongly felt.

The premise of divine grace (*Dei gratia*) became the basis for dividing the history of mankind into the periods *sub lege* and *sub gratia* – the first under the domination of the law, and the second under the dispensation of grace, a division exemplified by the Old and the New Testament. Man can gain grace through faith alone (*sola fide*) – a notion formulated by Luther on the basis of St Paul. In his *Sermon on Good Works*, published in 1520, Luther thus consistently rejected the importance of good works for salvation. He thereby questioned the primary driving-force of medieval religiosity, a force to which art was so indebted.

In this very abbreviated presentation of Luther's theological assumptions we have naturally ignored chronology, especially the course of well-known political events, and the origins of the process of organization of the new Church itself. Let us return now to the very beginnings of Luther's Reformation theology; that is, to 1516. From this period comes his first pronouncement on religious art.

In his university *Lectures on the Epistle to the Corinthians* he stated: 'to build churches, to adorn them . . . with images and everything that we have in houses of worship . . . all these are shadows of things worthy of children'. This is unquestionably a severe criticism of church art, though from a traditional position. There is no trace as yet of a future Reformation viewpoint, but between the lines one can infer a criticism of luxury and unnecessary expenditure. In the next two years he was to take up this theme several times. Yet he thought it fitting to tone down his criticism, stating in the same passage: 'Why should we fall into the heresy of the Beghards . . . and not tolerate any churches and ornaments? No!'[5] This passage is very characteristic of Luther, for one can see here in miniature, as it were, a foreshadowing of the same approach in the later *Lenten Sermons*, an approach defiantly defending art against doctrinaire thinkers who arbitrarily demanded its complete destruction. Luther probably had in mind not the Beghards but the Hussites. In 1516 Luther was still a loyal son of the Church, which accounts for his hostile attitude towards the Hussites, an attitude which was quickly to change.

In 1516–18 there were more remarks indicating Luther's initially hostile attitude towards religious art. In his *Lectures on the Epistle to the Hebrews* we read: 'God the Father created Christ to be the idea and sign which believers ought to transform into a [mental] image in order to turn away from the images of the world'.[6] Juxtaposing the incarnation of Christ – understood as the perfect intertwining of thought and sign – with the images of the world clearly has negative implications for art, especially when one considers how important Christological arguments were for Luther. Here Christ is compared with the supreme sign. A few years later Luther would abandon this dangerous line of reasoning because of the controversy over the Eucharist and the question of images.

From the *Lectures on the Decalogue* of 1516–17 one can infer that a good part of the arguments of the enemies of religious images was nonetheless unconvincing to Luther. Analysing the First Commandment ('You shall not have other gods beside me. You shall not carve idols for yourselves in the shape of anything in the sky above or on the earth below or in the waters beneath the earth'),[7] Luther indirectly opposed any iconoclastic interpretation of this passage. He distinguished between forbidden adoration of 'trees, stones, animals' and the cult due to God. 'Having images' was not forbidden in itself.[8] Moreover, basing himself on a well-known theological opposition *foris/intus*, Luther distinguished between exterior idolatry, which included the cult of images, and a more dangerous interior idolatry: namely, the idols which every person has in his or her heart.

The consequences of this distinction can be found a few years later in the discussion with Karlstadt on 'internal and external idols' and the order in which they should be removed. This was another premise of Luther's later position that inclined him to regard certain forms of religious art favourably. The importance of these trains of thought from his earlier period should not be exaggerated, however. They were muffled by his rejection of the cult of images and his generally unfriendly attitude towards matters of art. Social and ecclesiastical arguments of greater importance to him seemed especially in this period to incline him against religious art.

In thesis 50 of the ninety-five allegedly nailed to the church door in Wittenberg on 31 October 1517 Luther stated that St Peter's Church in Rome was being erected 'at the cost of the skin, meat and bones of the Pope's flock'.[9] In his *Explanations of the Theses* (1518) Luther expanded on the problem of the social costs of the cult of images. In the commentary to thesis 31 he stated: 'The first and main [good deed] is to help a beggar or one's neighbour in need. This ought to be done even at the cost of interrupting the construction of churches ... or interrupting the collection of contributions and offerings for the purchase of liturgical vessels or church decorations.'[10]

The most forceful, and at the same time the most fully considered approach to this problem is found in his *Sermon on Usury* (1519–20). Here Luther's sharp condemnation of unnecessary expenses for church decorations is tempered by the stipulation that certain elements of the 'visible Church' are necessary. 'But we ought to draw a boundary line and see to it that the cult is pure rather than costly. ... It would be better if we gave less to the churches and altars ... and more to the needy.'[11] Thus the question of the social costs of art – for that is what it should be called – had a considerable impact on Luther's approach to the question of images in the years 1519–22. Thereafter this issue resurfaced very rarely.

However, by 1520–1 the problems of art had become linked to certain theological conceptions in ways that laid a solid theological foundation for Luther's later pronouncements on art. Luther began to apply to idea of rejecting justification through works (*Werkheiligkeit*) to various aspects of ecclesiastical and social life. He started from the most immediate problem, that of indulgences, then moved through an intermediate stage, the fight against the cult and collection of relics, and finally arrived at the problem of art in the service of the Church: that is, art as an instrument in the efforts of each believer or of entire communities to acquire merit with God through which to earn salvation. Achieving salvation through works conflicted with the notion of *sola fide* and with the belief in the omnipotence of God's inscrutable will.

In his *Sermon on Good Works* Luther states that through endowing churches or images or through 'running to images' believers were only trying to buy their way into heaven. He emphasizes strongly the fact that this is the main driving force behind the cult of images especially in the case of religious pictures or statues. What was dangerous was not pure image worship – the belief that some emanation or even part of the sacred is immanent in a work of art (in Luther's opinion, few of the faithful believed in this) – but the misguided desire to gain salvation through endowing images and sculptures: 'This is why I have so often spoken against such works [endowing images] ... since among a thousand faithful it is hard to find even one who did not place hope in this, who did not want to gain the grace of God in this way.'[12]

An important role was also played by the publication towards the end of 1520 of his famous treatise *On the Freedom of the Christian Man*. Ostensibly its message was directed against the visual and ceremonial elements of religion. 'And that is why I greatly fear that few or no monasteries, nunneries, altars and church offices are Christian today; nor are fast-days or special prayers to some of the saints.' Once again Luther states that 'in all of this one seeks nothing else but one's own benefit: namely, when we believe that through this our sins will be absolved and salvation gained'.[13] The cutting-edge of the treatise was obviously directed against the existing practice of the faith, hence indirectly against the cult of images as well. Later in the treatise, however, Luther compares 'rites' to the scaffolding indispensable in the construction of a house; moreover, when he goes on to say that certain 'rites' are dangerous, he implies that to change them gradually rather than to reject them radically would be proof of the fortitude and steadfastness of a Christian, the real proof of Christian 'freedom'.

Such elements, which served to moderate the radical changes already under way, were surely not perceived either by the first Reformation theologians or by the mass of the faithful who succumbed to evangelical agitation, and who read in Luther's words a call to do away both with the abuses of the cult of images and with the images in the churches themselves. This attitude was encouraged by Luther's sharp attacks on places of pilgrimage and their indulgences, though his criticism was directed mainly against chapels, where the abuses had reached scandalous dimensions.

Let us return to the problem of the existence in Luther's early Reformation thinking – sometimes perhaps only in the form of a peculiar mental reservation – of certain theoretical 'safeguards' against extreme reductionism in matters of religious cult. I have already said that these 'safeguards' were not perceived either by the faithful in general or by people close to the reformer. Perhaps even Luther himself was unaware of their potential implications. It is characteristic of him that certain theological deliberations and trains of thought developed over a long period of time, and consequently the reformer himself was often unaware of the inner logic inherent in this process. Thus in the 'Catholic' Luther of 1512–16 we see a gradual increase of 'Reformation' elements, and in Luther the reformer of 1517–22 an increase of elements for which the term 'conservative' is perhaps not the most apt but which were certainly conservative in relation to later radical theologies. The theology of St Paul also threads its way through his entire work.[14] This theology was the source of Luther's rejection of salvation through works; it was also a logical bridge to the next stage, when Luther would refer to Paul's activities in Athens and to his tolerant attitude towards 'idolatrous ceremonies'.

In any case, it is hard to overemphasize the influence of the doctrine of justification on Luther's attitude towards art. At the same time, when one analyses Luther's use of this doctrine up to 1522 one can perceive through the reformer's eyes a remarkable gradation in the vexatiousness of the practices of the late medieval Church, practices which had grown out of a belief in the saving power of works. First and foremost came indulgences, then the cult of relics, and only later the misuse of works of art. However, the inherently iconophobic dynamics of the religious changes initiated by Luther would stir the minds and feelings of a widening circle of adherents, while the questions of indulgences and the cult of relics – problems that were much more clear-cut for the adherents of the new movement – would recede into the background.

From March 1521 Luther stayed under the disguise of 'Junker Jörg' at the Wartburg castle, in the solicitous care of the elector of Saxony. During this time Luther began his work on the translation of the Bible; he also corresponded with the group of activists in Wittenberg anxious to carry on the work of reform. From the middle of that year the process of change greatly accelerated in that town, gradually developing from strictly theological discussions to the implementation of practical reform in the community of the faithful. The eyes of all in Germany were focused on Wittenberg, where, because of the lack of clear directives from Luther, more radical elements began to come into prominence. Though they did not decisively gain the upper hand, they did radicalize some of the most prominent Lutheran activists and part of the citizenry.

Most important for the Wittenberg movement was the local Augustinian house, in which the situation gradually escalated during the summer and autumn of 1521. Friars from this monastery began to attack the sacrificial nature of the Mass ever more sharply, and soon they were demanding the abolition of celibacy, monastic vows, oral confession, and other things. From the middle of October the atmosphere suddenly became more fraught, and the first friars began to put off their habits. Ever louder voices called for the abolition of 'papist' ceremonies, among them even Melanchthon, who as late as October 1521 had defended the preservation of religious images.[15] From the beginning of November 1521 the movement was led by the theologian Andreas Bodenstein von Karlstadt as its theoretician and the Augustinian Gabriel Zwilling – by then already a renegade friar – as the instigator of direct action.

Various incidents took place during the few religious ceremonies conducted in the traditional manner. There were even cases of public desecrations of the Host. In December students from Erfurt joined the movement, fresh from the experience of storming monasteries in their native city (the so-called Erfurt 'Parson Storm' of 11–12 June 1521). On 3 December 1521 several of them demolished the wooden altar in the Franciscan friary. This was the first intimation of later iconoclastic behaviour. On 24 December Karlstadt administered communion under both kinds, and on Christmas Eve crowds attacked the parish and castle church, destroying church utensils. The city council vacillated in its reaction to these events under pressure from Karlstadt, Zwilling and their followers; its sole action was to excuse them to the increasingly concerned Elector Frederick the Wise.

Events in Wittenberg quickly moved towards a climax in which the validity of religious art became a major issue. Under the leadership of Zwilling, the Augustinians destroyed the images in their own house on 10 January, and the third iconoclastic incident took place at the end of January or the beginning of February.[16] Large numbers of Wittenberg burghers took part in this last event, which befell the parish church. Karlstadt did not participate personally, but he gave his support. The process of change culminated in the publication on 24 January of the Statutes of the City of Wittenberg, in which the city council approved the changes that had taken place. One passage in this document stated tersely: 'Both images and altars in churches ought to be removed in order to avoid the idolatry which such altars and images promote.'

On 17 January 1522 – as can be inferred from the date of the preface – Karlstadt completed his treatise *On the Removal of Images*, which provided a theoretical sanction for iconoclastic action, although it did not condone the use of force.[17] The measures undertaken by Frederick the Wise through the mediation of emissaries in February, especially in the second half of that month, were able to check the process of change but could not reverse it. Karlstadt and Zwilling were called to order, but only promised to stop preaching. Throughout February there was an unstable equilibrium between the two camps in Wittenberg. Matters remained in a state of suspension, as it were, though from the beginning of the month the more moderate or opportunistic reformers gradually began to distance themselves from Karlstadt and Zwilling. The townspeople felt the lack of a spiritual authority which could resolve the situation once and for all. This authority – and on this both the moderate and radical reformers and even some of the adherents of the old faith were agreed – could only be Luther. Only no one knew what position he would take.

I have outlined the events in Wittenberg in these momentous months in order to sketch the background against which Luther's attitude and actions at that time can be understood. In 1521, either independently or under the influence of Karlstadt, Luther had reached a similar position on many questions to the leaders of the Wittenberg movement. Hermann Barge, Karlstadt's biographer, could thus write quite aptly:

> The change that took place in Luther's assessment of the Wittenberg movement during January and February of 1522 will always remain a psychological problem. Until the first days of January he supported every step that had been taken in Wittenberg. From the very beginning he did not object to the marriage of priests.... The father-superior of the Augustinians, Linck, was agitating for actions that were a flagrant violation of monastic rules. The ears of the Wittenbergers were still ringing with the merry and wild shouts with which he inflamed their passions, urging them to reject the loathsomeness of the papist Mass, without any concern for the weak or those lacking strong religious foundations.[18]

Barge, who was not favourably inclined towards Luther, perhaps overemphasized psychological factors, as is understandable considering when his book was written (1905). Later scholars, relying on a wider range of Luther's works and using broader criteria for their evaluation, saw in Luther's decision of February 1522 the decisive turning-point that placed Luther on the side of a more conservative reform. According to this view, it was in early 1522, and not in 1525, that the split took place between the institutionalized, official Reformation and the 'radical Reformation' (as George H. Williams called it).[19]

In retrospect Luther himself also singled this date out as decisive; indeed, in his eyes the later disputes and differences with Karlstadt, the Anabaptists, other sectarians and the Calvinists seemed with hindsight to confirm the rightness of his own action. Luther's decisions were based on an intuitive rejection of radicalism, and at that time it was perhaps this that prevailed, rather than theoretical considerations, especially since a few years later he himself carried through almost all the changes in these months. The one notable exception was the retention of religious art. The theoretical reflections developed in his Lenten sermons give the impression that this exception was worked out somewhat later – perhaps at the end of February and beginning of March, when Luther had already taken the basic decision – being then only its ideological superstructure. Although both for Luther and his adherents precisely this theoretical argument later became binding, it is hard to say whether this was so from the very beginning. Luther knew that the position of the Elector of Saxony in the Holy Roman Empire was already a hazardous one and that the recent events in Wittenberg threatened the use of sanctions against him by the Imperial Regency Government. Luther also knew of the negative attitude of Frederick the Wise, who up to that time had been a loyal patron of the Reformation.

All of these factors, however, perhaps would not have caused the turning-point in Luther's attitude had it not been for two other events. The first of them was the arrival in the city of a group of radicals, the so-called 'Zwickau prophets', led by Niklaus Storch. As late as 13 January, Luther jested in a letter to Melanchthon that these dreamers would not sway him to an earlier return to Wittenberg, but towards the end of January he was greatly worried by the effects of their activities, although in reality their influence on the course of events was a minimal one. The second factor was to some extent connected with the first, since Storch and his followers were charged – as it seems without foundation – with iconoclasm. Luther probably heard about the iconoclastic riots of 10 January towards the end of the month. It was possibly because of them that he no longer vacillated in his position on the Wittenberg movement. Luther must have made the decision to oppose the Wittenbergers in the middle of February. Towards the end of that month negotiations began with Frederick the Wise on the conditions and circumstances of Luther's return to Wittenberg. Luther returned to the city on 7 March, and on 9 March he began a series of Lenten sermons which are known as his *Invocavitpredigten*: that is, sermons for the first Sunday of Lent. They were of decisive importance in defining Luther's attitude towards works of religious art.

Luther delivered the *Lenten Sermons* to the faithful assembled in the parish church in Wittenberg between 9 and 17 March: eight sermons were delivered, one day after another. They were printed as a whole a year later, but the section 'On images' was published immediately and had no fewer than seven further editions within a year.[20] This means that Luther regarded this fragment as the crucial part of the sermons and felt the need to popularize it.

In these sermons Luther took up the fundamental problem of the 'freedom of a Christian man', which could be reconciled neither with the normative, immediate abolition of certain sacral rites and ceremonies, even though they might already be antiquated (like the sacrificial Mass) nor with the obligatory introduction of new ceremonies (such as communion under both kinds), even though the new ones would be consistent with the spirit of the new theology. This interpretation of freedom, which required regard for the 'weak', for people who were horrified by the rapidity and violence of the changes and for whom the old ceremonies were necessary, recognized also, by a dialectical turn of argument, that one of the motors of the actions of those 'who wanted to turn freedom into compulsion', was the old justification by works. This remarkable leitmotiv runs through all the sermons. Five sections discuss in detail the innovations introduced during Luther's absence from the city and give examples of the calamitous actions of the Wittenbergers. These five sections are entitled: 'On images', 'On food', 'On the sacrament', 'On the two shapes of the sacrament' and 'On secret confession'.

The *Lenten Sermons* are unquestionably among Luther's most cohesive and convincing writings; they constitute a work in which the requirements of rhetoric are integrally intertwined with a clear line of argumentation. This double formal division – into eight sermons and five problems marked by separate subtitles – makes up two distinct homiletic and substantive arrangements, neither of which interferes with the other. The sub-chapter 'On images', which concerns us here, is part of the third and fourth sermons.

Apart from the merits of their contents, Luther's sermons are eloquent and – considering the tense situation in the city – tactful. Luther avoided directly antagonizing those groups which had participated in the iconoclastic riots; he skilfully measured words of condemnation in the course of the sermons. He managed to restrain his choleric temperament, a rare occurrence in his speeches and writings. He directly addressed his words of criticism to all the erring members of the community of the faithful. Only on one occasion – and then even very ambiguously – did he mention the names of Karlstadt and Zwilling in an incriminating context.

As though to mollify his readers, Luther begins by stating his personal attitude towards images. He states that he 'is not well disposed towards them',[21] for they are often a cause for 'idolatry', and for this reason – as he writes in another place – give many opportunities for 'abuses'. 'It would be better if we did not have them at all' is the next statement. In spite of its categorical nature, this is more of a rhetorical ploy than an intended declaration, for soon afterwards Luther puts forward arguments against the iconoclasts.

He begins by recalling the dispute over images in Byzantium, which he approaches ahistorically as a conflict between the Pope and the emperor. Though the Pope won, neither of the protagonists was right. 'They wanted to turn freedom into compulsion. This God cannot abide.' From the vast and complex subject-matter of the iconoclastic dispute Luther picked out the one particular aspect that he needed: namely, the inappropriateness of settling matters of art in a normative way. He did not yield to the temptation – which testifies to the discipline of his discourse – to condemn the papacy (an otherwise constant theme of his writings) for he focused here on other things. With this brief but forcefully expressed definition Luther shifted religious art from the domain of eternal religious truths to the domain of 'freedom', where all normative deliberations become an offence against God. This very approach, which appeals to the notion of freedom, really settles the theological position of religious art. And from this approach comes the definition of religious images that Luther gives towards the end of the chapter. Thus images are 'neither good nor bad'.[22] This is obviously a traditional definition, which stems from the notion of *adiaphora* (entities that are morally indifferent) in the philosophy of the Stoics, though this is not stated here directly. It is indirectly implied in the examples of the idolatrous adoration of the sun or 'abuses' as regards women and wine, presented in the most popular, simple and picturesque manner. In this second case Luther goes back to an old theme. In spite of their later popularity, the significance of these examples is not great. Their aim, through *reductio ad absurdum* of the 'substantial' attitude, was to show the limits of application of the *adiaphora* concept.

I have cited and attempted to delineate Luther's first line of argument. Significantly, the remark on the iconoclastic dispute is the only one in all Luther's writings and homiletics, unless one regards his later remarks on the 'superstitions of the Greeks' as a condemnation of the iconodulism of the Orthodox Church.

Luther's next line of argument was an assessment of the intention of patrons and endowers of works of art. Luther stated that the endowment of works of art, the placing of images in churches with the intention of earning merit with God, is entirely inconsistent with the doctrine of the rejection of good works and that this is 'the greatest, most important and most essential reason why images should be removed'.[23] He criticizes the Wittenbergers for not using this argument at all. This approach is consistent with what we know about the doctrine of justification in Lutheran theology as a whole: 'No merit is earned with God by setting up images.'

One might think that the application of the principle of justification by works to matters of religious art would have entirely negative consequences for the latter. Yet here Luther pursues a circuitous but in fact extremely consistent dialectical line of reasoning. With the well-known aphorism about extremes that meet in mind, Luther suggests that since it is regarded as improper to erect altars to earn merit with God the iconoclasts who destroy works of art might be guided by the same motives. This theme appears only between the lines – as though Luther was afraid to offend his listeners – and is only developed later.

For Luther the rejection of justification by works was so obvious (and in fact, as the equivocations of Karlstadt show, could not be solved on the basis of Lutheran theology in any other way) that he moves on to another question, which derives from patristic and medieval (Bernard of Clairvaux) criticism of luxury, a problem which in simplified form could be reduced to a somewhat demagogic contrast: money for the poor, or money to enhance the splendour of the Church. This problem had troubled Luther at the time of his Reformation 'breakthrough'. It resurfaced in connection with the changes in Wittenberg, since both in Karlstadt's treatise *On the Removal of Images* and in the Statutes of the City of Wittenberg, to which was appended the Statute of the Common Poor Chest, the questions of art and of help for the needy were juxtaposed. This might have given the impression that they were closely linked, and indeed in some cities costly liturgical items were confiscated and proceeds from their sale donated to the poor chest. This question seems to have caused Luther some difficulties, for it could not be resolved on the basis of theological premises alone. Once again, the problem of justification loomed. In fact, this was one of the reasons why care for the poor was institutionalized in Protestant communities – another example of a new social practice springing from theological premises. Once again using a simple, vivid metaphor, Luther emphasizes that it is better to give a golden gulden to a beggar than to raise golden altars to God. However, he does not pursue this theme; nor does he settle it in any categorical way. It even disappears from Luther's later writings, though we do hear echoes of it in certain works of the 1530s.

In the course of time the argument about the 'social costs of art' – as we might label this theme – was taken over by the 'radical reformers', the spiritual heirs of the medieval critics of the splendour of the Church who were in favour of a return to the simplicity of the religious forms and rites of the first Christians. Luther only wanted a doctrinal return to the times of the Apostles, and hardly saw art or civilization as malignant tumours on the body of the Christian community. That is why he seldom used this thesis of the 'simple beginning', which was a peculiar conglomerate of various, often mutually exclusive, aspirations, despite the fact that in its spirit one could read his motto *ad fontes*. Luther knew 'that the original church at one time did not allow the existence of holy images',[24] but since in his opinion the early Church was not as holy 'as might seem', this argument counted for little.[25] Thus his vision of Christianity differed from that of the circles of 'dreamers' (*Schwärmer*) and Anabaptists for whom aniconism was an indispensable condition of the happy state of Christianity of early, apostolic times.

The historical circumstances in which the sermons were read

are perhaps the main reasons why Luther had little to say on the right of religious art to exist. Having made a declaration of his supposed negative attitude at the outset – which as we know was rather a tactical measure – he could not make a complete volte-face. That is why the only argument – and a rather weak one, at that – in support of retaining images in churches was concern for the 'weak', for those members of the community who were horrified by the sudden changes or for whom the images could still contribute to their religious education. One can clearly see how Luther attempts to leave gates open for the future. He also used the argument on the necessity of suspending or rolling back reforms out of concern for the 'weak' with regard to all the religious reforms (such as the new form of the Mass or the abolition of confession) that had been carried out during his absence from Wittenberg. This was, of course, a defensive argument, which, into the bargain, was accompanied by the assurance that when the last simpletons awaken, these elements might be abolished or disappear (Luther preferred the latter) automatically.

In and of itself the argument of respect for the weak contained nothing that would seem definitive were it not for a mental construct connected with the concept of scandal (*Ärgernis*).[26] In a dialectical way Luther reversed what was a scandal to iconoclasts. What causes scandal is not a particular state (the existence of religious art) but the lack of faith of the iconoclasts who immediately try to make their doubts normative. This mental construct, which is analogous to his concept of justification by works, appears in the *Lenten Sermons* in a somewhat hidden form and does not strike the reader at once.

The iconoclastic events in the Wittenberg parish church were the spontaneous acts of the population, and despite the rapid intervention of the town authorities, various excesses were committed. All of this was done in 'tumult and violence'. Hence Luther's condemnation is categorical: events of this kind disturb the order of the community of the faithful: 'I state that you have erred . . . since this was not done properly. You will say this is consistent with the Bible, and I agree with this, but where is order? For this was done in a criminal way, entirely without order, giving offence to one's neighbour'.[27] Here one can already see how important the idea of order was for Luther – a notion whose most classic expression he found in St Paul's Epistle to the Corinthians (I Corinthians 14:33). As the years passed, emphasis on 'church order'[28] overshadowed for Luther most of the possibilities that resulted from the notion of Christian freedom.

Evaluation of the iconoclastic movements had to be entirely negative, however, because these movements often considered the spontaneity of iconoclastic action as a value *per se*. Even Karlstadt explained that his entire activity in removing images from churches was directed towards authoritative and orderly solutions that excluded the use of violence. Karlstadt himself also used the concept of order (*ordo*), but he used it in relation to the smallest units of Christianity, communes and parishes, laying the foundations of what was later called 'congregational Christianity'.[29] Luther in turn, to get somewhat ahead of the story, never made clear whether such actions as the removal of images – assuming that they were justified – could be carried out on the basis of the decision of a small community such as the local parish or only in accordance with that of a greater political unit. As supporters of the radical Reformation feared, following Luther's failure to be clear about this, these matters began to be decided by central political authorities. The *Lenten Sermons* are thus both a starting-point and a watershed here.

Much space in Luther's deliberations on images is devoted to a scrutiny of passages on art from the Scriptures. Luther here entered an area in which debates would take place throughout the entire sixteenth century: both for and against religious art. He employs four examples from the Old and two from the New Testament which supposedly demonstrate that neither the Jewish religion nor the first Christians categorically prohibited works of art and indeed that they made use of them themselves or tolerated them. The examples which Luther cites – the altars erected by Noah and Abraham (Genesis 8:20, 12:7), the cherubs on the Ark of the Covenant (Exodus 25:18, 37:7), St Paul and the Dioscur sculpture on the ship (Acts 28:11) – are not among the best examples of his deliberations on art. This is quite understandable considering the defensive tone of the entire passage. Luther defended himself more or less adroitly against the charges of the opponents of images. In this case he found himself perhaps defending not so much a lost cause as one difficult to maintain, since in those days there was a common belief in the existence of something like the 'Old Testament prohibition of images'.[30] Yet there were passages in the Old Testament that could be interpreted in a different way, and the moderate supporters of religious art

18

attempted to take advantage of this opening. Luther was aware that the First Commandment constituted an argument that was difficult to refute. Giving two ways of interpreting the entire passage – for and against images – he came out against any categorical interpretation. Referring directly to his pre-Reformation lectures on the Decalogue, he argued: 'What is forbidden here is the adoration and not the making of images . . . one can have or make images, but one should not adore them.'[31] Not until three years later, in passages in *Against the Heavenly Prophets*, does the train of Luther's hermeneutic interpretation end. According to him, the prohibition against making 'graven images' refers to the previous passage: 'You shall not have other gods beside me.' In the catechisms which he wrote or recommended, the passage about images is usually expunged from the First Commandment. Consequently, there is no doubt that he did not regard the discussion on the First Commandment as very important; moreover, he doubted whether the enemies of images could be convinced on this argumentational plane.

On the other hand, the story of the brazen serpent (Numbers 21:9) cited by Luther is among his best polemical arguments and contains also a deeper meaning. Luther grasped the most essential element in the history of this image. At the outset he mentions that Moses himself 'raised it', and so this great lawgiver also 'created an image'. But Luther did not stop with this rather casuistic argument, rightly stressing that King Hezekiah smashed the brazen serpent only when an 'abuse' occurred – that is, when the Israelites began to worship it – and not sooner. Luther's argument became a classic illustration of the 'abuses' of art. It suffices to compare his point of view with Karlstadt's interpretation (or, more correctly, absence of interpretation) of the same example of the brazen serpent in order to perceive a significant difference in the quality and logic of argument.[32] Luther also presented a well-thought-out exposition of St Paul's activities in Athens. For Luther this became a vindication of moderate tactics, for, as the reformer stated, St Paul refrained from removing the 'idols' by force and tried to convince the Athenians through discourse. The allusion to the iconoclastic riots is all too clear here.

The argument referring to St Paul's tolerant attitude in pagan Athens made a tremendous and, what is more important, an immediate impact on the Protestant camp. An additional factor was the fact that the Reformation was largely based on 'Pauline' theology. As early as 1522 the Lutheran Caspar Güttel, in his *Dialogue on How to Live Christianly or Evangelically*, referring directly to Luther, put forward as the only argument against the iconoclasts the story of St Paul's attitude in Athens: 'That is why one must give heed only to the evangelical fruits [i.e. faith and love]. This is not displayed by those who burn images and wooden sculptures. This does not serve the evangelical man. When St Paul came to Athens, he found many idolatrous altars. He overturned none of them . . . O, how often did St Paul spare the consciences of the weak.'[33]

The last essential problem of Luther's sermons in the part dealing with art is the question of the magical identification of the image with the supernatural reality of which it is supposed to be a reflection. It is one of the tasks of this study to determine what influence the fear of such identification had on the theoretical views of Zwingli, and to what extent awareness of such a danger pushed the mobs to the destruction of images.

Luther dismissed this question rather abruptly and very decisively: 'There are no or very few people who do not understand that the crucifix standing there is not my God – since my God is in heaven – but only a sign.' Towards the end of the 1520s Luther was to go even further. Referring to the First Commandment, he said: 'People were not so mad as to think that images, wood and stones are the real God.'[34]

We can believe that Luther was expressing his real convictions when he stated that there are very few people committing the error of identifying an image or sculpture with the sacrum. Moreover in a letter to Count Stolberg (1522) he even seemed in a paradoxical way to confirm the Eastern image theory that 'honour is paid only to the prototype', by stating that in his opinion most people are adoring the saints proper and not their images. He thereby clearly failed to appreciate the psychological power of images and the emotions that they were able to stir up. Despite his peasant roots, which the social rise of his father could not obliterate, and the fact that he was influenced by the rich imagery of late medieval popular culture, Luther was relatively free from notions about 'image magic' and the binary oppositions connected with it. Moreover, his nominalist theological education seems to have made him accept the fact that all imagery is a matter of social convention.

Luther displayed a remarkable psychological empiricism, and at the same time – except during his youth – he rejected the spiritualism represented by the movements of the radical Reformation and by some humanist circles. In Luther's theology, which was based less on intrinsic categories than on external categories derived from an analysis of humanity's relation to God, binary oppositions of matter and spirit were almost non-existent. It was also highly significant that on the basis of a New Testament theology Luther had overcome some of the dualistic solutions of the Old Testament. For the Old Testament preferred dualisms: severe oppositions of the body to the spirit, of the soul and the heart; or ethical dualisms for which, strictly speaking, no psychological explanation is ever given.

A scrutiny of Luther's sermons gives no definitive answer as to whether he had read Andreas Karlstadt's iconophobic treatise *On the Abolition of Images* when he was preparing them. In fact, these two works were written independently of each other. In April 1522 Hieronymus Emser published a treatise in defence of images directed against Karlstadt,[35] and in July of the same year Luther's well-known opponent Johannes Eck published his own treatise.[36] This was perhaps the most productive year in the history of the image controversy. It is worth trying to determine how they fitted into the chronological context of the first half of 1522. Luther did not take a position on Karlstadt's treatise. Karlstadt was obviously familiar with Luther's sermons, and although – as we shall see – his answer has not been preserved, we know that he did not renounce his views. When he was writing his treatise, Eck did not know Karlstadt's treatise or Luther's views, though he does mention Karlstadt's role in the Wittenberg riots and suspects Luther of complicity. Emser, on the other hand, had read Karlstadt's treatise and quotes from it, but he mentions Luther's divergent position only in the preface, remarking that this was only a tactical evasion on the part of the reformer.

The voice rising above the others in this quartet was Luther's. For his sermons were superior in their level of argument and their linkage with the structure of the new theology as well as in their sociotechnic effect – only Luther influenced the course of events with his words.

In April and May 1522 nearly all the changes introduced by the Wittenberg burghers at the beginning of the year were rescinded. The images were returned to the churches, though care was taken to prevent abuses. As regards other reforms in the so-called 'ceremonial sphere', here also there was a return to the former situation; however, this was really only temporary, since the process of evolutionary change, through which the 'ceremonies' disappeared one after another, continued until the 1540s (the elevation of the Host was abolished in 1542). Luther, together with the town council, was also instrumental in removing Karlstadt from all town affairs and making it impossible for him to influence the faithful. Under the pretence of polemic against one of his old enemies, the Leipzig Catholic Ochsenfart, the embittered Karlstadt attempted to attack Luther, but the censorship in Wittenberg prevented the publication of Karlstadt's treatise. The only passages of this work known to us are those recorded in the censor's report to the authorities. One of them concerns the problem of art.[37] It clearly shows that Karlstadt had not renounced his hostility to 'idols', though he began to be more interested in the Mass and Eucharistic problems. So the iconoclastic crisis gradually began to die out, and this problem would never occupy Luther's attention to such an extent in the future.

The period 1522–4 is a very important one in Lutheran thought. Summing up the conclusions of the March sermons, Luther once again took up the problems of religious art in his *Lectures on Deuteronomy*. The subject of iconoclasm came up again, but on a much smaller scale, in connection with the activities of Thomas Müntzer in Allstedt and of Karlstadt in Orlamünde. Despite all the differences that separated them, both these radical reformers attempted to realize at parish level the visionary and 'utopian' model of Christianity, a congregational Christianity based on strict scripturalism, one of whose essential components was the rejection of religious art. Their charismatic authority won them the support of the faithful, and Luther's fight with these two reformers gradually pushed him towards increasingly authoritarian solutions, towards a close alliance with political authority.[38] The rapidly accelerating process of establishing a Lutheran Church also played a role here. Notwithstanding the fundamentalist tendencies of the 'visionaries', this Church was to be a 'visible church'. Thus Luther gradually turned his attention to pedagogical aspects of reform, to various ways of influencing the souls of the faithful. Running parallel to this was a change in Luther's theology. The activities of the 'visionaries', who constantly referred to the prohibitions and commandments of the Bible, and who ostensibly followed the Lutheran principle of *sola scriptura*, confronted Luther with the problem of the validity of the Old Testament for his own time. This was very important for the history of the dispute on religious art, because most of the arguments of the opponents of art were based on Deuteronomy and other passages in the Old Testament. Luther's response was not absolutely clear-cut. On the one hand, he recognized the Old Testament or Law as superseded, invalidated by the sacrifice of Christ. This was especially true of Deuteronomy, which for Luther was a sort of *pars pro toto* of the Old Testament. 'Moses does not concern us', he wrote emphatically in the treatise *Instruction on how the Christians should use Moses*, published in 1527, but written in its main outlines in 1524–5. The Law applies only to the Jews; it was the price which this nation paid to appease God's anger. Luther called Judaizers those who, with varying degrees of strictness, called for fulfilling all of the injunctions of the Old Testament. On the other hand, according to Luther, many of the injunctions and commandments of the Old Testament still ought to be observed (e.g. the postulated marriage of a widow to her brother-in-law) if they are in agreement with natural law and are not a reflection of customs peculiar to the Jewish nation alone. Luther nowhere defines precisely what he means by natural law, being satisfied with the statement that this is what 'everyone has formed by nature and carries deep in his heart'.[39] The next passage is the quintessence of Luther's stance on this question: 'That is why images and the Sabbath and everything that Moses placed above natural law – since it does not contain natural law – is free, non-binding, and abolished.'[40]

In discussing the basic assumptions of Luther's Old Testament theology I have departed somewhat from my chronological exposition. The new direction in interpretation of the Old Testament appeared in Luther in a still unfinished form as early as 1524, as one can see from his short treatise *A Letter to the Saxon Princes on the Spirit of Rebellion*.[41] It was written in connection with Thomas Müntzer's activities in Allstedt, and once again, though on a smaller scale, touches on the problem of religious art. Müntzer as the preacher in Allstedt, inspired his followers to destroy the Marian pilgrimage chapel in neighbouring Mallerbach (24 March 1524). In the spring of that year Karlstadt, who was now active in Orlamünde, together with his parishioners removed images from places of worship. While Müntzer's adherents carried out their operation in an iconoclastic manner under the cover of darkness, Karlstadt and his supporters acted in accordance with the new order they had established and removed images peacefully and with the consent of the municipal authorities. News of both these events reached Luther almost simultaneously in July 1524, when Müntzer's and Karlstadt's activities had reached their apogee. Luther was strongly opposed to the model of ecclesiastical organization and Christian life which both of these reformers, each in his own way, were trying to create. Müntzer seemed to him more dangerous because of the intimate connection of his theology with social radicalism. That is why Luther published the aforementioned brochure, in which he unmasked Müntzer in no uncertain terms.

In a two-page passage on images, Luther identified the problem as not that of religious art, but that of the use of violence. 'Christ and his Apostles did not destroy temples, nor did they overturn images, but they captured hearts with the word of God, and then the temples and images fell by themselves.'[42]

At the beginning of August Müntzer was forced to leave Saxony. Luther concentrated his attention on his old antagonist Karlstadt. The fact that Karlstadt had distanced himself from Müntzer did not change Luther's negative opinion of him. On 22 August he had a bitter personal meeting with Karlstadt in Jena; on 24 August he disputed with his followers in Orlamünde.[43] This latter event provides a fascinating example of the divergent dynamics of the Reformation. The dispute between Luther and the theologically unlearned burghers of Orlamünde, who held very firm views of their own, primarily concerned the question of images, which had been removed there. Not surprisingly, Luther's adversaries referred time and time again to the Old Testament prohibition of images, while Luther with a certain hauteur tried to show that only 'adoration' of images is forbidden, not the making of them. In the scriptural arguments put forward by the Orlamünde layfolk, especially by a very fervent cobbler, we see visible traces of a folksy spiritualism (I would not, however, claim for the cobbler a status similar to that of his more famous colleague Jacob Boehme). In a very moving passage, the cobbler admitted that he too was once an idolator and that to forestall the danger for others all images should be abolished. Moreover, God himself, by saying in Scripture 'I want my bride to be naked', had given here a clear directive. Luther had no problem in ridiculing this somewhat naive interpretation of the topos of the

24

'bare, naked church' as the Bride. However, from a more modern standpoint the naive, unreflective Scripturalism of the citizens of Orlamünde strikes us as more sympathetic and in a certain way more authentic than Luther's arrogant theologizing. In such phenomena we can observe the parting of the ways between the Reformation of the elites and a more popular, radical Reformation.

The theoretical background of this confrontation, as seen through Luther's eyes, is contained in his great tract *Against the Heavenly Prophets, concerning Images and the Sacraments*, written in December 1524 and January 1525.

The part of this treatise devoted to questions of art is the second and longer fragment in Luther's works concerned with this problem. *Against the Heavenly Prophets* is a treatise of over a hundred pages which takes up many questions, especially concerning the theology of the Sacraments; with its polemical tone and numerous coarse personal remarks directed at Karlstadt, it lacks the clarity of exposition of the *Lenten Sermons*.[44]

In a brief introduction Luther once again defines the main tenets of the Christian faith. From the outset he unequivocally includes the matter of images, or religious art, in the realm of Christian freedom, calling them 'external things'. An interesting new accent in the introduction is the statement that the opponents of images are only practising 'external asceticism', demonstrating formal hostility to corporeal things. This is one of the few references to the spiritualistic currents that pertained to visionary movements. Luther, however, does not continue this theme, for these were problems which he never understood very well and rarely concerned himself with. He gave the chapter dealing with religious art *per se* a significant title: *On iconoclasm*.

Luther began by saying that Karlstadt had reversed the natural order for removing images: 'He removed them from the eyes, but left them in the hearts.'[45] This expression, based on an ancient literary commonplace which was especially popular in the late Middle Ages, itself became a commonplace in sixteenth-century discussion on images (as we shall see later). Zwingli, writing without reference to Luther, was to reverse the order, writing 'out of eyesight, out of the heart' (*ab Auge, ab Herz*). Since Luther wanted to highlight his own most important argument – namely, about 'proper' and 'improper' ways of introducing change, he states a few sentences later with disarming frankness, that he would defend religious art 'just to spite' Karlstadt and his

25

supporters. This statement also contains an element of a singular 'theology of contrariness' coupled with the idea of 'Christian freedom' and activated when the latter became threatened.

The rather startling accents in this part of Luther's deliberation are the statements that he would even tolerate 'the image of a saint'[46] and (on the following page but in the same line of argument) a 'Marian image'. However, this was only rhetorical contrariness, which had no consequences for his main argument.

Condemnation of the manner of carrying out change played a major role in Luther's deliberations. 'Another error of this iconoclasm is that it is conducted without order . . . that means, removing images in the manner of Karlstadt.'[47] Here Luther clearly links the actions of Karlstadt and Müntzer, despite his concession that Karlstadt is not a 'murderous prophet'.

Luther several times cautiously charged Karlstadt with causing riots in Orlamünde. A certain error on Karlstadt's part enabled him to do so. After being expelled from Saxony in September 1524, Karlstadt published a short treatise, *Whether One Should Step Lightly* at the end of October and beginning of November.[48] This is one of Karlstadt's more poorly conceived treatises, stressing first and foremost the necessity of immediate change. Though Karlstadt saw this as a task for the secular authorities, the publication of this work was a tactical error in the ongoing fight with Luther, supplying the latter with arguments justifying Karlstadt's expulsion from Saxony.

Even so, Luther did not directly take up the subject-matter raised by Karlstadt, addressing not so much the rapidity of the changes – which, as he surely felt, was the weak side of his practical theology – as the problem of infringing the rights of secular authorities through 'overturning images'. Citing examples from the Old Testament, Luther stated that where 'images and idols' were abolished (among the Israelites), this was done 'not by the rabble but the authorities' (*Obrigkeit*).

Luther referred several times to one of the favourite authors of the Reformation, St Paul, and especially to his famous Epistle to the Galatians, where he clearly rejects observance of Old Testament holy days. Both the injunction to observe the Sabbath – which Karlstadt postulated – and the ban on images are temporary 'ceremonial rules'. In Luther's opinion, idols were not harmful in the Old Testament as long as they were not worshipped: another reason for not burdening contemporary Christians with archaic laws. Luther constantly distinguished between two planes: the polemic about the ban on images in the Old Testament, which he continued to conduct, and ('let us talk evangelically about these things') the basic negation of the injunctions of the Old Testament for the free Christian.

The last problem which the reformer takes up in his treatise is the problem of the aims and function of religious art. He rhetorically requests the iconoclasts to allow Lutherans to retain holy images and crucifixes as 'mirror images' and 'mental signs'; such works serve 'to gaze upon, as a witness, to aid memory, and as a sign' (*zum Ansehen, zum Zeugnis, zum Gedächtnis, zum Zeichen*'). These are not traditional terms, though they had already appeared earlier in the theological vocabulary. Especially important here is the notion of sign. Luther had already used it in the *Lenten Sermons*. No elucidation of the semantic scope of this notion in the sixteenth century has been undertaken hitherto, but it was unquestionably used because, in a natural way, it demarcated the object and the image and counteracted tendencies to identify the image or representation with the prototype, to perceive the image as magical. Basing himself on St Augustine, Wyclif had, for the same reason, defined images as *signa sensibilia*.[49] In sixteenth-century theology the notion of sign had a singular reductive function in relation to the sacred. It would soon play a key role (a foreshadowing of this is already visible in *Against the Heavenly Prophets*) in the escalating controversy over the Eucharist.

Definition of the aims and function of art leads into the last part of Luther's deliberations. Though there are still a few evasions and polemics concerning the question of 'natural law' and the 'law of Moses', Luther's attention was already fixed on a programme – one would like to say a positive programme. He moves on to his last argument, which is supposed to settle the right of religious art to exist. Independently of his subjective will, man's thinking is figurative: 'Whether I want to or not, when I hear the name of Christ, there appears in my heart the image of a man nailed to a cross, just as my face appears in a mirror of water when I look at it.'[50] Hence 'faith from hearing', to use a well-known Lutheran term, is connected with figurativeness, both with the mental products of our imagination and – though to a somewhat lesser degree – with real works of art. God spoke to the faithful in images, especially in the Revelation of St John, in the Pentateuch and in the Book of Joshua. Luther, with great intuitiveness, has here grasped the remarkable imagery and vividness of these parts of the Bible.

There is a certain other aspect here as well. On the whole, Luther renounced exaggerated figurativeness or the use of allegories; sometimes his condemnations of allegory even give the impression that he regarded it as a kind of delusion, and he included the overcoming of this inclination among his famous 'tribulations' ('*Anfechtungen*'). However, Luther was concerned not with an antinomic opposition of reality vs. allegory, but with emphasizing the complementarity of thoughts, words and images and therefore changed his attitude. Sometimes he still gave words precedence, but elsewhere he even suggested parity for both means of faith – words and images. For Luther words were unquestionably more important both psychologically and theologically, but the important point is that the absence of images – and these changes take place in the pages of *Against the Heavenly Prophets* – becomes something unnatural, inconsistent with the special laws of religious experience.

After this statement Luther moves on to outline the scope of religious art. In brief, this is a programme for an illustrated Bible, though Luther clearly preferred great series of paintings on 'walls and houses' – as he somewhat enigmatically put it. In this formulation he made no direct mention of the interior decoration of churches, though obviously this entire programme was suitable for being applied to places of worship. The next point of Luther's iconographic programme applies to places of worship explicitly: namely, representations of scenes from the Passion of Christ, which were more important for emerging Lutheran doctrine than for traditional Catholic representation. Luther concluded this extremely important passage with one of his key statements: 'Would to God that I could convince the lords as well as the rich to have the entire Bible painted in detail on houses so that the eyes of everyone could see it; this would be a Christian work':[51] that is, nothing less than an open call for a new form of patronage in the field of ecclesiastical art. Luther here cleverly avoided the pitfall of justification by works, by calling this undertaking a 'Christian work' rather than a 'Christian service', and in fact his Protestant antagonists did not try to attack him on this particular issue. On this note his deliberations end – the reformer moves on to the sacraments and the Eucharist, which occupies the main position in the entire treatise.

The publication of *Against the Heavenly Prophets* concludes the main stage of Luther's deliberations on religious art and its function. By 1525, that turning-point in the history of Germany and Europe, Luther, after overcoming his initial doubts, was fully convinced of religious art's right to exist; he saw a place for it in the structure of the new faith, and what is more he began to formulate a modest programme of patronage and to consider questions of religious iconography.

That same year events took place which further strengthened Luther's conservative stance, his aversion to all sudden changes and to all manifestations of 'rebellion and riots'. Müntzer claimed leadership of the rebellious peasants in Thüringen, and in May 1525 he was defeated at Frankenhausen, tried and executed. Despite the different field of Muntzer's activities and the new issues they opened up, Luther saw his defeat as a direct consequence of his misdeeds in Allstedt, including iconoclasm.

After 1525 Luther's remarks on the subject of images are infrequent, and one can no longer speak of any clear development of his views, although a certain growth of interest in iconographic problems is discernible. From this time until his death in 1546, he spoke out on religious art with great interest, praised its educational merits, and recognized it as a genuine aid in the propagation of the Gospel. He even wrote about children and simple folk that 'they are moved more by an image and an allegory (*Gleichnis*) than by mere words or doctrines, as St Mark attests'.[52] Especially significant was his remark about 'images for children and simple folk'. This indirect reference to the famous pronouncement of Gregory the Great about images as 'books for the unlearned' was a clearly Catholicizing point of view in the dispute of the 1520s. For Karlstadt this would have been a 'highly papist' argument.

After 1525 Luther no longer debated with the enemies of images; he no longer directly rebutted iconophobic views or actions. When writing against the Anabaptists in Münster he did not mention their iconoclastic rampages. Morever, he did not refer to Zwingli's or Bucer's iconoclastic actions. Even taking into account that he was not well informed about the situation in Upper Germany and Switzerland, he must have heard about the more notorious iconoclastic events, such as those in Basle in 1529 which so terrified Erasmus. His attitude of allowing the appropriate political authority to decide the question of images – even against them – cannot fully explain his neutrality on this point. It is therefore surprising that he did not take up the question of images during the numerous meetings and negotiations with the Zwinglians. These meetings began with the famous debate in Marburg in 1529 and lasted until 1536, when all hopes were finally dashed of reaching agreement on the question of the Eucharist.[53] The problem of the Eucharist probably became so paramount in Luther's thinking that he failed to make any use of the charge of iconoclasm in his dispute with the Swiss. At the beginning of the Marburg Colloquy (1529) Luther listed seven differences separating his followers from those of Zwingli but the problem of images was not mentioned. Not surprisingly, therefore, the image question was only indirectly touched upon, in point 14 of the Marburg agreement between Wittenberg and the Swiss in the section on the liturgy, where it was postulated that changes in liturgy should be made gradually so as not to undermine the faith of the weak. This formulation had such a Lutheran flavour to it that Zwingli even had to justify himself on this score after his return to Zurich. Neither side attached much importance to it, however, as it was a by-product of protracted negotiations on other matters. During a second colloquy in Wittenberg in 1536, Martin Bucer raised on behalf of the Swiss the issue of the 'continuance of the cult of images in Wittenberg'. However, he received only a brief and evasive answer, from Johannes Bugenhagen. More importantly, the famous Confession of Augsburg of 1530, the basic credal statement which was intended to unite all Protestants, did not raise the issue of images, thus relegating it, rather prematurely, to insignificance, as subsequent events were to show. Four Upper German cities presented their own rival confession in 1530, the so-called Tetrapolitan Confession, which called expressly for the removal of images; this document was also in fact primarily involved in the ongoing dispute over the Eucharist and the Real Presence.

With an increasingly positive attitude towards images, Luther had apparently lost interest in the matter. Earlier he had complained, not just rhetorically, that too much attention was paid to 'ceremonies'. Nonetheless, Luther's idea had a considerable indirect influence on the liturgy and visual forms of religion in central and northern Germany, via ecclesiastical statutes influenced by him.

From the late 1520s onwards nearly every independent territory or imperial city issued its own ecclesiastical statutes (*Kirchenordnung*). Luther had a role in the creation of only eight such statutes, and rather unimportant ones at that. However, he gave his support and blessing to the statutes drafted by his closest collaborator in Wittenberg, Johannes Bugenhagen, known on account of his birthplace as 'the Pomeranian doctor'. Exemplary for many others were those drafted for Brunswick (1528) and Lübeck (1529), which were especially influential in Pomerania. These laws usually regulated the decor of churches. Closest to Luther's views seems to be the relevant passage in the Brunswick statutes, that there are still a lot of 'false images' but, those which are not the object of idolatrous practices should be retained 'in churches, since we do not wish to resort to iconoclasm to destroy images'.[54] The Brunswick statutes contained the significant proviso that in future such images as had become the object of idolatry should be removed.

PROBLEMS OF ICONOGRAPHY

This book focuses its main attention on the question of images and deals only in passing with iconographic problems; nonetheless Luther's views on this subject do merit some reflection. Luther's scattered iconographic comments and references are – as has already been shown – less than clear in intention, and no longer passage exists that gives explicit directions on their content. The changes that took place in the decoration of churches, as well as the themes of an emergent Lutheran art, were the result of the fundamental assumptions of Luther's theology, of his stance on the question of images and of his exposition of certain scriptural themes which made no direct mention of the possibility of representation as an image. The demise of a whole range of themes in religious iconography thus had no tangible connection with Luther's comments on iconography. Conversely, we can observe in Luther's iconographical comments how his fundamental assumptions shine through even in trivial instances.

In his iconographical comments Luther was guided by, first, his penchant for the literal reproduction of a text – the 'word' of Scripture; and, secondly, his basic Christological interpretation. For example, in speaking about the representation of the 'Horned

Moses', Luther was well aware of why the Vulgate speaks about Moses' 'horned visage' (painted erroneously with two horns instead of rays),[55] but he was willing to accept this representation as permissible in an allegorical sense, since it made visible the awe which Moses justly inspired as the personification of Old Testament law. If this was consistent with Luther's basic understanding of biblical theology, he was also willing to allow deviations from the principle of literal illustration of the Bible, i.e. illustration 'according to the Word'.

In particular this applies to his few remarks about representations of Christ. Fundamental for Luther was the image of the crucified Christ, which was intended to show the fundamental aspect of Christ's work – the redemption of the faithful.[56] In various comments on this subject he did not produce any suggestions which went significantly beyond the existing iconographic tradition. He did not opt expressly for a naturalistic portrayal of suffering or, on the other hand, for more idealized representations (though on the whole he emphasized the suffering more than the idealized Christ). As he stated in commenting on the Resurrection, he would leave to the painters how they would represent Christ's suffering. The crucial point here for the Christian beholder was to understand that this is really a 'consoling image': that Christ's death on the cross was suffered 'for me and for us'. Luther knew and accepted images of Christ on the cross, along with the instruments of Christ's Passion, as well as late Gothic allegorical representations of Christ in the wine-press. In accepting such depictions, tainted by excessive medieval devotion, he nonetheless always referred to the historical and concrete Passion of Christ. In the final analysis he felt free to opt for a wider, semi-metaphorical understanding of the historical facts of Christ's Passion, for the material and spiritual inseparability of the person of the Saviour, the cross and the church itself. In order to show the paths that Luther's thinking followed in Christological iconography, we could cite his comments on yet another theme: 'Painters paint the Infant Jesus with a cross on his back. I don't want this. I would prefer that they paint the entire Church on his back, for nowhere will we find the Christian Church if we don't see the one which lies on Christ's back.'[57]

Luther took the identification of Christ with the Church so far that he allowed representations of St Christopher, obviously not as a historical representation but as a symbol (he expressed himself as follows about the legend itself: 'unquestionably one of the greatest legends and greatest falsehoods'). In carrying Christ, St Christopher was bearing the 'entire Church' on his back. Hence Luther's thought turned on the artistic designation of the 'Church' in close connection with the figure of Christ, but it is obvious that he could not find an equally skilful designation for the Church to that he created in hymnology, when he formulated the brilliant metaphor of the 'mighty fortress'.

The natural culmination of Christ's Passion – especially in optimistic Protestant eschatology – was his Resurrection. Luther emphasized the victorious power of Christ in exceptionally strong words ('Christ the Victor'); his description of this subject is extremely dynamic. For Luther, the image of the risen Christ trampling death underfoot ('He was such a great enemy of death that he trampled it under his feet') has the same message as the representation of Christ's Harrowing of Hell. In this last motif Luther stressed the intensity of Christ's struggle with the devil and stated categorically that this scene should be painted with all the naturalistic elements inherent in the fierceness of that action.

The theme of the Last Supper, crucial in all Christian iconography, also played a vital role for Luther. Moreover, if any single scene had to be chosen for an altar, then Luther chose the Last Supper, a scene which in his words would be surrounded by large gilded inscriptions. This latter suggestion shows how vividly Luther still recalled aesthetic features of late Gothic art. Though Luther's marginal remarks hardly reached any wider audience, one can say however that Lutheran art after 1550 faithfully reflected his preferences in this regard. The typical Protestant altarpiece in this later period contained three scenes: the Last Supper, the Crucifixion and the Resurrection.[58] However, it is rather hard to see here a direct contribution of Luther as iconographer. It was more a reflection of more general Lutheran theological assumptions.

The reformer's position on devotional images cannot be explicitly defined either. He rejected some devotional representations like Veronica's cloth, but he did not reject such popular types of Christological iconography as the 'Man of Sorrows'. He clearly preferred 'historical' subjects such as the Last Supper or the Crucifixion but did not oppose continued representation of the thematic cycle of the Way of the Cross, not even in the workshop of his friend Lucas Cranach. The theme thus passed only gradually into oblivion in Lutheran art.

As a consequence, Luther's influence on the Christological iconography of the new confession was not that great. He did certainly contribute by the themes he rejected to the abolition of some particularly irritating subjects from the doctrinal point of view: for example, the so-called double intercession of Christ and Mary. On the positive side his role is still somewhat nebulous. This can be seen in the problem of the intellectual authorship of the so-called 'Law and Grace' theme.[59] This was the most important new Protestant iconographic formulation. Cranach's woodcut from c. 1530 and two somewhat different versions in paintings in Gotha and Prague disseminated this motif throughout Reformation Europe. Though almost all elements of the scene had appeared in Luther's sermons and writings of the 1520s, his role, that of Melanchthon and of course Cranach's own contribution to the iconography of that theme still await final clarification.[60] The same is true of Luther's role – probably somewhat overrated – in formulating a programme for the illustrated Wittenberg editions of the Bible.

Luther's attitude towards the cult of saints and how to depict them changed in accordance with the evolution of his theology.[61] In the initial phase of his intense fight with late medieval devotion Luther vehemently rejected the cult of saints on the basis of his doctrine of justification, as he did the cult of images. Around 1520 he stressed mainly the deplorable abuses of the cult of the saints. Later – sometime after 1524/5 – he tried to sketch the outlines of a new attitude towards the cult of the saints which did not entirely reject it, but he avoided anything which might link that cult to the question of images. Needless to say, his approach here differs from that of the iconophobic theologians for whom these problems were intrinsically linked, but within the framework of his theology there is a development analogous to that of his views on the question of images: the subsequent stages were quite similar in both.

From the very beginning Luther also rejected uncompromisingly the associated cult of relics. He did not even hesitate to criticize his patron, Frederick the Wise of Saxony, for collecting relics on a grand scale.[62] However, he did not link this question with the problem of images, so that they remained separate issues in the Lutheran tradition.

34

Luther's starting-point in this question was once more the formula of *Christus solus*, a point of departure used in considering images of St Christopher, whom Luther regarded as an allegory of the Christian man and tolerated only because of his connection with Christ. Luther knew that many of the saints and the cultic forms associated with them were of fairly recent vintage and believed that the early Church did not know any such cult. However, this argument – like the one about the lack of images in early Christianity – was given little weight by Luther, who opposed all ideas of a simple return to the condition of the primitive Church. Thus, he rejected the abuses occasioned by the cult primarily while giving less thought to the authenticity of particular saints or to the verisimilitude of their legends. The real novelty in Luther's attitude towards the saints was his different interpretation of the meaning of saints for Christians: 'The saints are given to us as an example not for their deeds but for their faith.' Thereby all attempts to imitate their action were groundless. Here Luther cut the life-line sustaining the cult but also relativized the importance of the saints themselves, thus laying the foundation for their demise in the Lutheran tradition.

In order not to yield any ground to the iconoclasts, Luther defended the legitimacy of the images of saints, while admitting that many of them could be revered in idolatrous ways. When he comes to concrete themes and images, a critical tone prevails. Thus Luther vehemently criticized images of St Thomas Aquinas, St Barbara, St Francis or Ursula and the 11,000 virgins. Luther argued that these were all 'false images', but he rejected even more strongly all iconographic versions depicting the 'conformity' of the life of a particular saint with that of Christ. An altar in Lüneburg where the life of St Francis was depicted as parallel to that of Christ was condemned in no uncertain terms.

Thus Luther's Christological approach prevailed, and in conjunction with the lower status of the saints fatally weakened both their cult and its pictorial manifestations. Thus neither the relative tolerance of the Lutherans for old images of the saints nor isolated cases where new images were created, mostly of Christopher and some local saints, alter the fact that after 1540 saints (with the exception of the Apostles and Evangelists) do not appear at all in the religious iconography of Protestantism. The older pictures of the saints gradually vanished from the churches.

Luther's pronouncements on Marian images[63] could not be other than negative. The last flowering, around 1520, of the cult of miraculous Marian images – for example, the 'Beautiful Virgin' of Regensburg[64] – was vociferously condemned. Lutherans were also vehemently opposed to any form of Marian pilgrimage. But the iconoclastic challenge also changed Luther's attitude here. I have already mentioned the passage in which he states that he will defend Marian images to spite the iconoclasts. An additional motive was provided by the fact that Müntzer and his followers had destroyed a Marian chapel. There are even a few remarks after 1525 in which Luther seems to encourage looking at Marian images. However, even in these more positive comments the Christological point of view dominates completely: 'The Infant Jesus sleeps in the arms of the Mother of God: when he awakens, he will ask us what we have done and how we have behaved.'[65] On the other hand, Luther sharply attacked Marian images which seemed to deny the primacy of Christ: for example, the representation of Mary as Mother of the Church. His description of the subject differs somewhat from the contemptuous sneers of Zwingli, but he rejects it in no uncertain terms. In a much milder manner he came out against images of Mary representing her as a queen in full glory. In the latter case he even went so far as to present an iconographic proposal, suggesting that Mary be shown rather in 'her great poverty',[66] as a person uniting 'the glory of God with her own insignificance'.

Despite Luther's relative tolerance of them, Marian images vanished from Protestant iconography and from Protestant churches after c. 1550. In this sense Christocentric Protestant theology caused the disappearance of an entire pictorial theme, tainted in the eyes of many Lutherans by the excesses of the Marian cult, while Luther's suggestion that the Mother of Christ be depicted as 'Poor Mary' elicited no response.

Hence Luther's stance on existing iconography and his attempts to lay down guidelines for change were full of contradictions. Above all, he did not devote a single cohesive passage to this subject. His scattered remarks played no important role in contemporary disputes about art. Luther's pronouncements also show us that he always thought in terms of the image's conformity to the Bible and did not display any greater understanding of its aesthetic dimensions.

CONCLUSION

To a certain extent Luther's attitude towards art was a matter of pure chance, a result of his shocked reaction to iconoclasm and of the logical consequences of the position he took towards it. In many other respects, however, his attitude was a consequence of his mode of theological reasoning.

Let me indicate some other aspects of this question. The argument of this chapter is that Luther rejected any dogmatic position in the dispute over images and supported a more nuanced approach. For him, both ontologically and iconographically, it was less important what a work of art was than what it meant for the Christian believer. There is a clear convergence here with the general assumptions of Luther's Christology. For every believer Christ is, first and foremost, 'there for me' (*pro me*). Questions about Christ's essence are of lesser importance than the role of the Saviour in the life of a Christian. Thus, Luther rejected all Trinitarian speculation. The radical conclusions that could be drawn from Luther's statements seem to point in somewhat different directions, but they are united by his tendency towards a practical relativism. In a passage in the *Great Catechism*, Luther stated: 'only trust and faith of the heart make a god or an idol'. Gerhard Ebeling has called this 'an extremely dangerous' statement.[67] It really is, for it opens up lines of thought that lead right up to the nineteenth century, seeming to combine a docetist emphasis with an anthropologism of a Feuerbachian type. However, the radicalism of these words is an isolated example within the overall context of Luther's writings. Yet in seeking words to visualize Christ's role, Luther used concepts which are not entirely consistent with Reformation Christology. On the whole, this aspect of Luther's theology is perceived even by modern Protestant theologians as somewhat problematic. Characteristic is the commentary of Pinomaa, who speaks of Luther's incredible 'boldness',[68] when in fact we are faced with a clear acceptance of docetism as a legitimate intellectual construction: 'What difference does it make whether Christ is a God or not, whether he was a body or only a fiction, whether he had a soul or not.'[69] This obviously does not mean that Luther's theology in its essentials can be linked with docetism or anthropologism in accordance with the nineteenth-century understanding of the term. Rather, it is a proof of the latitude in thinking Luther allowed himself in his struggle to demonstrate the role of the Saviour in human salvation.

In the reformer's approach to the problem of religious art we perceive the same emphasis on the *servitude* of the object, the thing experienced. Luther refused to reflect on what religious art is and what it could be; he only asked whether it could serve the 'weak' in their religious education. Art is a medium which lacks its own inherent sacrality. Hans von Campenhausen concluded his discussion of the attitude of the reformers towards art by saying that 'art is a language for Luther'.[70] But he seems to have underrated the qualitative difference of these two potential carriers of religious truths. For Luther language was 'the sword of the spirit': that is, a medium capable of absolutely unmistakable meaning. Art, on the other hand, was a much more ambiguous sign, which could conceal some unrecognized error. Despite this, both art and language were means of transmitting religious truths and in theory should be 'transparent' by their very nature.

It would surely be a very interesting task to study Luther's attitude towards the problem of images within the framework of his Christology. Indeed, one might even discern a certain model for solving theological problems, which for the sake of simplicity we might call 'relationism' – a model which continues to operate even when the starting-point is diametrically different. For example, among the arguments in defence of images we do not find the traditional statement of iconodules that man himself has been made in the image of God, for Luther rejected this assumption. According to him, Original Sin was responsible for the loss of any likeness. Yet this reasoning seemed to be contradicted by the evidence of the Bible (Genesis 9:6) so Luther made a characteristic relativizing modification. There remains in humanity a certain remnant of likeness precisely thanks to the relation with God, to the fact that mankind is subject to God's plan of salvation. In reference to our subject-matter, the *tertium comparationis* here is without doubt the notion of image: for both in his stance on images and in the problem of 'man as the image of the Creator' one can clearly perceive Luther's tendency to relativize the process in which the reality of the image becomes the analogy of the reality of salvation. According to Luther, humanity lost its similarity to God while retaining a vestige of it in the form of God's actions on its behalf. Nor did religious art have such an autonomous value for Luther. The aptness of this analogy in the context of the subject-matter under discussion seems to come from the very notion of image, and in this regard it is doubtless a convergence of a special kind.

Luther's strength was without doubt the fact that in his theoretical argument he used concepts in their dynamic aspect. Through his favourite method of *reductio ad absurdum* and a scrutiny of the entire field of semantic meaning he strove to put them into practice. Making full use of the dialectics of 'offence' and the 'rejection of works' he brought his reasoning to a conclusion that he had already assumed a priori.

Typical of Luther are his recurrent justifications of simplicity (*simplicitas*) in exegetic, literary and artistic work. We find these apologies both in his glosses to illustrations and in an alleged utterance of Dürer quoted by Luther in his *Table Talk* (as noted by Aurifaber): 'Doctor Luther once said that Albrecht Dürer, the famous painter, used to say: "I like pictures that are painted as simply as possible". . . . Likewise I would like to deliver the simplest possible sermon that every believer could understand.'[71]

Elsewhere Luther praised the Pentateuch for its succinctness. He made an interesting analogy here with the famous artistic topos of the painter Timanthes, about whom Quintilian remarked that in the scene of the sacrifice of Iphigenia he showed her father with a covered head because such great pain could not be portrayed.[72] The allegories which Luther so eagerly used in his homiletic and literary writings he constantly renounced in theory, either on general principles ('beware of allegories') as leading to a falsification of the Scripture, or on the grounds of their supposed ineffectiveness in straightforward religious debate ('mysteries cannot fight'). However, this singular cult of simplicity, which might have pushed Luther towards ascetic reductionism in diverse fields, was tempered either by the principle of 'church decorum' and appropriateness or by Luther's own mental predispositions, which induced him often to use rich figurative metaphors and comparisons.

The talents and personal predispositions of great people become historically relevant only when they are congruent with the evolutionary structures and temper of their time. This is also the case in the unavoidable comparison between Protestant music and the figurative arts. The reformer liked music very much and cultivated this branch of art himself.[73] Even though church music – like images – was part of the broadly neutral field of *adiaphora*, Luther not for a moment entertained the thought of abolishing it. (Lack of space here prevents me expounding on the negative Calvinist attitude towards organ music, which shows some similarities with the battle over images). In fact, both Luther's work on hymnology and under his inspiration, the organization of choirs, the nucleus of Protestant musical life (to exaggerate somewhat), have no counterparts in the approach of the great reformer to the visual arts. This was congruent, however, with the inner logic of the Reformation process: the Protestant community conceived as a congregation needed music as both a sacral and a secular communal bond. Not surprisingly, therefore, Luther's attitude towards music – especially his beloved domestic music – became an important part of his biographical legend and part of the cultural tradition of Protestantism: a tradition that Protestantism manifestly lacks in the visual arts.

When we sum up Luther's attitude towards the question of images and the problem of a new Protestant art we are struck – despite his many pronouncements – by a certain fragmentariness of his legacy. His pronouncements on artistic matters and architecture could be only of very limited use to the patronage of nascent Protestant church art.

Luther left no clear guidelines on church architecture. To be sure, he did stress that certain adornments are appropriate in a church. He thereby toned down remarks that were especially prevalent at the beginning of his theological work, where he stated that no particular church building had any sacrality. When he opened in 1544 the first Protestant house of worship 'not infected with papism' – the castle chapel in Torgau[74] – Luther initiated an interesting type of a small Protestant church, which engendered a long series of imitations up to the middle of the seventeenth century, but this was not the standard of an urban church. What is more, Luther did not address the question of church decor in a way that would have been binding for Lutheranism. As early as the 1520s he stipulated that the pastor stand behind the altar facing the faithful (which obviously would have ruled out any retable), although he later qualified this view. The abolition of side altars took place, as we know, somewhat automatically as a result of the break with the previous practice of the Mass and a reduction in the size of the clergy. However, this gap soon began to be filled by the endowments of the rich patriciate and middle class, which commissioned elaborate tombstones and epitaphs with a particular theological message. Luther was never aware that, owing to the lack of other elements, most of the works of art defining the artistic as well as the theological image of the church building would be somewhat voluntaristic. Nor was he aware of the fact that the shape and the appropriateness of tombstones involved an implicit assumption of 'justification by works', not to mention the theologically questionable form of the so-called 'epitaph-altar'. 'If we wanted to honour graves in some way, it would be more fitting to paint or write on walls good epitaphs or passages from the Bible, so that they could be seen by those going to tombs or to the cemetery.'[75] This really is Luther's only pertinent, and very general, comment on a subject which would play a crucial role in Protestant art after 1550.

On the other hand, it is hard to judge how much Luther influenced two other matters of great importance for Protestant art: the inclusion of inscriptions in pictorial representations or the placing of inscriptions on the walls of churches, and the appearance of the so-called 'altar-pulpit'. Luther did suggest, at least in the passage quoted above, putting inscriptions on the walls of churches, and he proposed placing around the representation of the Last Supper a golden inscription with a quotation from the Bible; but these were only casual utterances. Inscriptions in churches became more the preserve of the Calvinists, while the process of including inscriptions in Protestant pictures had already begun – as an autonomous artistic phenomenon – in the early 1520s. The altar-pulpit came into being a long time after Luther's death, and it is hard to imagine that he could have foreseen this form or in some prophetic way defined its theological context. A passage from the *Sermon on Baptism* (1534) shows rather that he was a supporter of a symmetrical arrangement of the altar, pulpit and font; on the other hand some of his statements expressed the view that the particular elements of a church could be placed anywhere. For example, one could preach in a barn or in the town-hall, while a baptismal font could be found even 'by the Elbe'. Hence Luther's legacy in this field was highly ambiguous. Declarations of absolute freedom were interlaced with utterances and actions that moved in the direction of an ever stricter organization of the 'visible Church'.

On the other hand, Luther influenced the development of the conception of the Protestant cemetery, which in turn seems to have played a significant role in the modern history of the cemetery as an urban-artistic form. This suggests the general principle that the influence of the Reformation turned out to be strongest and most enduring in those artistic forms of religious and social life in which the aspect of utility was dominant (e.g., cemeteries, town-halls, alms-chests, altar-pulpits, but also Reformation broadsheets in mass editions). This is consistent with what we know about the Reformation as a movement developing from religious motives and for a long time guided by religious fundamentalism, but whose historical influence on the civilization of Western and Central Europe should be assessed primarily in social terms.

Institutional problems of art were of no interest to Luther. Despite his justly praised sensitivity to social and economic matters, he failed to perceive the rapidly deteriorating economic situation of artists after 1517. Even his friendship with Lucas Cranach did not arouse Luther's interest in their professional condition, although contemporary sources were full of artists' laments about their increasing pauperization following the collapse of religious patronage. Perhaps the figure of Cranach, a resourceful and well-to-do burgher, in whose person Luther probably saw the ethos of the Reformation come to life, hid these problems from the great reformer.

Luther obviously did not defend the legitimacy of religious art for its own sake. Art was primarily useful in promulgating the Word of God. What is more, the question of banning art was coupled in such a way with an entire complex of theological views inimical to Lutheranism that its defence was simultaneously a defence of Lutheran principles.

2

The iconophobes: Karlstadt, Zwingli and Calvin

Es hasst die Kirche, die mich auferzog
Der Sinne Reiz, kein Abbild duldet sie,
Allein das körperlose Wort verehrend.

(Schiller, *Maria Stuart*)

One of the characteristic features of the theological development of the early Reformation was that many intellectual processes seemed to run on parallel lines. In reality the interdependences as well as the great reformers' knowledge of one another's doctrines were not as great as they seem now from a historical perspective, which tends misleadingly to unify certain events and aspects. We have already mentioned the treatises of 1522 on the image question, which were produced largely independently of each other. A similar conclusion also seems plausible with regard to the views of the three great reformers to be discussed below. The connections between their systems were weaker than might be supposed and they hardly influenced one another at all on the image question. They arrived at similar positions by very different paths, thus showing the wide range of problems and references characterizing the 'image question'.

IMPATIENT REFORMER: KARLSTADT

The main stages in the development of the views and work of Andreas Bodenstein von Karlstadt (1480–1541) unfolded until the mid–1520s in close connection with the activity of Luther. The fight against images took up less than four years (1521–4) of Karlstadt's theological and political career and reached its climax in the Wittenberg riots in January 1522 and the dispute with

43

Luther in August 1524. Owing to these events, however, Karlstadt, who since 1517 had been collaborating with Luther and in 1519 took part as Luther's equal in the famous Leipzig debate with Johannes Eck, in only two years found himself pushed into the extreme left wing of the Reformation.

A closer scrutiny of Karlstadt's theological evolution shows that some conflict with Luther was unavoidable. It would surely have erupted after 1525 over the problem of the Eucharist. At that time, however, the dispute would have run along different tracks, although Karlstadt's ultimate fate as a fellow-traveller of the Swiss reformers would probably have been the same. Things evolved differently, and thus the image question acquired a special importance, for it caused the first real split in the Reformation. It also generated the popular formulas that were used by both contemporary and later polemicists to define Karlstadt's theological stance and activity.

The Wittenberg events of December 1521 and January 1522 were thus the climax but not the beginning or the end of Karlstadt's interest in the image question. From the 1521 treatise *Instruction on Vows* up to the short treatise *Whether One should Step Lightly*, published three years later, the image question was one of his main subjects of deliberation. In the interval between these two treatises Karlstadt's position characteristically stiffened. Whereas in the former Karlstadt, after briefly condemning religious images, singled out 'internal idols' as more dangerous (a similar position was taken a year later by Luther but in a more rhetorical context), in the treatise of 1524 he constantly reiterated that religious images should be removed immediately and utterly failed to consider the merits of the case. That is why the treatise of January 1522 *On the Abolition of Images* (*Von Abtuhung der Bilder*)[1] deserves greater attention here as the central exposé of Karlstadt's view on the image question.

This short work lacks, however, both the clarity and the logic of Luther's *Lenten Sermons*. Problems and arguments recur in a rhetorically simplistic way that tends to obscure the theoretical foundations of Karlstadt's conclusions. This obscurity is also due to Karlstadt's overuse of the controversialist device of reasoning by contraries, inferring far-reaching conclusions from a reversed argument (the Bible speaks about listening to the voice of God, so it does not speak about images, etc.). The treatise lacks cohesive lines of argument, which have to be educed from a mass of disparate comments and scattered remarks. The greater emotional tone of many passages, when compared with Luther's texts, hardly gained thus the desired results of its author's polemical strategy.

Karlstadt began his treatise with three basic arguments: '1. To have images in churches is contrary to the first Commandment, Thou shalt have no other gods before me. 2. To place idols on altars is even more devilish. 3. Therefore, we should put them away in obedience to Scripture.'[2]

At the outset Karlstadt refers to the First Commandment, to the principal argument which will come up time and time again throughout the treatise. This was naturally the strongest weapon of the opponents of images and Karlstadt vehemently fixed his attention on the idolatrous practices of the cult of images – the bowing-down and burning candles before images and the kissing of them. In his view, these practices furnish an irrefutable proof that images are inherently evil, that they are changing the church into a 'den of murderers'.

At one point Karlstadt even states[3] – in a tactically dangerous argument which could be easily used against him – that the Jews, who did not tolerate images in their temples, conducted themselves much better than Christians, since the latter place various votive offerings in houses of worship – here he gives a long list – and expect help from them. All the images 'raised by people' are bad.

Karlstadt also addresses sharp words of criticism against the teaching of Gregory the Great that images are the books of the laity. From pictures the laity can only learn to esteem 'fleshly desires'. Continuing this strand of argument Karlstadt arrives at radically spiritualistic assertions: 'For example, from the Crucifix you learn only the physical suffering of Christ, how he drooped his head, etc. But Christ said "The Flesh profiteth nothing and only the spirit makes alive".'[4] It would be difficult to find anything more opposed to Luther's views.

The reverse side of medieval image worship appears quite clearly in the treatise: namely, a genuine fear of images. Karlstadt himself admits this in a very personal passage. He was pushed to radicalism not only by his theoretical awareness of the inappropriateness of images but also by his own fear, which was an offshoot of the magic of images: 'and I have in myself a harmful fear, which I would fain be rid of, but cannot.'[5] It is well known that not a few iconoclastic movements were based on this sort of motivation. At the moment of the rejection of its sacrality, the image had to be destroyed in an almost ritual way, for otherwise by tempting with doubled force it would have caused even greater harm.

While Karlstadt derived the motivations for his views primarily from theoretical arguments, a subjective factor is clearly evident in the way he justified carrying out changes. This subjectivism is of a different kind from Luther's, though it was certainly candid. Karlstadt was unable to justify his behaviour tactically in broader categories. Luther declared himself initially to be a professed enemy of religious images, making concessions only for the sake of the weak. Karlstadt, with almost suicidal candour, confessed that the mass of the faithful lagged behind his own development towards iconophobia. Without applying present-day categories, it must be said that Karlstadt's remark about the sick seeking consolation in crucifixes and images and about the necessity of mercilessly combatting such deeds is a striking example of theological and intellectual dogmatism (Karlstadt, much more than Luther, was an intellectual of a rather modern type, prone to espouse 'forced utopias'). It would obviously be hard to decide which of the leaders of the Reformation was the most doctrinaire (certainly not Luther), but Karlstadt unquestionably had the least tactical sense, which in the conditions of a revolutionary movement is probably more important than simply being right.

In arguing against an image-friendly interpretation of St Paul's actions in Athens, Karlstadt used a method which anticipated hermeneutic interpretation, attempting to demonstrate that St Paul was an enemy of images.[6] However, his main efforts were directed towards proving, on the basis of an analysis of manifestations of the image cult, that holy images serve as objects of idolatry. He turned the cutting-edge of his attack mainly against images of St Christopher, showing clearly what controversies this cult inspired at that time.[7]

Let us return for a moment to the basic features of Karlstadt's theology – especially its theocentrism – since these elements influenced the argument against images in various ways. Calvin's theocentric approach to the image problem was based on the use of the notion of 'the hidden God' in the understanding of transcendence and permanence; Karlstadt's theocentrism, on the other hand, had a less intrinsic and more external foundation through its accent on the Law of God. Consequently, a similar conclusion (ban images) and similar basic theological elements were educed in a somewhat different way, separating Karlstadt not only from

Calvin but from other theologians as well. This difference manifested itself in the concept of 'offence'. Here a difference in dialectical reasoning appeared which was to have far-reaching consequences for the tactics chosen by Karlstadt and by other reformers. To quote Ulrich Bubenheimer:

> For Karlstadt there exists an 'offence in faith' if something is objectively in conflict with divine Law. This state of things 'offends', in that it stands in the way of real faith, even though the erring believer may be unaware of this. For Luther 'offence' (*Ärgernis*) is engendered by a situation in which someone is subjectively offended by something offending his conscience. Then a situation could arise in which the faithful could have to act against his own conscience. The state of things that gives rise to 'offence' may even be a bad one, objectively speaking, but the faith is weak. That is why the removal of images causes 'offence'.[8]

In the logical order of things, for Karlstadt even the smallest liturgical and practical problems became a domain subject to the divine Law. In this way he lost much of the freedom of manoeuvre that Luther retained when settling similar matters. By thinking and acting in the categories of a 'congregational Christianity' Karlstadt seemed to deny the necessity that all religious ceremonies within a given territory should be uniform. This fact explains both the exceptional hostility of the elector of Saxony towards Karlstadt and the fact that – notwithstanding certain theological differences – Karlstadt found a more suitable field of activity in the politically very fragmented regions of Upper Germany and Switzerland where a notion of the urban commune was dominant which could be equated in theory – though as a rule not in practice – with a congregational Christianity.

We should be cautious, of course, not to apply our present understanding of the concept of 'freedom' or 'Christian freedom' too closely to these problems. The historical consequences of Luther's position, whose initial liberalism gave way, because of its inner contradictions, to the authoritarian model of a rigidly state-controlled Church are well known. As regards Karlstadt, it is significant that an Anglo-Saxon scholar from a civilization with a long, but hardly freedom-loving, Puritan tradition of congregational Christianity perceived clearly the authoritarian consequences of Karlstadt's position. Gordon Rupp's distinction between the 'evangelical "may"' of Luther and the 'legalistic "must"' of Karlstadt[9] (viewed against the background of the Puritanical movements and their hostility to all form of religious art) provides a much-needed challenge to the trend of Reformation historiography initiated in 1905 by Hermann Barge's imposing monograph on Karlstadt,[10] which was often uncritically apologetic towards both Karlstadt and some of the more radical reformers.

The strict understanding of the divine commandments exerted such an influence on Karlstadt's theological judgement in the domain of liturgy and images that it pushed into the background, to the role of ancillary arguments, the antithetical concepts of 'spirit vs. body', which otherwise were an essential component of his theology of the spirit in the years 1522–9. What is more, this rigorous concept of God's Law constituted Karlstadt's direct response to Luther's concept of neutral, value-free objects – the *adiaphora*. From the point of view of the inner logic of his system, the lack of the latter concept hardly weakened Karlstadt's position.

Karlstadt's treatise also contains formulations that were not very fortunate from the point of view of nascent Reformation theology. Basing himself on an incorrect interpretation of a scriptural passage, Karlstadt tried, in a rather clumsy argument, to negate the role of images of the Saviour and thus seemed to reject the mediation of Christ.[11] Lapses of this kind, unintentionally smacking of Arianism, later gave Luther the pretext for the blatantly untrue charge that 'Karlstadt does not believe in God'. The fact is that Karlstadt's Christology, which in the end remained within the limits of Protestant orthodoxy, had a somewhat different, more summary nature. Karlstadt wrote little about the activity of Christ: he always emphasized the person of Christ within the totality of God's plan of salvation.[12] His Christ was never that inordinately concrete Lutheran Jesus *pro me*, and he also rarely referred to Christ as an example for imitation. More important for Karlstadt than the activity of Christ was the memory of Christ's sacrifice. This also influenced his Eucharistic doctrine, by negating the real presence of Christ in the sacrament.[13]

These differences in Christology led in the direction of a tendency that began to dominate strongly in Karlstadt's thinking after 1522 and lasted to the end of the 1520s: namely, to spiritualism. Karlstadt's spiritualism was, however, of a special kind. It was not coupled with social radicalism and found its fullest expression in deliberations on Christian morality based on a specific procedure of the internalization of religious experiences which Karlstadt called 'resignation' (*Gelassenheit*). While the links between his spiritualism, which was greatly influenced by the medieval German mystic Johannes Tauler, and the other parts of his doctrine were of varying intensity, clear connections exist between his Eucharistic teaching and his enmity towards images. Karlstadt took from Tauler the notion that the soul has to become detached from inner images. In a peculiar mixture of medieval mysticism and traces of Neoplatonic thought Karlstadt rejected such inner images as inimical to man's similarity to God. This similarity – weakened by Original Sin – man has to re-establish by the said procedure of resignation, in a long process of expelling outer and inner images until the heart admits only the image of Christ and the 'image of good law'.

Curiously enough, in his doctrine Karlstadt avoided most of the archetypal ideas connected with the concepts of the 'poor church' and the 'primitive church'. Here too, in my opinion, resides the basic cleavage between his position and that of the radical Reformation. In the 1530s this led him to join the Zwinglians.

In his treatise against images we find few explicit traces of Karlstadt's spiritualism. On the one hand, the problem of ceremonies is treated here from the angle of God's law – by counting up God's commands to destroy idols. On the other hand, the conviction of their inherent harmfulness is expounded with monotonous insistence. Only at the end of the treatise, as though sensing intuitively one of the directions of Luther's attack, does Karlstadt place a logically cohesive passage in which he discusses from a different angle the problem of the validity of the commandments of the Old Testament in relation to the New: 'Some kissers of images say: the Old Law prohibits images, the New does not. We, however, will be obedient to the New and not the Old Testament.'[14] Having reduced to this minimum the position of the opponents of Old Testament law, Karlstadt presents a further line of argument based on the statement: 'we do not follow obligatorily the Old Law but we agree on it jointly'[15] since Christ changed nothing substantial in the Old Law. Going even further, he tried to show that St Paul's teaching can be reconciled fully with the Old Testament. For Karlstadt the 'signs' of the Old Testament are something more than mere foreshadowings and prefigurations of Christ. Once again, in a polemical fervour that transcends the bounds of his own fundamental theology, he states that 'Christ himself is contained in the will and message of the Old Testament'.

It is not just such controversialist stratagems that seem to reveal a cleavage between his arguments and his own fundamental assumptions. A further argument, based on his favourite method of *reductio ad absurdum* – if the Old Testament were not valid, then killing would be permitted, and concluding with the dramatic statement that worse than breaking the law not to kill is the adoration of images – is a telling example of his polemical extremism. On the same question, Luther, who also sometimes used the method of *reductio ad absurdum*, was as we know, much more subtle.

Karlstadt was never a 'Judaizer' in the strict sense, but the radicalism of his arguments (which was attended by much less extremism in the doctrine) made him, in the opinion of his contemporaries, and also of many Reformation historians, a classic representative of sectarian fundamentalism. His treatise against images and his role in Wittenberg in 1522 and later in Orlamünde linked his name once and for all with iconoclasm. However, his influence on the debate over religious art was not great. Neither in Zwingli nor in Calvin do we perceive his inspiration. On the other hand, Karlstadt did influence the short treatise of the young Swiss reformer Ludwig Hätzer, *The Judgement of God . . . on how One ought to conduct Oneself with Regard to Idols and Images* (Zurich, 1523).[16] Hätzer was initially a supporter of Zwingli but gradually became more radical and moved towards Anabaptism. He was theologically unprepared to take up such a complex problem as the image question. Both in its biblical hermeneutics and even in particular expressions his treatise repeats many of the themes and terms (e.g. calling churches with images 'pits of murderers') of Karlstadt's *On the Abolition of Images*. However, some elements (definition of 'idol', the attack on the corporeality of religious images) received independent treatment. Hätzer placed an even stronger emphasis on the polemic with Gregory the Great's idea of images as 'books of the laity'. The convergences predominated, however. Let us quote one typical example. Karlstadt stated: 'Even if all the images of the world are assembled, they will not help you in one sigh for God'; while Hätzer varied this as: 'All of the images on earth assembled together cannot make you by even a hairbreadth more like or closer to God.'[17]

ZWINGLI: ICONOPHOBIA AND POLITICAL MANOEUVRING

The great Swiss reformer Ulrich Zwingli went through his reformation turning-point in 1518–19 and by 1520 already occupied a separate position of importance in the Reformation movement. If we had to define his theology by one basic concept, then 'humanistic spiritualism' would be probably the most apt definition. Earlier contacts with humanists had deepened Zwingli's philological interests and inclined him to study not only the Bible – which he considered as the only foundation of the Christian faith – but also patristic and classical literature.[18] He emphasized more strongly than Luther the necessity for complete abolition of the Mass. The dominant feature of his position, however, was a special kind of spiritualist theology, though different from the one espoused by Karlstadt. In Zwingli's view, nothing based on corporeal elements can lead to salvation. Zwingli's spiritualism manifested itself primarily in his Eucharistic doctrine, but also left a visible imprint on his doctrine of justification and his many deliberations on the liturgy.

Of all the reformers Zwingli was the most political. For him the Gospel was a call to practical action. Though embroilment in politics was to be the cause of his defeat and death in the battle of Kappel (1531), he was until then quite successful as a politician. In the very complicated situation created by the image controversy in Zurich, Zwingli managed with great acumen gradually to implement his programme.

In the years 1518–22 various reformation problems began to take shape in Zwingli's mind. The view of most scholars, who saw in Zwingli a similar theological development to that of Luther, was challenged by Fritz Schmidt-Clausing, who stressed the primacy of liturgical problems over the questions of fundamental theology:[19] a position to which I do not subscribe. Moreover, there existed in Zwingli up to a certain moment a peculiar hiatus between doctrinal changes and their liturgical consequences; this concerned primarily the cult of saints and of the Virgin. In the second phase of his evolution, from January 1523 on, this hiatus began to shrink dramatically, largely under the influence of the increasing role of spiritualism in Zwingli's thought.

Let me return to my starting-point and state that Zwingli rather quickly worked out his doctrine of 'justification by faith', which rejected the attainment of salvation through works. Closely connected with it was his rejection of the cult of saints and all its appendages, a cult that in his view was based less on idolatry pure and simple than on the vain hope of attaining justification thereby.[20] Despite this, Zwingli saw in the cult of saints also a further problem: namely, its connection with the notion of the 'intercession of saints', which negated the mediating role of Christ. At the beginning of 1523 Zwingli began to be interested in the image question. Around that time he was asked for advice in the case of a certain Frau Göldli from Lucerne.

This story,[21] which will be discussed in more detail in Chapter 3, can serve as a paradigm of the consequences for the question of images of Reformation justification doctrine. In the eyes of Zwingli the fact that Frau Göldli tried to attain salvation by erecting the statue of a saint weighed more heavily than the fact that she thereby furthered the cult of saints. In this early phase he was thus inclined to see the phenomena of the cult of saints more from a fundamental perspective and less under the category of idolatrous abuse. The Göldli incident also opened his eyes to the whole tangle of pragmatic problems connected with an eventual abolition of religious images. Zwingli was thus better prepared than the other great reformers to consider the juridical aspects of impending changes (such as the right of donors to withdraw endangered objects which they had donated).

In the summer and early autumn of 1523 several iconoclastic incidents took place in Zurich and its vicinity (in Stadelhofen).[22] Zwingli had come out publicly in the summer against the cult of images and now saw the spectre of an emergent revolutionary iconoclasm. In these months Ludwig Hätzer's treatise (discussed above) also appeared and, under the circumstances, unquestionably helped to inspire iconoclastic actions. Zwingli was absolutely determined not to allow uncontrolled iconoclastic outbreaks which might have played into the hand of the still powerful, if progressively weakening, Catholic faction. Public debates were sometimes used in the Reformation to resolve a conflict or defuse a tense situation. Zwingli was thus the prime mover among those who proposed a public debate on the question of images. The debate was held on 26–28 October 1523, with the participation of the clergy, leading reformers and a large number of Zurich burghers.

The dispute was initiated by Leo Jud,[23] a friend of Zwingli's. He was followed by Ludwig Hätzer, one of the most radical of the Reformation activists, who called for a ban on all images without exception – an extreme standpoint which brings to mind Muslim aniconism. The next speaker was the pastor Heinrich Lüti, whose role in this well-staged and pre-planned debate was to play the devil's advocate. He recited the traditional casuist arguments which defended the legitimacy of images on the grounds of the existence of 'images' in the Old Testament (the brazen serpent, the cherubs on the Ark of the Covenant). He admitted, however, that idolatrous abuse did take place in regard to such images, though he characteristically chose the most extreme example of the adoration of the golden calf. Reference to these biblical examples provoked a response from Leo Jud, who devoted considerable attention to the image of the brazen serpent. Looking at it from a prefigurational standpoint, he put forward the view, unquestionably influenced by spiritualist ideas, that thanks to Christ's Redemption immortality had replaced mortal things, and internal cult had replaced external forms. The latter was a reference to the antithetical pair 'internal/external' often used by iconophobes in the image debate. Christ, as the 'living serpent', had taken the place of the brazen serpent; this was another overt reference to antithetical concepts. Jud thus regarded the physical presence of Christ as having put an end to the need for religious painting and to its legitimacy. The cherubs on the Ark of Covenant Jud deftly characterized as a kind of ornament without the status of images. After Jud came Konrad Schmid, who concentrated on the images of saints and emphasized that faith in their intercession was unacceptable. He did stress, however, that one should refrain from too sudden a reduction of the visual forms of this cult.

Zwingli, who was the last to speak, thus already had a ready frame of reference. He argued rhetorically against any delay in the removal of images. Referring to the arguments of Schmid and taking up the problem of St Paul's liberal position on pagan ceremonies in Athens, Zwingli stated that tolerance of the customs of pagans was one thing and leniency in the face of the errors of the 'weak' another. For the latter, statues and images were a great danger.

The dispute ended with apparently no clear decisions but with an indication of the line to be followed: Zwingli was asked to write a statement on the issue, which he did in November 1523 (A Brief Christian Introduction). In December that year the participants in the disputation met once more and issued a memorandum (*Advice on the Mass and Images*) advising the demolition of all altars, the abolition of processions and that donors be asked to retrieve works donated by them or their families. The town council hesitated to take the final step and Zwingli – sure of his final victory – did not persist in the matter. The final decision to remove all images in Zurich was taken on 15 June 1524, and in two momentous weeks in July all Zurich churches were purged of 'idolatry'[24] – without, however, any actual iconoclasm – and became thus as Zwingli put it 'beautifully white'. Only the stained-glass windows survived. The whole, seemingly hesitant, process was a masterpiece of moderate tactics.

Zwingli expounded his views on the image question in many publications and shorter statements, of which the *Brief Reply given to Valentin Compar* (1524/5) provides the most lucid and pertinent analysis.

Zwingli categorically states that images are against the First Commandment, since they primarily weaken faith in one God. He also questioned the Lutheran analysis of the First Commandment, with its distinction between a prohibition of 'adoration' and a permissible 'making' of images. But then he shifts his attention away from the law of Moses: like Calvin later, Zwingli realized that the core of the matter in the question of images resided in the necessity of placing one's faith in God alone. Karlstadt's preoccupation with the Old Law was alien to him.

The Swiss reformer started from a dynamic understanding of the notion of idolatry. For him – and here a certain convergence with Luther may be discerned – idolatry is the result of a subjective process. Though he began with the assumption that all people by nature have a certain inclination towards idolatry, only some of the internal images become real 'idols' as a result of human actions. Zwingli's position here did indeed vacillate: sometimes he was inclined to condemn unequivocally internal images, while at others he was willing to relativize his judgement.

Zwingli devoted much attention to the images of the saints, and his starting-point here was pronouncedly theocentric: 'this is idolatry of the maddest kind, diminishing the glory of God and depraving consciences'.[25] Moreover, this cult inspired the greatest number of idolatrous acts such as prostration or the burning of votive candles before images: 'Let us take the image of St Anne in Stammheim. Did people go to visit it before it hung there? No. And now, after it has been burned, do they visit it? Certainly not.'[26] Zwingli here manifestly underestimated the specific auratic attraction of miraculous images such as that of St Anne in Stammheim. As many sources confirm, pilgrimages to places where such miraculous images once existed continued for decades after their iconoclastic destruction. The cult of saints, Zwingli continued, has no basis in the Scriptures and 'we have ascribed to these pious deceased Christians what is due to God alone'. This constitutes an injury not only to God but also to the saints: 'Was it right that you should have had recourse to the help of St Peter, Michael, Gertrude or Barbara? No, you ought not to make idols of them!'[27] Zwingli indicated that there was some similarity between the cult of saints and the cult of ancient gods and heroes, suggesting the fictitious origins of many saints. A few years later his collaborator and successor Heinrich Bullinger, basing himself on the writing of Lactantius, would state emphatically that 'what Jupiter, Mars and the other gods were for the pagans, the saints are for us Christians'.[28] Pursuing a byway of the problem, Zwingli also attacked the 'indecorous' representation of saints: 'Here stands Magdalene so voluptously painted that she incites licentiousness ... there stand Sebastian, Maurice and the pious John the Evangelist looking like lords, warriors and pimps.'[29] Continuing his remarks on the transgressions of the doctrine of decorum, Zwingli condemned the frequent degradation of saints to the role of figures holding coats of arms.

In Zwingli's polemics against the abuses of religious art, we find also numerous remarks about the purpose of expenditure on church art. In the first place this money should go for the needs of the poor, since only the clergy (and, some of Zwingli's supporters added, the artists) gain by the cult of images. He also devoted some attention to the motives of the donors, which he viewed sceptically, stressing the peculiar mixture of pride and vanity involved. Moreover, he related their deeds to the specific theological category of hypocrisy. As a politician, however, he took these matters most seriously and recognized the right of ownership originating from family foundations and donations.

One of the basic points of Zwingli's theology was the dramatic question 'God or creatures?'. This question also jointly determined the distinction – in which the cult of images played a major role – between true and false religion. 'If we put our trust in creatures (persons, human works), then we cease to trust God.'[30] Here Zwingli's spiritualism resurfaces.

Typical of this attitude was the strong Nestorian fear of uniting the divine and the human, which characterized Zwingli's Christology and led him to draw sharp distinctions between the 'spirit' and the 'flesh' in his debate with Luther over the Eucharistic presence, between the sign and the 'visible' and 'invisible' church in his ecclesiology, and between the 'inner' and 'outer' word of Scripture.[31]

In a letter to Martin Bucer (3 June 1524) Zwingli uttered the famous phrase 'What you give the senses you take away from the Spirit'.

Zwingli's spiritualism also had clear consequences for the Christological context of the image controversy. Harking back to the arguments of the Byzantine iconoclasts, Zwingli categorically stated that neither crucifixes nor other images of Christ should be placed in churches. This problem, however, caused him serious doubts and he admitted that the argument referring to the Incarnation could be the 'greatest obstacle' for the opponents of images. Zwingli, however, was of the opinion that Christ ought not to be represented, since divinity cannot be shown. The most important things in Christ thus cannot be shown.[32] On the other hand Zwingli did not want to push this rigorism too far. He felt the weakness of this line of argument and therefore partially loosened his prohibition by allowing in private homes images depicting the humanity of Christ (though in later Swiss practice this was to turn out of little importance). He was wholly unwilling to tolerate crucifixes. The problem of the Incarnation was to trouble the adherents and allies of Zwingli for some time: Bullinger reiterated Zwingli's view that after the Resurrection Christ could not be corporeally depicted; Martin Bucer on the other hand proclaimed in his (pantheistically conceived) works a spiritual vision of Christ that would have made any religious images superfluous.

Zwingli introduced a fundamental distinction between images in the home and those in churches. In homes one can keep images 'of a historical nature', and this also applies to the category of 'biblical histories'. In churches every work of art, with the exception of 'ornaments' (though Zwingli, perhaps intentionally, never specified the exact meaning of this term) becomes an idol. Zwingli was ready to make an exception only for the stained-glass windows very popular in sixteenth-century Switzerland. (However, a century later the English Puritan William Prynne was to warn sternly: 'Popery may creep in at a glasse-window'.[33]) A sculpture of Charlemagne inside a church becomes an idol (like Luther, Zwingli did not examine the question of tombstones) whereas placed outside on the tower of the Great Minster it will not become an object of adoration. To qualify somewhat the negative resonance of his remarks he felt constrained to state emphatically that 'pretty pictures and statues as such give me much pleasure'.[34]

From these views, with spiritualism as the ever-present background, a specific gradation of the harmfulness of religious art can be deduced, a gradation which characteristically depends on the specific material illusion projected by the object. The least questionable are the aforementioned stained-glass windows, then come pictures, and then sculptures, which are the worst of all. The difference separating Zwingli from Karlstadt and Calvin – who would not have deigned to consider such a gradation – are clearly perceptible here, as well as his unintentional proximity to the practices of the Eastern Orthodox Church with its total ban on church sculptures.

On the other hand, Zwingli treats 'idolatrous abuse' as a category *per se* and ascribes to it a certain role – though a much weaker one than does Luther – especially in deciding whether a given work is an 'idol' or not. So we can find words in Zwingli that Luther might have written: 'If you understand that one should not seek help in sculptures, images and allegories, in represented things and should not worship them, then the war is already won.'[35]

On the basis of the sources cited, we might be inclined to see the reformer's stance on the image question in the context of a certain humanist spiritualism (a term which should be used with considerable caution, however), partially derived from Erasmus. But even within this complex of ideas Zwingli's evolution after 1522 takes a special direction. For Erasmus, both the ceremonial religious practices of the late Middle Ages and the cult of images were primarily evidence of 'false views': that is, the result of ignorance caused by a decline in education. Without questioning Erasmus' diagnosis, Zwingli, however, was inclined to see in ceremonial and liturgical rules disrespect for divine laws.

The change that appears here in the qualitative evaluation of the human condition is closely connected with the new humanistic form of education, in which the Protestant law became the real will of God understood existentially. That is why pushing it aside by 'human law' is recognized as an especially flagrant offence against the will of God.[36]

Zwingli smoothly moved to a new position and never broke with Erasmus as drastically as did Luther. For our subject-matter the differences outlined here are important in so far as they show how many different paths – often loosely connected with one another – lead to iconophobia.

It is rather surprising that the image problem was not on the agenda in direct contacts and theological disputes between the Swiss reformers and Luther and the Wittenberg circle. For this period, however, we have a detailed description of Luther as seen by Zwingli. This characterization was written in 1527, just before Zwingli became entirely absorbed by the dispute over the Eucharist. Despite the fact that the image problem was by then past history both for Zurich and for Wittenberg, there is a clear reference here to Luther's position on this subject. Zwingli begins with an almost ecstatic encomium on Luther's personality and recognition of his crucial role:

> no one in the entire camp of Israel cared to oppose the enemy openly. . . . Then you yourself, as the faithful David . . . took the weapon in your own hand. You yourself were Hercules, who appeared at a time of need, where there was danger. It was you who killed the wild bull, crushed . . . Antaeus and punished Cacus. Speaking briefly, if you had also removed the images . . . if you had not eaten corporeally in the bread an imagined body . . . then not only would you have cleaned the Augean stables but you would have carried heaven on your back.[37]

It is significant that the image problem comes first. Zwingli was never really aware which religious images Luther was willing to tolerate, but he suspected him of accepting rather too many 'papist' pictures. Worse still, in Zwingli's eyes the lack of clear directives led in Saxony to a paradoxical situation: 'In Saxony one man throws images out of the church, another carries them back to the church, one steals pictures, another turns them with their face to the wall and a third one overthrows them'.[38]

Zwingli's conception of *adiaphora* was very narrow[39] and had many qualifications attached, primarily the assertion that idolatrous practices and abuses absolutely preclude the possibility of granting even this status to 'innocent' objects like unidolatrous pictures. The notion 'abuse does not invalidate use' (*abusus non tollit usus*) was alien to him. Characteristically, even where he allowed the existence of religious images (as in the case of biblical paintings at home or of stained-glass windows) he avoided calling them adiaphorist solutions. This logical inconsistency was criticized by the moderately iconophobic Martin Bucer, who pointed out that images outside the church should in any case be designated *adiaphora* or else be banned too.

When it came to general reflection on the position of the image question in the whole complex of Reformation theology, Zwingli shared with other great reformers the conviction that its importance was grossly inflated. The fact is that Zwingli, to a far greater degree than other reformers, was interested in the domain of liturgy proper; moreover, he wanted to abolish the Mass immediately. In Zurich the potentially dangerous image question blocked the process of change in these matters for a time. Zwingli saw this rather clearly and lamented the fact. He would thus certainly subscribe theoretically to Luther's view that too much time was being devoted to the image question. Zwingli's views considerably influenced the removal of images in many Swiss cantons as well as in some cities of Upper Germany; his dilatory tactics, however, were less often followed. His collaborator and successor Heinrich Bullinger, in particular, was to popularize these views and represent the Zwinglian position in the question of images.[40] In his writings we find a stronger historical basis, especially in many passages relating to the cult of images in antiquity and the Byzantine image controversy. However, he added little of theological substance.

JOHN CALVIN: THEOLOGIAN OF THE INEFFABLE, DISTANT GOD

In presenting the views of the great French reformer John Calvin (1509–64) on the image question the biographical–historical aspect will be almost entirely omitted. On the image question Calvin was perhaps the only one of the great reformers who did not find himself under the pressure of events – Geneva had already abolished religious art in 1535, and he was not forced to proceed tactically. Calvin's theology unfolded as a logical, self-contained system with only few references to the works of other reformers.

In the question of images there are no references to Luther, Karlstadt or Zwingli. Calvin valued Luther highly, although he differed from him on many points. On the other hand he had less regard for Zwingli, being repelled by the lack of order reigning in his theological writings.

Being a very rigorous thinker himself, Calvin worked out in the famous *Institutes of the Christian Religion* (1536–59) the most systematic theological exposition in Protestantism. Except on the Eucharist question, on which he took a position similar to Zwingli's, Calvin's theological views did not evolve much after his espousal of the Reformation; nor did his view on the question of images.

Calvin's theological system was perhaps less original and differentiated than Luther's, but it was more cohesive. In the popular view of it, his system can be reduced to a rigid predestinarianism. This is obviously an oversimplification, but we can take this concept as the starting-point of a short presentation of the directions of Calvin's thought, for it did exert an important influence on his theological approach to the image question. To a lesser extent than Luther, Calvin referred to non-intrinsic constructions, though they sometimes appear in his system and – as the concept of corruption – modify the rigidity of his general assumptions and premises.

The Genevan reformer was first and foremost a preacher of the authority of God. For him the commandments of the Scriptures were primarily expressions of God's majesty based on his possession of eternal truth. Calvin's rigorous concept of predestination (discernible also, in a much less binding form, in Luther's pronouncements) turned the notion of 'faith' into an immanent value not confirmed by the relation of the believer to God. The Lutheran dialectics of justification by faith, in which the German overcame theological rigorism, was rather alien to Calvin, who understood 'Christian conscience' and 'Christian freedom' very statically as a specific agreement with the commandments of God contained in the Scriptures.

Especially characteristic of Calvin's views was his understanding of the role of Christ:

> With Calvin Christ is always examined together with God, they form an objective whole, we can approach Christ through spiritual meditation. On the other hand, in Luther

Christ is seen first and foremost from the side of his relation to the individual believer... here too traces of predestinarianism are to be seen in Calvin.[41]

Both the abstract stability of his system and his lesser interest in Christology influenced Calvin's approach to the image question. We can also connect Calvin's interpretation of the concept of *adiaphora* with his dislike for intermediate concepts. He did not apply the concept to the image question at all, and in the other cases where it suggested itself as a solution he either dramatically restricted its application or rejected it totally. Indifferent, intermediate elements have to be abandoned if there is the slightest danger of their giving offence. Luther, as we know, in a different and much more skilful way took up the problems of Christian conscience emerging here. As a rule Calvin gave the notion of 'ceremony' a negative connotation. His lack of tolerance for liturgical diversity also had its source in strict adherence to the Bible. Despite this, Calvin did not succumb to the temptation of resting upon the directives of Old Testament 'ceremonial legislation' but connected his views on the question of these ceremonies to an overall theocentric perspective.

The theocentrism of Calvin's theology was also manifest in a problem indirectly connected with ceremonies: namely, the organization of Christian communities. Here as well, starting from premises different from Luther's, especially from the question of the form of God's power over people, Calvin with greater consistency and clarity presents an authoritarian model of a 'particular church', which owes its ultimate shape to the direct interference of God in human affairs. What is more, by relating all matters to the concept of the glory of God, Calvin insisted on subordinating all ceremony to that notion. Though he concentrated only on the problems of the Geneva Church, he also expressed the hope that Geneva would become the model for the universal church in all things.

For these reasons the spiritualistic elements in Calvin's theology (contained *in nuce* in his approach to ceremony and Christology) were completely stifled by his peculiar type of 'spiritual realism'. That is why one cannot really speak of spiritualistic elements in the context of Calvin's approach to the image problem. Ernst Saxer[42] was unquestionably right when he rejected an antithetical pair of concepts suggested by Alexandre Ganoczy,[43] namely, body vs. spirit, as the decisive key to the theology of the young reformer. Saxer proposed an entire series of other oppositions to define Calvin's theology, quite righly noting that the aforementioned pair of concepts first and foremost would serve as a link with Zwinglianism, which would be untenable both from the historical and from the fundamental theological point of view. Saxer's observation is fully confirmed in a scrutiny of Calvin's attitude towards the image problem.

In Calvin's theology the notions of the majesty and glory of God (*soli Deo gloria*) were fundamental. Whereas with Luther the 'visibility of God experienced through the Passion and cross' enables the believer to give up attempts to grasp the 'invisible God', with Calvin Christology – viewed through the prism of the doctrine of predestination – even deepened the ultimate mystery of God. The most beautiful and fundamental passages of the *Institutes of the Christian Religion* are those in which Calvin praises the omnipotence and greatness of God, while at the same time emphasizing his immeasurable distance from us.

Hence Calvin's pronouncements on religious art refer in the first place to the relationship of God to humanity, which, however, is a static one. The making of images is primarily a misunderstanding of the essence of God:

> We are similar to God only in our souls, and no image can represent him. That is why people who try to represent the essence of God are madmen. For even their souls of little worth cannot be represented. God is spirit – says the Scripture – and yet they want to give him a body. . . . Since God has no similarity to those shapes by means of which people attempt to represent him, then all attempts to depict him are an impudent affront . . . to his majesty and glory.[44]

Calvin put this even more forcefully in the *Sermon on the First Letter to the Corinthians*:

> So here we have the source of all the idolatries that have ever come into being, and this happens when people believe that God will not become close to them if they do not have some visible sign. Why is it that the Papists cannot do without images, statues and similar things? Because it seems to them that God will move away from them if they do not have there [in the place of worship] some figure.[45]

Calvin here gave a characteristic injunction to maintain distance, which can be best described by the German term *Abstandsbefehl*, and applies this not only to art. God in his essence is imperceptible and cannot be described: 'All the signs that he has ever chosen for showing himself to people had this feature, that they made people aware of the imperceptibility of his being.'[46]

Calvin here makes perhaps the most characteristic use of the argument concerning the existence of an image (cherubs) on the Ark of the Covenant. This, which was repeated many times over by iconodules, meant little until then and really did not go beyond an ordinary 'casuistic' biblical argument. While the iconodules happily argued that it showed that 'religious images' as such were allowed in the Old Testament, the iconophobes tried to classify the cherubs not as an image but as a kind of 'ornament'. Calvin attempted a new interpretation, which went beyond these assertions. The placing of the cherubs on the Ark of the Covenant was really like a veil protecting the majesty of God from the eyes of the people:

> through this covering of the Ark they stopped the human
> eye from contemplating God[47]. . . . If the Papists say that
> there were images of cherubs on the Ark, this really refers
> to . . . the necessity of closing our eyes when the need comes
> to have recourse to God and of not approaching him except
> through the mediation of his voice.[48]

The role of this Old Testament exemplum in Calvin's theory (he returned to it several times) can be compared only with the role of the brazen-serpent passage in Luther's discourse. The majesty of God, according to Calvin, is 'too remote for people's gaze'. Calvin condemns the belief that elements of the divine *energeia* are found in some statue or image less than the far worse sin of merely attempting to compare God and objects – the glory of God is incomparable.[49] The reformer consistently sharpens the concept of God to those limits in which neither human 'similarity to God' nor even the signs of God in the Old Testament can become a pretext for his visual representation: 'For God forbade . . . the making of any images representing him, since they would falsify his glory and change his truth into falsehood.'[50]

One could multiply quotations from the *Institutes of the Christian Religion* and other writings testifying to the importance for Calvin of the concept of the 'glory or majesty of God' – a concept which, by contrast to Luther, he did not understand as a relation. The glory of God is being thus belittled and denigrated by images and idolatrous cults; a similar idea can be found in Martin Bucer's tract against images of 1530, *That No Kind of Image is Permissible* (*Das Einigerlei Bild*).[51] For Calvin the concept of divine transcendence also spoke against attempts 'to enclose' God in the institutions and forms of the 'visible Church'. 'God is not contained in the visible Church, but is above all the heavens.'[52] Incidentally, it might be added that the evolution of Calvin's views on the Eucharist also started from reflections on the problem of defining on the concrete 'local' presence of Christ in the Sacrament.

Calvin, by contrast to Luther, but like Karlstadt and to a lesser extent Zwingli, was not inclined to show any leniency towards the 'weak in faith', either in theory or in practice. As we can see from a discussion he conducted during the Berne dispute over predestination in 1551, he simply did not recognize this category of the faithful at all. That can explain the fact that he so forcefully attacked the Gregorian argument on 'images as books for the unlearned'. For Calvin this is not an important argument at all, as it was for Zwingli, for it was situated on the level of practical theology. Nonetheless, even in denying it he used arguments that went beyond the topic of 'books for the laity': 'Their final subterfuge is the statement that these are books for the poor in spirit . . .; I do not see what advantage simpletons could derive from images, unless it were that they would become anthropomorphizers . . . and that they would image a corporeal God.'[53] In rebutting this argument Calvin referred both to the inscrutability of God and to the affirmation of the role of the word (in the entire gamut of its meaning in those times: i.e. from the Word of God to the spoken and written word as a means of communication), since it is by means of words that God 'descends to the level of common people'.[54] At the same time, in his remarks on images we also find an opposition of the body to the spirit characteristic of Zwingli – that is, of spiritual religion contrasted with the tendency of sinful man to anthropomorphize it; but this is only one of several lines of argument, and hardly the most important.

Thus the opposition of the word to the image gains a special significance. The word, being obviously a synonym for Scripture and religion as a whole (in Calvin there is even a certain sharpening of Luther's 'faith from hearing'), is opposed to the 'dumb statues'. It is in the image question, among other places, that we find in

Calvin a remarkable 'apologia for hearing', which perhaps
Giuseppe Scavizzi defined most precisely in this context:

> In Calvin the ear seems to acquire an almost divine conno-
> tation, the eye only a human and earthly one, both on
> the level of philosophical deliberations and ordinary mental
> associations. In fact for Calvin the ear stands for the soul,
> the eye for the senses.[55]

The condemnation of 'Roman pomp' went hand in hand with the
condemnation of the 'cult of the external', which was contrasted
with 'spiritual knowledge'. Also connected with this was an apologia of simplicity.[56] Art itself easily can become one of the instruments of Satan that he uses to deceive people, who by their nature
are prone to pomp, the cult of the external, and anthropomorphization of God's truth. Calvin looked at the entire cult of images
theocentrically as a negation of the attributes of God, and for this
reason he was not inclined to devote much attention to attempts
to relativize the ban on images.

Calvin's analysis of the Second Commandment plays an inordinately important role. Probably independently of the Zurich circle,
Calvin also adopted a way of enumerating the Commandments
which was different from the traditional list being followed by
Lutherans. Thanks to this change, the ban on images being classi-
fied as a separate Second Commandment, the importance of the
Old Testament prohibition of religious art became very clear.
Calvin had decided to make the analysis in such a way as not to
be accused of succumbing to the prohibitions of Old Testament
laws. That is why he emphasizes several times that the divine
prohibitions of the Old Testament always contain something more
than what flows from their mere letter: that they are only a
starting-point and that their interpretation must be made in the
context of the entire Bible. For this reason Calvin makes a longer
analysis, whose conclusion – after stating that the Second Commandment without doubt refers to 'idolatrous images' – says:
'God should be adored in spirit' and not through material things.
It is characteristic that Calvin in equal measure quotes passages
from the New Testament (John 1:18; I Timothy 1:17) in support
of the ban on images.

In his analysis Calvin emphasizes arguments based on external
factors more strongly than might be expected. In this context he
states that the ancient pagans were aware that they were adoring

a material thing and not God and that this practice was opposed by the law of Moses. Calvin thereby undermined the Nicaean distinction between *latria* and *doulia* ('adoration' and 'veneration'), and – starting from this statement – he strongly accented the inappropriateness of all symbols of God made by human hands:

> Neither do I want to pass over the fact that they [the papists] try to use an imagined distinction. They state that the adoration which they show to images is not real adoration (*latria*) but only veneration of a lower order (*doulia*). According to them, this veneration or service to images can be given or shown to images without affronting God. They regard themselves as innocent, since they are only servants and not worshippers of images. As though service were something less than adoration – in reality it is even the reverse. . . . In fact they differ in nothing from the idolators whom in this way, as though under compulsion, they want to condemn. But in this way they cannot cut themselves off from idolators . . . for, as though in competition with them, they invent new symbols which, in their opinion, represent God and they create them with their own hands.[57]

As has been said above, Christology is accorded less importance in Calvin's theological system. This appears nowhere so clearly as in the image question. Calvin speaks the whole time about the affront to God, while very rarely mentioning images of Christ. He firmly rejects representations of Christ and the crucifix ('the devilish form of Christ'); however, he puts less emphasis on the fact that the divinity of Christ is impossible to represent and treats such images more as an assault on his 'divine majesty'. The question of incarnation as an argument does not appear in Calvin's frame of reference. For him the 'whole Christ' was contained in the Resurrection and the return to the Father, since we no longer know the corporeal Jesus and can only grasp him 'spiritually'; Calvin completely rejected the Lutheran Christ *pro me*, understood as an attempt to visualize the earthly Christ.

In Calvin the lack of a Christological frame of reference is responsible for the fact that his remarks about the traditions of the iconoclastic dispute and patristic revocations are occasional and unsystematic. Calvin quotes the alleged pronouncements of the participants in the Council of Nicaea (in fact all of them in a distorted form) on the basis of the less than iconodulic *Libri*

Carolini. These decisions of Western theologians in the period of Charlemagne, which distanced them to some extent from the excesses of the Byzantine cult of images, were discovered in 1549, and Calvin hurried to use them as arguments in the latter editions of his *Institutes* (conversely, the Roman Catholic Church put them temporarily on the Index). Calvin pointed to the low theological level of the Council; he attacked the Nicaean resolutions[58] most strongly for what he thought was a blasphemous attempt to recognize the image as the equivalent of the word. His other quotations from patristic literature mostly concern the anti-image commandment in the Decalogue, or the fact that the first 500 years of the Church were aniconic. From the traditional repertoire of iconophobic texts we find in Calvin references to Ephiphanius of Cyprus and to the small anti-image synod in the Spanish town of Elvira.

Calvin did not treat the notion of Old Testament ceremonies as a cohesive whole. He could accept some of them, but most ceremonies he rejected as inadequate to the majesty of God or as evidence of 'Judaizing'. To this whole domain he applied also his conception of 'corruption': that is, of the tendency of people to distort God's commandments, an inclination which in a large measure resulted in the anthropomorphization of religious concepts. According to Calvin, it was in the biblical story of the erection, adoration and subsequent removal of the brazen serpent that people's inclination to 'corruption' was revealed.[59] While Luther emphasized that only the deplorable fact of 'cultic abuse' caused and justified the removal of the brazen serpent, Calvin on the other hand stated that this episode had to end that way owing to mankind's innate tendency to anthropomorphize and visualize religion, and that this was the logical fate even of forms instituted by God. In the rich exegetic tradition of this biblical passage – a minor *locus classicus* of the image controversy – Calvin's approach is distinguished by its rigid consistency.

Calvin revealed a similar understanding of 'corruption' in another theological concept: namely, the notion of 'miracle'.[60] For some astounding reason Calvin did not negate miracles on principle; however, the extent to which he subjected this concept to limitations and provisos of verification was tantamount to suspending its validity in theological terms. With special insistence, he tried to demonstrate that 'image miracles' are the product of a 'corrupted cult' and a by-product of the special category of 'superstition'. Referring expressly to the 'papists' image-miracles', Calvin also attacked all the miracles connected with the cult of saints' relics.

Calvin also did not reject totally the concept of the 'visible Church'. Despite many reservations, he upheld its validity, if somewhat defensively. Aware that the opponents of this concept were to be found chiefly among the radicals and Anabaptists, he took care that his fight against images should not be interpreted as a total negation of that metaphoric construction. Sometimes he went further than that: he even expressly allowed 'decoration' as such to grace the buildings of the 'visible Church'. In a time when many Protestants, even moderate ones, regarded all kinds of 'ornament' as superfluous, Calvin stated that 'some ornaments consistent with divine worship are not useless in church if they incline the faithful to practise holy things with humility, devotion and worship'.[61]

In Calvin's position we find a fusion of two concepts which thread their way through the entire sixteenth-century image dispute: namely, 'idolatry' and 'superstition'. The latter was rather more important for Calvin, for it better showed how human misconceptions grow up around the cult. Hence it served him as an operational concept. 'The manner in which Calvin uses this concept shows that he is more inclined to regard superstition as the product of the active practice of idolatry', wrote Ernst Saxer.[62] Generally speaking, however, the semantic scope of the two terms largely overlapped.[63]

More essential in this context, however, would be a scrutiny of Calvin's interpretation of the Old Testament. We can generally say that Calvin differs from Zwingli primarily as regards the attitude towards spiritualism; while the attitude towards Old Testament laws is the main element that sets him apart from Karlstadt.[64] It is not so much the rigorous interpretation of biblical laws that has Calvin maintain his ban on images, as a fundamental evaluation to be detected in the Decalogue – of mankind's perpetual inclination to degrade the service of God to a service of idols. In this sense, paradoxically, Calvin's point of view is both theocentric (the glory of God as the main determinant) and anthropocentric. However, the anthropocentric moments outlined here were not able to counterbalance the theocentricity of Calvin's doctrine, which manifests itself also in his anti-image stance.

With Calvin the motif of the condemnation of luxurious art,

the fight against luxury and 'indecency' (obscenitas) did not figure largely in the context of the image dispute; on the other hand – and this is where his pragmatism showed itself – it played a more important role in his few remarks and commentaries on church architecture and decoration. The fight against 'Roman pomp' and 'fallacious ceremonies' should, however, be separated from this strand, though there were close connections here which Calvin pointed out:

> In what manner will the temple of God be properly used? . . . This will not happen when various rites are celebrated with great pomp, when the temple is full of gilding, gold and silver . . . for the glory of the temple of God does not consist in this. . . . God cannot be grasped in visible houses of worship, magnificent altars or ceremonies.[65]

In this question Calvin alludes to the Lutheran concept 'in the sight of God'. Since pomp achieves nothing in the sight of God (on the contrary, it is an attempt to embody the spiritual relation man/God), one ought to bridle 'pride and vanity'. Despite this, Calvin skilfully avoids certain dangerous antithetic concepts that could link his theology to radical currents. To be sure, he did say: 'You are too preoccupied with the walls, seeking the Church of God in the beauty of the building.'[66] Then followed a longer argument on the necessity of moderation in the decoration of buildings and of allocating money to help the poor and needy. At the same time, however, Calvin, who opposed the radical Reformation, clearly cuts himself off from the ideal of the apostolic poverty and rejects the notion of 'apostolic simplicity'. As his controversy with Theodore Beza shows,[67] Calvin was very wary of patristic arguments, even though he espoused the view that the first five centuries of Christianity were aniconic. He undoubtedly shared with Luther a conviction about the many mistakes committed by the early Church. To eschew any similarity to the radical Reformation, Calvin never referred to the motif of the 'church in a barn' which Luther used, somewhat rhetorically, to explain his doctrine of the congregation of the faithful.

Apart from some rather general exhortations to moderation, Calvin did not leave behind many concrete instructions on the construction, structure and outfitting of churches. He probably shared Luther's belief that in the first place they should be 'adapted to preaching'. They should contain no images or crucifixes whatsoever. The only furnishings were to be inscriptions from the Bible: 'We ought to have the Law of God in writing, we ought to have sentences on the walls like pictures; but let this not be done to justify ourselves – as though we were paying off God.' Inscriptions were for Calvin the manifestation of the voice of God; his directives in that matter were to exert a profound influence on the decoration of Calvinist churches. The particular formulation about 'paying off God' vividly demonstrates that Calvin too used this fundamental Protestant assumption to negate the donating of religious images. Going beyond the subject of religious art, there is an interesting strand in Calvin's thought about architecture. He stressed the importance of 'elegance and splendour' in the construction of a city; moreover, he emphasized the necessity of 'conformity' between the structure of a city, the spirit and manners of the inhabitants and its architecture. What make his remarks all the more interesting are the clear references to the topos of the 'heavenly Jerusalem' combined with rather veiled references to Geneva itself. Calvin stopped short of proclaiming that Geneva represented an earthly model of the heavenly city. On a slightly different level he probably would not understand the concept of a 'utopian city', so popular in sixteenth-century literature and thought, since this would mean a deplorable secularization of the idea.[68] In the Protestant world, models of utopian cities – to mention only Johann Valentin Andreae's famous *Christianopolis* (1619) – became popular only after Calvin's death. Nonetheless, there obviously exists a certain affinity between the special atmosphere of the isolated Geneva, rigorously governed both in the religious and in the cultural sphere,[69] and models of utopian, social and architectonic order – an affinity which should be further explored.

The practical consequences of Calvin's stance can be grasped quite clearly. Calvinist churches were stripped of visual elements, only tablets with inscriptions from the Bible remaining. Though Calvin, somewhat contradictorily, allowed the keeping of holy images in private homes, his numerous negative pronouncements and the impact of his whole system predetermined their reduction in this case too. On the other hand, he left an open field for narrative biblical scenes – especially from the Old Testament – and for secular art. Of decisive importance was the removal of works of art from the sacral sphere, from places of worship; in profane places an image took on an entirely different meaning.

Some decades after Calvin's death his north German followers went so far in the so-called *Bremen Confession* as to recognize the right to keep images of Christ in private homes, for there was no danger of such images becoming the object of a cult. This was surely a logical development of Calvin's thought, though one which for doctrinal reasons he himself probably would not have supported. Calvin stated his position clearly: 'Certainly, it is permissible to make use of images; however, God wishes his temple to be freed from images. If in a secular place, however, we have a portrait or a representation of animals, this is not harmful to religion . . . even idols kept in such places are not worshipped.'[70] Thus in homes or public buildings of a secular type the faithful could keep or exhibit 'biblical stories'. This notion, which in the artistic practice of the sixteenth century exhibited a peculiar mixture of semi-secular and semi-religious subject-matter, is in reality the only one of this kind appearing in Calvin's deliberations on art, since 'histories'[71] have in his understanding certain educational merits which purely devotional pictures totally lack. What is more, in combating Roman religious cult, Calvin felt compelled to attack images of this kind hanging in churches, less on account of the fundamental ban on images than from the professed fear of their 'abuse'. 'Why do the Papists place images in the temple? Do they do so in order to learn about history? Not at all. It is not for history that the Papists have images, but only so that people will kneel here.'[72] On the other hand he emphasized that 'histories', and especially their pictorial realizations, could be often inaccurate – which, in his opinion, was an even stronger argument for restricting them to the secular sphere.

Calvin gave also a short definition of the scope and goals of art. His definition has a simplicity and laconic emphasis that is rarely encountered in the writings on art of that period. 'Hence all that we see can be imitated by painting.'[73] In the *Institutes* Calvin gave a more detailed account:

> As regards what can be painted or engraved, it is permissible to represent 'histories' as a memorial, or figures, or [to create] medals of animals, cities or countries. Instructive things or remembrances can be derived or depicted from them. As for the rest, I see no other purpose they can serve except pleasure.[74]

Thus Calvin regarded 'histories' or landscapes as the two main subjects of pictorial art. A similar view was espoused by Zwingli's successor Heinrich Bullinger in his tract against images of 1539, *On the Origin of Divine Worship and of False Images*.[75]

This specific configuration has understandably fascinated many scholars and cultural historians in the twentieth century. In their work Calvin appears as a kind of spiritual director of the realistic current in the painting of the Calvinistic Low Countries (Bullinger remains virtually unknown).[76] Whether his brief suggestions for painting landscapes were that much read or conscientiously followed remains another matter. After all, the realist tradition in the Netherlands culminating in the great age of Dutch seventeenth-century painting had iconographic and formal antecedents running all the way back through the sixteenth century.

Moreover, the influence of Calvin's directives proved to be not that great in Geneva either. The processes he had started there were not conducive to art at all. Thus in 1580 all biblical images – even in printed books – were banned. The great Calvinist historian of art Waldemar Deonna had to admit that the 'Calvinist conception very much hampered the development of art in Geneva'.[77] The few paintings executed before the eighteenth century, when Liotard put Geneva back on the artistic map, were mediocre, utilitarian works not deserving the epithet of realism. Of course we have to remember that Geneva even before Calvin had no great artistic tradition comparable to the Netherlands: it is a truism that without a suitable level of development of artistic culture, no directives of any kind can have a proper effect. That Dutch art on a general level profited, however, from the secularizing current inherent in Calvinism is, of course, another, quite well-known, matter.

In one specific artistic field Genevan Calvinism did exert a very profound influence: I am thinking of sepulchral art. Here, in fact, the few directives of Calvin – and still more the ostentatiously ascetic forms of his own funeral – resulted in a complete elimination of both the ceremonial itself and of all forms commemorating the departed through sepulchral artistic objects.[78] Genevan cemeteries were characterized by almost anonymous graves. That is the more striking since in the German territories under Calvinist influence we do not find such a total reduction. As regards Lutheran practice one can say that it was very different, in terms of both the often elaborate tombstones and the even more magnificent cemetery complexes in some Protestant cities (e.g. Halle).

As can be inferred from a scrutiny of the writings and documents in Geneva at that time, the ostentatious ascetism of the forms of burial was commonly regarded as consistent with the doctrine of the rejection of works, and as a fight against inappropriate luxury. Extant reports and protocols of the meetings of the Company of Pastors on this matter certainly make an unpleasant impression on us today, considering the bureaucratic and autocratic pedantry of their regulation of funeral ceremonies. In the context of the European situation of the sixteenth century, however, they are marked by a somewhat ostentatious, but unquestionably honest, egalitarian tendency.

EPILOGUE

When stating that Calvin did not have to take decisions on the question of images under the pressure of iconoclastic acts, I referred to the young and middle years of the Genevan reformer. In a cruel sequel, which put an end to many of his illusions, Calvin was confronted in the last decade of his life with iconoclasm and its destructive consequences. In 1561 news of the great iconoclastic campaigns in France began to reach Geneva. Calvin was shocked both by the fact of widespread, armed iconoclasm and by the many scandalous episodes connected with it. At that time Calvin's collaborator Theodore Beza was engaged in negotiations between moderate French Catholics (the so-called *politiques*) and French Huguenots concerning the question of images. A special Protestant–Catholic colloquy devoted to the problem of images was held in Saint-Germain (January 1562) which, although it ended without any formal agreement, showed that some Catholics were ready to make far-reaching concessions on the image question.[79] Calvin was thus rightly convinced that Huguenot iconoclasm was corrupting morals and, worse still, harming the cause of the Reformation in France. His reaction was unequivocal and forceful. Having learned about iconoclast destruction in Sauve, in 1561 he wrote with indignation about the attitude of the local Huguenot pastor:

> We speak of the foolish deed which was performed at Sauve in burning idols and pulling down a cross. We are very much surprised at such temerity in a man whose duty it was to moderate and restrain others. For, as we have heard, he

not only gave his consent to the deed (which was already too bad a thing) but he stirred up the people, being the most mutinous of all ... to maintain that he acted so in good conscience is an example of intolerable obstinacy.... God has never commanded the casting-down of idols, except to each in his own house, and in public to those he arms with authority.[80]

The last sentence reminds us of Luther's polemic with Karlstadt; there is also a clear distinction between the public cult and images in private houses. Calvin went even further: taking up a motif used mostly by Catholic polemicists, he declared that iconoclasm leads also to the illegal appropriation of public property: 'It is a double crime to plunder public property', as he formulated it. When commenting on the great iconoclastic disturbances in Lyon (13 May 1562) he stated with bitterness:

There was an inconsiderate zeal in devastating the temples as they have done, but ... it was done in the heat of passion.... But what can they say of plunder? By what title is it lawful to take away by force things which do not belong to any private person? ... We have been told that the booty which was taken from St John's church has been offered for sale to the highest bidder and sold for 3,600 livres.[81]

The emphasis Calvin puts on 'authoritarian' solutions to the iconoclast crisis is fully understandable in the light of what we know about the rigidly controlled Genevan theocracy. However, in France that solution was not possible, although the iconoclastic disturbances there played into the hands of Catholic extremists as Calvin rightly feared. In French Huguenot iconoclasm the fissure between fundamental reformation theology and the dynamics of mass action appeared very distinctly. The reformation process within a city could be controlled and iconoclasm averted: Luther in Wittenberg and Zwingli in Zurich had shown the way here. A mass movement on great territories with local leaders and a penchant for rituals of denigration and destruction could not be induced to moderation by the letters and interventions of even an impeccably iconophobic great reformer. That bitter lesson Calvin was to learn in the last years of his life.

3

Iconoclasm: rites of destruction

> But now may we see
> What Gods they be,
> Even puppets, maumets and elves.
> Thrown them down thrice,
> They cannot arise,
> Not once, to help themselves.
> (William Gray, *Fantasy of Idolatry*)

The iconoclasm of the Reformation was not only the by-product
of theological controversy; it was a remarkable historical and
cultural phenomenon with a complex structure. It brings up many
problems, not all of which can even be mentioned in this chapter.
The difficulties start with the term itself, for iconoclasm is both
a forceful and a somewhat ambiguous expression. In the strict
sense it means hostility to religious images (including sculptures),
a hostility that manifests itself in their destruction through a more
or less ostentatious public act. In this sense, obviously, a large
number of the events in Protestant lands cannot be regarded as
iconoclasm. We can speak only of a partial reduction of the use
of images and sculptures in the decor of churches in Lutheran
lands, and their complete elimination in Calvinist territories. If
these changes were carried out in a peaceful way – that is, if the
images and sculptures were taken off the walls and not destroyed
at once; if this took place under the supervision of superior
authorities (a point which was strongly emphasized by many
reformers) and did not take the form of a tumult or an ostentatious
destruction of the physical substance of the work – then these
changes were not iconoclasm in the strict sense. In spite of this,
iconoclasm is such a forceful term and so rooted in polemical

rhetoric (I exclude here, however, its more metaphorical context, now quite common in English usage) that it is hard not to use it even in reference to such actions as the removal of images carried out in stages in Zurich under the supervision of Zwingli, a process whose peculiar character I analysed in the preceding chapter.

There were many attempts to steer iconoclastic actions and to change them into the gradual elimination of interior decoration from churches – in other words, transform them into a type of limited action which could find the support of the majority of the faithful. Specific stratagems were used both in iconoclastic acts and in more moderate actions. For example, at a meeting of Polish Calvinists with envoys of the Czech Brethren in Secemin in 1556,[1] one of the participants advised the noble patrons of churches to act slowly and to prepare the simple folk gradually for the removal of images. First, the altars were to be closed and the images covered with sheets; and then, without haste, they were to be withdrawn from the main nave and concealed in the less open spaces of the church. In other cases the process began by turning the face of the image to the wall. On the other hand, in fifteenth-century Poland the act of turning images to face the wall had a definite iconoclastic, Hussite connotation and was regarded as the prelude to the act of destruction. In Polish sources we read about persons who turned images upside-down and face to the wall 'in the manner of heretics' (as at Pyzdry in 1446).[2] All of this shows the difficulties of classifying iconoclastic acts.

Their diversity is astonishing. Let us start with the quasi-ritual public burning of images and sculptures at the stake or their more frequent destruction *in situ*. Sculptures evoked greater aggression both for theoretical (reminiscences of heathen idols) and for rather obvious psychological reasons. The decapitation of sculptures – perhaps the most frequent type of damage – and the breaking of their limbs possess an obvious symbolism. As David Freedberg has emphasized, the intention was not always to destroy the entire statue: 'The aim is to render images powerless, to deprive them of those parts which may be considered to embody their effective-ness.'[3] That is why particular fragments of sculptures were so often maimed (heads, limbs, noses, ears and eyes; in the case of statues of saints, their attributes).

These damages can be connected with semi-magical beliefs expressing a peculiar fear of images (*Bilderfurcht*) but obvious analogies appear here also to medieval acts of punishment. Martin

Warnke saw in the iconoclastic practice of meting out punishment to those parts of the figure representing sensory organs the symbolic counterpart of real corporal punishments.[4] This procedure implied the necessity of preserving the damaged statue as a symbol of the punishment experienced or of the humiliation of its authority. Warnke put forward his hypothesis on the basis of examination of sculptures damaged by the Anabaptists in Münster. Other acts took place with the clear intention of mockery. For example, in Laventie in the Netherlands a certain Baiert in 1566 attacked the statue of a saint 'and broke off the beard in the manner of the Guizes.[5] Images were broken, run through with swords or (in Poland) sabres; the eyes on pictures were gouged out;[6] this last operation had its direct antecedents in the attitude of the Turks to Byzantine mosaics. For example, the figure of Christ was cut out from a painting of Holbein's,[7] and then the eyes of the figure were gouged out. There were still other kinds of damage and desecration. Images and sculptures were smeared with filth or with cow's blood – a concrete symbolism of mockery. Other gestures of degradation that might be mentioned include throwing images of Mary into latrines or the more popular throwing of images and sculptures into wells, rivers and lakes.

Another criterion was, so to speak, the religious status of a work of art. As a rule the first targets of attack were the most worshipped images or those famed for miracles. Here tactical considerations intertwined with the symbolic meaning of such actions. In Strasburg for a long time the town council was content (especially in 1524–6) with gradual removal of the 'most dangerous idols', but then in 1529 all images were destroyed.[8] In the case of the removal of interior decoration or of iconoclasm carried out in a single step, the iconoclasts usually started with the most famous works – as though they wanted to show that even the 'great idols' were not capable of an anti-iconoclastic miracle in their defence. However, there were also cases, especially in ritual burnings at the stake, in which the prominent 'idols' were destroyed at the very end, as a kind of grand finale.

It is necessary to stress, however, that in none of the major Reformation theologians do we find explicit praise of the use of violence – though Müntzer comes quite close to it – namely, in the sense that such a ritual act of destruction would acquire an intrinsic religious value of its own. At most, the use of force was an accepted by-product of the exigencies of the reformation process. From this it was still a long way to faith in the special symbolic values of the *auto-da-fé*, as in the Spanish Inquisition especially as the symbolic understanding of fire was different in Catholicism and in Protestantism.[9] The Catholics understood fire as a purifying element, the Protestants first and foremost as a trial.

Psychological reactions to concrete actions were also uncommonly diverse. Sometimes iconoclasm was treated in a semi-ironic fashion as a 'war against the idols'. Quite often the deadness, the lifelessness of images was emphasized, the fact that the images which were allegedly all-powerful, or at least supposed to visualize the sacrality, did not defend themselves against physical aggression. A prime example of this attitude is the shout of one of the Basle iconoclasts in 1529 as he threw the crucifix from the Great Minster on to the fire: 'If you are God defend yourself, if you are human bleed.'[10] (In this case an additional complication is the fact that a representation of Christ was involved. Certain analogies with Eucharist iconography, as examplified in the famous theme of the *Mass of St Gregory*,[11] do appear here, since the iconoclasts demanded a similar miracle from the crucifix.)

We find a somewhat different attitude in the autobiography of Thomas Platter, who in his youth had been a Zurich iconoclast:

> One morning, Zwingli was to preach in the church of St Mary, and when I heard the bells calling to the sermon, I thought to myself: I have no wood, and there are so many idols about which no one is concerned standing in the church; so I went to the church, to the nearest altar, and I grabbed John and returned to school with him. I threw him into the stove and said to him: 'Johnny, bend down now, you've got to go into the stove.' When he began to burn, there was a great hissing and cracking from the oil paint.[12]

In attempting to rationalize this act of destruction, Platter tried, through a naive story, as it were, to discharge the emotions of those times years later, reducing the old motivations, aggressions and irresolutions to a pleasant anecdote – which is significant in itself, as a psychological process of displacement.

Seen in the aspect of historical circumstances and effects, iconoclasm is a problem that is difficult to define and classify precisely. More than other events of the reformation process, it was a projection of crowd psychology and collective emotions, a phenomenon that was dependent on the state of progress of the reformation process, the resistance put up by the old faith and the amount of control over the crowd exercised by charismatic leaders or the town council. The state of research on the Reformation in towns in Central Europe still does not allow us to create a model of iconoclastic actions as a component of the whole process of change.

As a mass movement iconoclasm was subject to the dialectics of the revolutionary process. On the one hand it could have acted to speed up the process of change, but it could also document a process that had already taken place. This aspect was emphasized most forcefully by the Basle iconoclasts, who said that in one hour they had done more for the Reformation – by destroying images – than the town council had done in three years of dilatory deliberations.[13] On the other hand iconoclasm of this kind was the easiest, most spectacular, and therefore the most superficial, phenomenon and it often (but not always) created the appearance of a revolutionary leap forward. This is especially true of the attempts to Protestantize Eastern Orthodox areas, where iconoclasm turned out to be an empty and harmful gesture. That is why the iconoclasts often had to suffer the bitterness of defeat, especially when emotions began to subside and the Reformation began to devour its own, radical, children.

Thus an explosion of iconoclasm could mean that in a given place the Reformation was moving to a higher, more radical stage, but in some cases, especially in upper Germany, actions carried out under the supervision of town councils could serve to discharge tensions and to channel the actions of the more radical elements. The iconoclastic actions in January 1522 in Wittenberg serve as a classic example of the discrediting of radical circles, which – thanks to Luther's prestige and skilful tactics – were removed from leadership of the movement. These events were the first signal – the next and much more dramatic one was to be the peasant war of 1525 – of the polarization of the Reformation into a moderate and a radical wing. From such a viewpoint, we obviously do not distinguish between intentions and effects; but this is also due to the lack of a model. Almost always, however, iconoclasm meant the crossing of a particular point of no return in relation to the old faith. The fact of the matter is that this point happened to vary in accordance with the course of the Reformation in each town. Sometimes iconoclasm accompanied the taking-over of the first churches; more often it marked the watershed when the Protestants appeared as the stronger confession; sometimes it symbolically demonstrated their final triumph, which usually happened when the town council decided to expel the rest of the Catholic clergy from the town.[14] If we accept a kind of 'social control' (a concept suggested in this context by Robert Scribner)[15] as the key element of the tactics of the town council in the period of the reformation process, then iconoclasm appears to us as one of the basic problems of social engineering within this concept.

The social composition of the participants of the iconoclastic riots is very hard to determine; in many cases we lack reliable sources. In the nineteenth century, with its optimistic view of cultural progress, there was no place (even among Protestants) for any understanding for iconoclasm, so that there was a well-formed opinion on this subject: the iconoclasts were for the most part the mob or town rabble, a few fanatics, and young people. As regards young people, their disproportionate participation in riots of this kind is obvious and often confirmed by the sources (Stralsund, 1525; the first riots in Riga in March 1524; Basle, 1529, and many other cases).

So much for youth. The question of social stratification is, however, much harder to answer. In many actions the common populace dominated (as in Stralsund in 1525),[16] but we also know of many cases in which patricians (for example in other Baltic cities) or even the mayor (as in Braniewo) participated. In Pernau in Livonia in 1526 a group of middle-class townsmen wanted to overthrow the mayors by inciting iconoclastic riots. We also know that the clergy participated in iconoclastic actions (Wittenberg, 1522) and artists as well, including those who only a few years earlier had created the 'idols' (among them Jörg Breu the Elder and Niklaus Manuel Deutsch).[17]

The social composition of the iconoclasts has been studied most thoroughly for the Low Countries. This has been facilitated by the documents of numerous so-called 'councils of disorder' which were appointed by the authorities to punish the rioters. The documents clearly show the wide participation of the middle classes in iconoclastic acts – burghers, artisans, and some merchants. Relatively few participants belonged to the Netherlandish aristocracy. To be sure, in accordance with the policy followed by the Spanish authorities and the duke of Alba, representatives of the more affluent groups were more severely punished; moreover, their participation was easier to determine – a fact which might have somewhat distorted the proportions. It must be stated that both in the Netherlands and in Riga, for example, there was also a proportionately greater participation of newcomers from other cities, regions, or countries (in Riga the so-called *Schwarzhäupter* or 'Black Heads'). From the Netherlands (especially the south) we know also about bloody clashes between the local populace which adhered to the old faith, and wandering groups of iconoclasts.

Iconoclasm as a rule took place in a tense situation, when the city was already seized by a fever to act. Often the direct impulse to iconoclasm was some dramatic attempt to preserve the old faith, most often a procession or an aggressive sermon, which was automatically taken as provocation. Sometimes even a minor incident, the intentional or even accidental damaging of a sculpture or image, sufficed to attract a crowd and trigger acts of violence. In Stralsund in 1525 anticipatory action – the attempt by a private patron to withdraw an object from a church – served as the signal for attack.[18] There were also many cases of private iconoclastic actions. Often these were break-ins by small groups into the church at night for the purpose of destroying several objects; the perpetrators perhaps intended an ostentatious call for more resolute reformatory actions. Thus iconoclasm was a kind of declaration, both individually and collectively. Like every act of this type, it had its own dramatic, sometimes even tragic, aspect. The deed of the Moscow barber Foma Ivanov (which will be discussed later), who, surrounded by hostile clerks and investigators, publicly destroyed an icon in a church, had something about it of ritual suicide.[19]

Iconoclasm was also susceptible to actions of a provocative nature. In Poland during the rise in strength of the Counter-Reformation there were cases where crucifixes were intentionally placed in the area of villages belonging to heretics so that the removal or destruction of these holy objects could serve as a pretext for the church–state machine to undertake repressive measures. It is characteristic that the last stage of the history of the famous seat of the Polish Brethren, Raków, began in 1638 with such a cleverly exploited incident, involving a crucifix destroyed perhaps by chance.[20] The boundary line between complete provocation, the instigation of iconoclastic actions and opportunism, or on the other hand intentional iconoclastic damage is obviously fluid and hard to determine across the centuries. Like everything connected with provocation, these things are vague. For there were cases in which the Reformation authorities, in secret and often at night, caused the destruction of the interior decoration of churches and chapels. (The wider, quasi-official sanction separated these actions from similar ones carried out by groups of a few persons.) The city authorities did not admit their complicity; nor was the restitution of the outfittings allowed. Finally, somewhere in the collective subconscious there glimmered during such events the memory of the frequent alleged 'desecrations of the Host', especially in the fourteenth and fifteenth centuries, which were taken as pretexts for anti-Jewish incidents.[21]

Our chief interest here is in towns, for – as has been emphasized many times – the Reformation in Central Europe was primarily an urban phenomenon (in Poland it was somewhat different). To make a somewhat superficial analogy, the most intense iconoclastic actions in Russia took place in Novgorod, which was culturally and socially the most advanced city in Russia. On the whole, peasants were supporters of the cult of images. There were numerous cases of the resistance of the rural population both to the reduction of interior decorations of the church and to attempts to remove them completely. This is true for the territories of the Holy Roman Empire and – as Waclaw Urban's studies have shown[22] – for Poland as well. This resistance was not limited to Catholics. The Lutheran rural and small-town population strongly resisted attempts to impose Calvinism from above. In the great German Peasants' War of 1525 more than one church (and especially monasteries) fell prey to devastation or plunder, but this happened in the course of wartime operations and pillaging. Nonetheless there are some cases in southern Germany and Switzerland where peasants undertook iconoclastic actions, especially in the case of hated convents. However, we should not overrate these incidents. For the peasants, by contrast to the inhabitants of the towns, the image question was not a problem of 'anguished lay piety' (to cite a very pertinent expression of Steven Ozment). In peasant culture sporadic acts smacking of iconoclasm (for example, punishing the statue of a saint who failed to meet the hopes placed in him) belong only to the category of causal–instrumental actions. During the German Peasants' War a unit of local peasants destroyed the furnishings of the church belonging to the monastery of the hated monks in Anhausen, but spared the altar donated by the rural populace. (In towns it was just the opposite: iconoclasm in Riga began in March 1524 with the ostentatious destruction by young members of a confraternity of the altar that their brotherhood had endowed in the past but they did not touch other images.) Despite the fact that Müntzer had, as we know, been more or less directly involved in iconoclastic actions in Mallerbach in 1524, many of the peasant units put religious images on their ensigns.[23] In any case, it is a truism that common folk have a longer attachment to visual forms of religion.

It has several times been emphasized that iconoclasm, despite its semantic forcefulness, is not a very precise term as far as social practice and reception are concerned. Much here depends on the form and the intended ostentatious effect, but much also depends on other, marginal circumstances. The boundary with mere vandalism has to be delimited.[24] Wars, uprisings and urban disturbances often resulted in the destruction of churches without intentional iconoclastic effects. Zwingli was labelled by his opponents as a stormer of churches and images invoking the tradition of the 'Parson Storm'. Although Catholic propaganda soon became aware of the deep differences separating the Lutherans and Calvinists on the image question, for a long time it called all Protestants iconoclasts.

Special forms of iconoclasm also involved the confiscation (or sometimes simply theft) of liturgical equipment. The followers of the old faith sometimes called these acts iconoclasm. There were also removals, confiscations or appropriations of the most valuable works of art; the criterion of choice was the commercial value of the material used.

The territorial scope and the chronology of iconoclasm are thus clearer than its concrete role in social practice and in individual urban reformation processes. Its political effects are also quite clear. Iconoclasm started in 1521 in the territory of Germany and Switzerland, on the whole (apart from Baltic areas and the Wittenberg episode) in areas which – at least in the initial phase – were connected with the Reformation of the Swiss type and not with the Lutheran one. For example, iconoclasm did not affect Nuremberg, and thanks to this this Lutheran city preserved priceless Gothic and early Renaissance monuments.[25] Also, the iconoclastic events in the cities of upper Germany and Switzerland in most cases did not undermine the authority of already formed reformation groups. The extremely drastic iconoclastic events in France in the years 1559–62 greatly impeded the effort of the royal court at mediation and deepened the gulf between the two faiths. It is significant that as late as 1561 the moderate Catholics from the party of so-called *politiques* were supporters of a considerable reduction of the cult of images. The excesses of iconoclasm opened the way for extremists in both camps.

The great wave of iconoclasm that swept through the Netherlands in 1566 and destroyed many works of painting and sculpture was of a somewhat different nature. To a large extent it was a national–political rebellion and marked the start of the decades-long war of the Netherlands (later only of the United Provinces) for independence.

On two other occasions iconoclasm would have a considerable influence on political decisions. In the winter of 1619/20 the removal of images and sculptures from the cathedral of St Vitus combined, so it seems, with their ostentatious public destruction, estranged many Czechs from the rule of their new monarch, Frederick V, the so-called 'Winter King', and in some ways was unquestionably one of the causes of his isolation and his defeat in the battle of the White Mountain.

In England the isolated iconoclastic acts of the 1630s inspired by the anti-Stuart opposition were transformed during the Civil War into a mass campaign directed from above which, as one can surmise, cemented the ranks of the Puritans. As in Münster in 1534, Cromwellian iconoclasm was directed in the first place against symbols of religious and political authority (though of course it also expunged all 'Laudian' residues from the churches). The English Bishop Gardiner had warned of such a turn of events a century earlier, when he stated that iconoclasm directed against images must inevitably transform itself into an action against the aristocracy and the king, even when it was itself initiated by the royal court (in this case that of Henry VIII).[26]

Iconoclastic incidents also played an important role in the so-called 'Second Reformation': that is, the process of a forced Calvinization of Lutheran territories in the years 1560–1619. The aforementioned Prague episode of 1619 belonged to that group. Church visitations ordered by the authorities were the chief weapon in achieving the sought-after 'idolless' state. But circumstances changed: starting with the Amberg riots of 1566 there developed a whole series of conflicts between Calvinizing political authorities and the predominantly Lutheran population. Riots or small-scale disturbances broke out in the Upper Palatinate (1581–9), Marburg in Hesse (1605), Sonneborn–Lippe (1606), Danzig (1590), Silesia (1616) and Berlin (1615).[27] In the majority of these incidents the Calvinist authorities scored a somewhat pyrrhic victory and the fierce resistance of the local population was to presage the Lutheran–Calvinist divisions of the Thirty Years' War. Needless to say, in the long run these conflicts considerably weakened the Protestant camp.

In the face of widespread opposition the Calvinists changed their tactics in the second decade of the seventeenth century. In 1614 the famous Calvinist preacher Abraham Scultetus formulated a new strategy in an advisory letter to the elector of Brandenburg, Johann Sigismund, who had just converted to Calvinism. The Calvinist rulers should refrain from reforming Lutheran churches and removing images everywhere.[28] They should, however, purge their court church or chapel of all idols and thus set a shining example of true faith for all their subjects: one day the population would follow of their own accord.

The ensuing 'court church iconoclasm' forms a fascinating chapter in the history of both iconoclasm and politics. For the strategy did not succeed: limitation to the domain of the court did not bring a relaxation of tensions. The Lutherans refused to accept a self-contained iconoclasm; they acted from the outset on a principle of opposition. The reaction of the Lutherans and of course the Catholics to three instances of such court church iconoclasm following one upon another (Berlin 1615, Güstrow 1618, Prague–St Vitus 1619)[29] was even more hostile than before. In 1620 alone almost a dozen pamphlets condemning the Prague iconoclasm and singling out the negative role of Abraham Scultetus (who was then chaplain and advisor to Frederick V of Bohemia) were written by Catholics and Lutherans. Scultetus' pathetic efforts to point out that Frederick had actually refrained from a Calvinist takeover of the Prague churches made no impression – the reckless deed estranged many moderate Lutherans from the first Protestant king of Bohemia. The demonstrable potential of iconoclasm was so great, and the chosen church so prominent, that any rationally conceived model of a contained, self-limiting iconoclasm was bound to fail: especially if the removal of images included acts of wanton destruction, as in all three incidents.

However, the idea that a court church or, in a more limited

way, a court chapel could be exempt from the general rules and liturgical strictures prevailing in a given country could also be applied in the opposite direction. Both the chapel of Elizabeth I, where a crucifix could be found,[30] and the later chapel of Queen Henrietta in Somerset House in London, with its rich imagery, differed from the generally aniconic outfittings of the English churches.

To return to the problem of iconoclasm's link with a concrete territory: it must be noted that there were two models of iconoclasm in Europe – the upper German and the Dutch. The region of upper Germany, the mainstay of the urban Reformation, was characterized by a great diversity of Reformation processes. We cannot speak of an iconoclastic psychosis in this region, since every case of iconoclasm had its own local genesis and was approached in a different way. In the Netherlands in August 1566 a sudden iconoclastic revolution extended across the entire country in two weeks. Apart from certain exceptions, iconoclastic incidents occurred here in successive regions, as if by contagion,[31] and the characteristic feature of this movement was the irrelevance of the boundaries between town and country.

A completely blank page in the history of European iconoclasm is seen in the events that took place on the Baltic coast in two waves (1524–6 and 1529).[32] They are hard to understand because they occurred in areas where the reformation had taken a Lutheran turn. They had a dual role in the reformation process: in the western basin, where iconoclasm – generally in organized form – took place later (1529), they put the seal, as it were, on victory over the old faith. In Livonia, in the Pomeranian cities of Braunsberg (Braniewo), Stolp (Slupsk), Stettin (Szczecin), Stralsund (though in the strict sense it lies more in the western basin) and Stockholm these incidents marked the culmination of the first period of the fight with Catholicism and symbolized the first determined attacks on the old faith.

While the incidents in the western basin and Stralsund are closer to the urban model of upper German iconoclasm, the iconoclastic incidents in Livonia in 1524–6 constitute such an essential element of the local Reformation process that one can speak of something intermediate between the upper German and the Dutch model, though the countryside was not affected by iconoclasm. In all, we know of ten serious explosions of iconoclasm, embracing Riga, Reval, Dorpat, Pernau, Fellin and Werden. They took diverse forms, and I have attempted to present some of them in this chapter.

Independently of the significance of iconoclasm in the Reformation and thus also in the history of Livonia, Baltic iconoclasm played an important role in the unintended process of antagonizing Eastern Orthodox neighbours. Half a century after these events the Lutheran churches on the Baltic coast were once again full of pictorial epitaphs and had been adorned with splendid main altars and pulpits decorated with images. Few people remembered the incidents, but in neighbouring Russia it was believed that every Protestant was an iconoclast.

Without depreciating the mass nature of iconoclasm and its instrumental value, it must be noted that it generated new problems — let us call them problems of individual conscience — which in the course of time would, thanks to Protestantism, become the main features of European civilization. On this subject-matter we have the very interesting account of the case of Frau Göldli, a townswoman from Swiss Lucerne, and the role played in this case by Zwingli.[33] Frau Göldli, who had fallen seriously ill, took an oath that if she recovered she would endow an image of St Apollinaris for the church of the Beguine community in Lucerne. However, these were the years when the Reformation was on the upswing, and after a certain time Frau Göldli became one of its supporters. She then recognized that she had committed an act inconsistent with the principles of true Christianity: namely, putting faith in the intercession of saints. Thus she went to the church, took the image, and burned it. For this act the Beguines brought charges of blasphemy against her before the town council, and Frau Göldli was sentenced to pay a small fine and restore the image of St Apollinaris. She paid the fine but categorically refused to have a new image made. For this reason she faced serious punishment.

When asked for his advice towards the end of 1522, Zwingli suggested to Frau Göldli that she seek compromise solutions (letter to Myconius of 22 December 1522). He saw a way out in paying to the Beguines a considerable sum as compensation (in addition to the fine paid). However, if the Beguines were still to insist on Frau Göldli's direct participation in the making of a new 'idol', then she ought resolutely to refuse on grounds of conscience, even if the consequence were to be the death sentence. A few passages of Zwingli's letter, in which he outlined Frau Göldli's line of defence before the court, deserve to be quoted:

> As regards . . . the replacement of the image with a new one, then I implore you, be fatherly, that is, do not compel this unfortunate woman to do something against her own conscience and to have to repeat the senseless act which she had done in the past. Show your favour to St Apollinaris in such a way that my soul will not be sentenced to eternal damnation. . . . And so that you believe this, I am declaring my willingness to pay to the Beguines an amount of money equal to the price of the image; they can do what they wish with this money.[34]

It should be noted that we do not know the final outcome of this case, though it could not have been very favourable, because Lucerne was one of the bastions of Swiss Catholicism.

This episode reveals in a dramatic way the new spiritual world of the Reformation. Only on the surface – as one commentator has put it – was Zwingli's counsel impractical, since with Frau Göldli's money the Beguines could have had a new work made themselves. In this strict separation of the legal–financial from the religious and symbolic aspect there appears the new civil–legal thinking, as it were, of the Reformation. This thinking accepted the world of private legal obligations, but at the same time it clearly drew the limits of compromise.[35] In the manifest way in which Zwingli speaks of an eventual martyr's death we see that admixture of level-headed realism and uncompromising adherence to principles that a few decades later would be characteristic of the Genevan theocracy led by Calvin.

Hence iconoclasm brought with it new problems in the field of individual psychology and at the same time possessed concrete social references. This very precise dialectic explains the diversity of its epiphenomena. The Frau Göldli incident is perhaps its most emphatic but not its only manifestation. We know of the request in the 1530s of the patrician and patron of the village church, Konrad Roth of Ulm, to wait another day or two for changes in his church 'until my aged mother dies'.[36]

Another characteristic situation arose in Hamburg, where the altars were removed from the chapel of the hospital of the Holy Spirit (c. 1525). In response to the protests of the old chapter, the town council stated that additional hospital beds could be put in the space thereby obtained.[37]

Iconoclasm as a cultural phenomenon also played a role in changes in the status of works of art. It gave rise to the cult of a considerable number of new miraculous images in both Catholicism and Orthodoxy. The miraculous Częstochowa painting of the Black Madonna is perhaps the best-known example here. There were many legends about weeping images or about immediate punishments meted out to criminal iconoclasts: for example, being struck by lightning, paralysis, etc. (the so-called *contrapasso* motif). A popular motif about some images or sculptures had it that they were endowed with miraculous powers to resist iconoclastic acts – they did not burn, or could not be destroyed with sabre strokes. It is interesting that even the Lutherans invented legends about incombustible pictures of Luther.[38] The remark of the Calvinist polemicist Grzegorz of Żarnowiec on the other hand attempts to invert this strand: 'for God often strikes with lightning those carved images that they call crucifixes.'[39]

On the other hand in some cases the iconoclastic threat to a concrete work brought about attempts to explain more precisely its status as a means of transmission, something which was not possible in the medieval conditions of an all-encompassing sacralization. It became a special practice to place inscriptions on some images. These inscriptions gave theological explanations or, even more frequently, called upon the faithful not to worship these works. In an extreme case – the writing of the text of the Ten Commandments on an altar picture of Hugo van der Goes – this was rather a demonstration of an aniconic attitude combined with reference to the prohibition of the Decalogue: the episode was sharply condemned by the great historian of Dutch art, Carel van Mander.[40]

In accordance with the new civil–legal Reformation attitude in property matters, there were cases when endowed images or – more often – decorative epitaph shields were spared. They were not destroyed, but returned to the donors or their families. Leaving aside the case of Frau Göldli, we repeatedly meet with an official acceptance of the right of the endower to dispose of the work he had endowed, or even to destroy it. Finally, one of the first manifestations of the modern cult of works of art north of the Alps took place in the course of the iconoclastic events in the Netherlands in 1566. The Ghent altar of the Van Eycks was first walled up in the chapel of the church and then, through the efforts of the town authorities of Ghent, removed to the town hall to save it from raging crowds. Regardless of what prevailed in this particular case – real admiration for artistic merit, an undefined feeling for the values of 'something old', or local patriotism – this was the harbinger of a new attitude towards works of art.

Iconoclasm as a complicated historical–religious phenomenon possesses a set of various cultural–symbolic connotations. I have already mentioned the background of magical–symbolic acts of degradation; there are obvious tracks leading from this to the practice of hanging in effigy and other 'rituals of humiliation' and 'denigration rituals', and finally to the belief in witches and sorcery. I shall leave aside here the first, most obvious, connection with the practice of punishment in effigy – that is, the ontological status of a work of religious art – for iconoclasm in the most general sense was a form of struggle in effigy with the entire system of the old faith. In many cases this was a substitute for dogmatic controversy or – at the opposite pole – for a direct physical attack on the representatives of Catholicism. This latter argument was often put forward by French Huguenots (we attacked statues – the Catholics attacked and killed people) to excuse Reformation violence. Our interest here is in the most concrete, individual references to the ritual of punishment or to a fight using effigy procedures. Hanging or burning in effigy[41] was a part of the degradation rituals, and, leaving aside the legal aspect of this procedure, it has to be said that these rituals constituted an object of great interest and attraction to the people of the sixteenth century.

During his journey to Rome in 1510 Luther came across a political fight conducted by the method of degradation in effigy, and from his account[42] we can see how fascinated he was by this phenomenon. During Ash Wednesday in Lucerne in 1523 Zwingli's portrait was burned in effigy. It is hard to say whether this act was supposed to be a symbolic response to Zwingli's iconoclastic tendencies.

An image of St Francis was hung on the gallows in 1524 in Nebra (Saxony). We know that a year later in Wolkenstein the sculpture of St John was hung upside-down on the gallows.[43] In this last case inversion, with which we are already familiar from earlier iconoclastic practices, was added to the ritual of punishment in effigy. Loosely connected with the effigy ritual was also the specific practice of putting idols in the pillory. In Königsberg in 1524 a statue of St Francis was treated thus;[44] the same happened to some idols in Xanten in 1566.

The logical consequence of accepting the form of a ritual execution of the idol was the participation of the public executioner in the ceremony. During the iconoclastic riots caused by the Huguenots in Agen in 1562[45] the crowd of townspeople preparing the pyre for the images was joined by the town executioner, who said that it was 'his duty to ignite the pyre'. We know that in Herford (1531) and in Basle (1529) the executioners took part in the riots, though their exact role is unknown. It seems plausible to assume the participation of the town executioner in the hanging of idols in effigy, though we have no direct accounts. To continue this inventory of pseudo-juridical rituals, I shall refer to the 'trial' of images in the Dutch town of Den Briel in 1567.[46]

The above-mentioned cases of acts of degradation performed on images of St Francis exemplify interesting parallels between German and Scottish Reformation history. In both countries an astounding number of early iconoclastic attacks seems to have been directed against images of St Francis, perhaps reflecting the intense political struggle against the friars (whom Luther called 'that pestilential sect'). In Zwickau in 1524 an image of St Francis wearing ass's ears was set up contemptuously on the town fountain and then burned. Two decades later in far-off Perth (in January 1543 or 1544) three men were sent to the gallows for 'hanging up the image of Saint Francis on a cord, nailing of ramme's hornes to his head and a kowe's rumpe to his taile'. One of the earliest iconoclastic incidents recorded in Scotland concerned two men who were sought by the authorities in Dundee and Perth in 1537 for the crime 'of hanging of the image of St Francis'. A similar incident occurred in Aberdeen in December 1544, where again the ritual was parodied (or, conversely, applied literally!) when two men hanged the 'image of St Francis'. Since no direct influence is realistically imaginable in such coincidences, a certain general pattern of symbolic responses begins to emerge across Reformation Europe.

Thus the ritual of destruction was conceived as a symbolic inversion of existing popular devotional rituals. Works of art connected with such rituals were to receive an inordinate amount of iconoclastic attention. This holds true in the case of processional crosses or figures, but even more so in the case of the famous

'Palm Sunday ass' (*Palmesel*). The *Palmesel* consisted of a wooden cart on which was fixed a statue of Christ seated on an ass. This image was drawn through the town in the colourful Palm Sunday procession. In a whole sequence of picturesque iconoclastic incidents recorded from Switzerland and southern Germany in the years 1523–31 the *Palmesel* was burned, derided, thrown into the water or brought to 'dishonourable places'.

That punishment in effigy applied to a statue was somewhat ambiguous (it could mean the concrete statue, it could aim at a 'false' iconographic type represented by the work, or it could aim at the prototype itself) has already been said. In the case of the crucifixes subjected to punishments of the effigy type it was of course the 'idol', not the prototype, that was debased. In Waldshut in 1524 Balthasar Hubmaier – who was to become a famous Anabaptist – pulled out the crucifix on a rope from the church in an unsurpassed pre-execution debasement.[47] In Riddagshausen (Lower Saxony) in 1551 the crucifix was first decapitated and then hanged on a tree.[48]

In the case of crucifixes iconoclastic fervour sometimes unleashed very special actions, whose characteristic features included a clumsy re-enactment of the iconography of the Passion. In Dorpat in 1525 the iconoclasts reportedly struck at the crucifix with swords and spears. In Portsmouth around 1550 'an image of Christ crucified was so contemptuously handled as to have the one eye bored out and the side pierced'.[49] Both in Saint-Jacques (1566)[50] and in Armentières (1566) the Flagellation was re-enacted. Though it was the 'deceptive idol' that was punished, the rites chosen here bordered on blasphemy.

Iconoclastic acts also make evident the connection between ritual degradation and denigration and rituals of punishment and purification. The point of crystallization in this case was the problem of witchcraft, since the not uncommon invectives directed against the 'sorcerous idols' incline us to seek possible connections between the entire complex of ideas concerning witchcraft and iconophobic sentiments. We possess a good account of the linkage of iconoclastic acts with the fight against witchcraft. In Riga in 1524[51] the iconoclasts sacking the cathedral denounced a hitherto especially venerated image of the Mother of Christ as the image of a witch and subjected it to the traditional trial of ducking in the river, from which the painted panel, of course, emerged victorious. Hence, in accordance with the procedure of a witchcraft trial, it was proclaimed a witch and solemnly burned at nearby Kubsberg, the traditional place of execution of witches.

The identification of iconoclasm with the fight against witchcraft and demons was the subject of a completely forgotten debate between two historians of the Reformation in the Baltic countries, Otto Pohrt and Leonid Arbusov, in 1928.[52] Pohrt saw a deeper meaning in the fact that the greatest iconoclastic riots in Riga had broken out on 16 March and then, after half a year of calm, once more on 8 August 1524: that is, on two days devoted to St Cyriacus, who in medieval tradition was known primarily as a tamer of demons. Pohrt also connected a further episode from the iconoclastic disturbances in March, in which Easter songs were sung after the destruction (with still two weeks to go to Easter), with the understanding of iconoclasm as a symbolic equivalent of the Easter triumph over hell and the forces of evil. Although Arbusov criticized Pohrt's hypothesis on the basis of a dissenting scrutiny of the sources (which are somewhat enigmatic), in my opinion Pohrt's intuition appears quite plausible, and it can be corroborated by further comparisons. Thus in Geneva two of several iconoclastic actions took place on 8 and 24 August 1535. The latter was St Bartholomew's day – this saint was also a tamer of demons. St Bartholomew's day 1559 was celebrated in London with great bonfires in which roods with their statues of the Virgin and St John, were 'burned with great wonder'.[53] Could a similar motive of a struggle with demons have shaped certain symbolic strands in the Catholic reception of the night of St Bartholomew in 1572? Astonishingly, this question has not been raised in the many studies concerned with that fateful event.

The rites of destruction often assumed forms pertaining to archetypal symbolism. A prominent part is played by so-called rites of passage: by being brought down from the sacred to a 'low', profane sphere[54] the idols had to lose their auratic power. An incident from the great iconoclastic riots in Stralsund in April 1525 shows very vividly a symbolic sequence based on debasement and these rites. The miraculous statue of Mary of the Seven Sorrows was taken out from the Johanniskirche, stripped of its adornment and then hacked to pieces. The rump was brought to an inn (a 'dishonest place') asked to perform a miracle in its defence and finally burned.[55]

The concept of symbolic inversion referred to above, in its most simple context of turning the image or sculpture upside-down, might have linked iconoclasm as a cultural phenomenon with the carnival and similar ceremonies and with the topos of the 'upside-down or topsy-turvy world'. The connection between carnival rites and iconoclasm was suggested in a pioneering article by Robert Scribner.[56] Of course, carnival celebrations could sometimes serve as a vehicle of social protest, though more often they stabilized the system by letting off steam and 'mocking revolution'. In Basle in 1529 the iconoclast riots started on Shrove Tuesday (9 February); the crowds sang carnivalesque songs and heaped abuse on the idols which were carried away from the churches. The debased images and statues were brought to a great pyre and duly burned on the next day, Ash Wednesday; the intended symbolism is obvious. Images were also burned on Ash Wednesday in the north German town of Einbeck (1530 or 1531)[57] and in the Dutch town of Den Briel (1567), in the latter case after a public 'mock trial', as mentioned above.

A very interesting sequence of episodes connecting carnival with iconoclasm took place 1531 in the small town of Lippstadt (Westphalia).[58] The Lippstadt incident was a by-product of a protracted power struggle in the town. However, because of its peculiar structure, this provincial and politically insignificant episode might serve as a textbook illustration of the dynamics and symbolic rites of the 'Reformation in the cities'. The town council still clung tenaciously to the old faith, while the common folk, among whom (characteristically) there were 'very many young people', organized during the carnival of 1531 a mock procession, carrying great puppets of the Pope and emperor through the city. Then the ceremonies connected with the cult of relics were parodied. Afterwards the crowds went on the rampage through the churches of the city and everywhere struck off the noses of the statues. The obvious political motive behind the iconoclasm, the wide participation of youth, the choice and the sequence of the denigration and debasement rites, including the very popular (second only to decapitation) form of statue mutilation, all make it a little paradigm of iconoclast context and symbolism.

Iconoclastic incidents during carnival, but also during Lent, where the symbolic context is less obvious, also took place in many other cities. Often they took the form of a mock carnival procession, as in Biberach, where after iconoclasm in 1531 statues of saints were carried through the city.[59] In Hildesheim in 1543 a statue representing Christ as the Lord of Suffering was carried in the Carnival on 4 February (*Pfaffenfastnacht*) on a kind of city tour, stopping here and there in inns.[60] Mock processions were not, of course, confined to the carnival sphere. In Braniewo (Braunsberg) in 1525 there were many cases of parodies of the Mass by the increasingly aggressive Lutherans, and on Christmas Day that year the mayor, Rabe, along with several townsmen dressed in bearskins, as though imitating the so-called 'Turon procession' burst into church and ostentatiously began to destroy images.[61] Perhaps the carnival tradition had also to do with a fact recorded in 1628 in the Lublin province of Poland, where the young Sobek cut the eyes, ears and nose out of the image of the Virgin and put it on his face as a mask – a deed for which he was swiftly punished.[62]

There is also a certain connection between the tradition of celebrating the 'world upside-down' and an event in Poitiers (14 March 1559), where the furnishings of a church were destroyed by a group of women and small children.[63]

One should, however, be very wary of a watertight, all-encompassing linkage of these phenomena. Neither the sources nor our theoretical knowledge allow us to do so. What is more, the astounding career of Bakhtin's vision of carnival, coupled recently by Robert Scribner and Emmanuel Le Roy Ladurie[64] with the history of the Reformation period, could, if not subjected to strict rigour, create a certain haziness of concepts: despite the aforementioned incidents and other episodes, one cannot see in the carnival the symbolic essence of all the changes and conflicts of the period. The same applies to another, now modish concept: namely that termed 'antibehaviour' and popularized by the Tartu circle of semioticians as an essential, though paradoxical, element of the religious culture of old Russia. A conclusion that one of the so-called 'Holy Fools' (*Iurodivyie*), who shocked the faithful by their 'antibehaviour', could commit a real iconoclastic act would be extremely misleading in view of Russian anti-iconoclastic phobia. This can be proved by a tale about a paradoxical deed committed by one of the most famous 'Holy Fools', Basil the Blessed, who, as the account goes, before the eyes of the startled faithful smashed with a stone a famous miraculous picture of the Virgin.[65] It turned out, however, that under the level of paint of the holy image a figure of the devil was scratched on the board. So this pseudo-iconoclastic deed really belonged to the culture of paradox peculiar to some strata of the Eastern Church and was not tainted by heresy.

To the domain of wholly paradoxical acts, where the element of completely unmotivated madness is very evident, belongs the attack of Don Quixote on a procession with a Marian feretory. From the manner in which Cervantes treats this motif one feels a certain sensitivity on the subject – the iconoclastic sixteenth century had just passed; however, through a skilful ending, the story is imbued with poetic, phantasmagoric qualities and the tension is thus discharged.

Iconoclasm is also the projection of a certain fear deeply rooted in the people of that time: namely, the quasi-magical fear of figures coming to life, fear of the very principle of showing the sacredness in an image that aspires to be a likeness. This 'fear of images', to which Karlstadt himself admitted, was more deeply embedded in the people of that time than we can probably imagine. Accepting an image as the bearer or means of transmission of the sacred assumed a certain type of symbolic acquiescence or submission to the force of tradition. Some scholars see one of the causative forces of iconoclasm in the disappearance – which took place around 1500 as a result of the evolution of North European art – of the specific conventional barrier of signs between the image and the beholder. The huge, life-sized statues of saints, which, thanks to new artistic techniques, 'looked alive', are supposed to have aroused in the residents of the countries north of the Alps unused to the mimetic principle of art (but not, understandably enough, in Italy) a subcutaneous, unreflected inner fear which found an outlet in psychologically liberating acts of iconoclastic destruction upon the advent of the Reformation. This is one of several possible explanations of the peculiar form of iconoclastic acts only a dozen years or so after the zenith of image worship.

This explanation would fit into the conventional view of iconoclasm as a commonplace, though sometimes violently bizarre, reaction of people to the fallen symbols of the previous order and as the embodiment of a tardily perceived, but therefore the more strongly expressed, feeling of being deceived and misled by the cult of images. This would conform with well-known schemata of human psychological reactions in times of upheaval.

Although the past decade has seen a veritable explosion of studies on iconoclasm, we are still a long way from an authoritative picture of either the causative elements or the effects of Reformation iconoclasm. It even seems that research positions have undergone further stratification. Depending on the line of research taken, different, though not always diametrically opposite, emphases appear. For scholars examining the Reformation and its culture from the angle of a clash between an elitist and a popular culture, iconoclasm appears an especially difficult problem. The French scholar Solange Deyon perhaps best expressed the research perplexities of this trend:

> Iconoclasm is . . . a process in which both an encounter takes place and a hiatus begins between the doctrinal solution and its acceptance by the faithful: the reformers often had little understanding of the deeds which, as it might have seemed, were the result of their direct inspiration. Simple people and those who were literate did not use the same language, and that is why perhaps in iconoclastic acts we catch the moment of the parting of the ways of the religion of the people and the religion of elites. First and foremost in the iconoclastic gesture we see something like taking someone at his word, something that begins to weigh on the theological controversy itself; but at the same time we also see other inspirations, chiefly the desire to make a break, which can only be done through the ritual of sending to destruction. This is a ritual symbolized by the pyres on which, without any order whatsoever, are thrown crucifixes, sculptures, liturgical vestments, and altar settings.[66]

Deyon's analysis would explain much of the theological debate between Luther and the burghers of Orlamünde.

A leading historian of the urban Reformation, Bernd Moeller, sees the causative mechanisms and antecedents of the iconoclastic movement differently:

> In this sense . . . the phenomenon of iconoclasm must be recognized as one of the elements of the self-affirmation of the Lutheran movement, though it might be rather hard for us to understand the implications of this motivation. Though in the course of iconoclasm elements of the public representation of the wealthy were also smashed, the more important phenomenon was the rupture with the previous system of salvation, which now began to be regarded as erroneous and

harmful. So in consequence of evangelical sermons, people destroyed the medieval society based on 'religious perform- ance' to which in a sense every one of the iconoclasts belonged; and so each time the iconoclasts also destroyed their own past.[67]

This in turn might serve as a commentary on Frau Göldli's action. One thing seems certain: there can be no simple, monocausal explanation of the forms, intensity and character of the iconoclasm of the Reformation. We should not, however, forget that most people did not harbour such intense feeling against images; they probably opted or would have opted for an orderly, administrative solution or for a gradual withering-away of the cult. Many felt an acute sorrow and grief for their beloved 'idols'. It required a special combination, indeed, of religious, political and historical circumstances for *some* of the former endowers and donors of images (*Bilderstifter*) to turn into passionate iconoclasts (*Bilder- stürmer*), to use once more Hermann Heimpel's now classic word- play.[68]

2 Unknown artist, *Christ on the Palm Sunday Ass*, Cologne. c. 1500. An iconographic type intrinsically connected with the devotional rituals of the Late Middle Ages – frequently attacked by South German and Swiss iconoclasts in the 1520s.

1 Heinrich Vogtherr the Elder(?). *The Idolatry of the Israelites*, woodcut, Strasbourg edition of the Bible published in 1532 by Wolfgang Köpfel. One of the many depictions of Old Testament idolatries during the Reformation.

3 Michael Ostendorfer, *The Pilgrimage to the Image of the Beautiful Virgin in Regensburg, 1520*, woodcut with a handwritten comment by Albrecht Dürer below it (1523), condemning this idolatrous practice.

4 Unknown artist, engraving, *c.* 1540, showing Karlstadt as Rector of
Basle University. Karlstadt was the only great reformer to become exclusively associated with iconoclasm to the detriment of his other, no less
distinctive, theological views.

5 Unknown artist, etching showing Russians taking an oath before a household icon, from Adam Olearius, *Vermehrte Neue Beschreibung der Moskowitischen und Persianischen Reise*, Schleswig 1656. An ironic Protestant view of everyday Russian iconodule practice.

Rex iratus facerdotes interficere iubet, Danielq3 Belum cum templo subuertit.

6 Anonymous artist after Maerten van Heemskerck, *Destruction of the Temple of Baal*, engraving, 1565. Depictions of Old Testament narratives with anti-idolatrous overtones were very popular during the Reformation, this one predating the iconoclastic outbreak of 1566 in the Netherlands.

7 Franz Hogenberg, *Calvinist Iconoclasm in the Netherlands on 20 August 1566*, engraving, published in Michael Aitsinger's *De Leone Belgico*, Cologne 1588. In his famous engraving Hogenberg shows the iconoclastic destruction of a church, particularly the pulling down of statues.

8 Anonymous author, portrait of Calvin, engraving, French loose-leaf print, Paris/Lyons, 1611. Iconoclasm as one of the four negative by-products of Calvinism is shown in the top left section of the four scenes surrounding the portrait of Calvin.

9 Unknown artist, woodcut showing iconoclasts plundering and destroying a sanctuary, from Thomas Murner, *Vom Grossen Lutherischen Narren*, Strasbourg 1522.

10 Burning of crucifixes and 'papistical' books in England in 1643, by an unknown artist. As time went on, crucifixes and crosses became identifying symbols of popery and idolatry.

11 Heinrich Füllmaurer (?), central part of the so-called Mömpelgard Altar, around 1540. This demonstrates the importance of written inscriptions (often biblical texts) for early Protestant art – although not all the examples use them as excessively as here.

4

Icon and pulpit: the Eastern Churches and the Reformation

The subject of this chapter is among the most interesting aspects of the image dispute in the sixteenth century, though the events described below took place on the peripheries of the European world of that time and for this reason are not very well known. Despite this, from the point of view of the methodological assumptions of this work, I deem it advisable to devote considerable, perhaps even disproportionate, space to them. The comparison of such diverse movements and diametrically different religious and aesthetic attitudes will bring certain elements of the Protestant doctrine into clearer relief. The encounter with Eastern Orthodoxy had to be a litmus test for all reductionist tendencies in religious art (to which the various forms of the Reformation unquestionably belonged); and though this test did not decide the rightness of decisions on ceremonial matters, it very clearly showed their consequences both in liturgical practice and in the wider relations between the two confessions.

In considering the mutual relations between Protestantism and Eastern Orthodoxy, it must be stated that this was really a collision of two cultural systems with such different structures that the same measure of historical time cannot be applied to them. Though none of the great world religions is characterized by rapid evolutionary change (with the exception of the period of its birth), it is hard to imagine a greater contrast between the rapid development of Protestantism in the first half of the sixteenth century and the static, long duration of Eastern Orthodoxy. A certain turning-point in the history of the latter (though only for Russian Orthodoxy), though not very deep and not interrupting its main lines of development, were the reforms of Peter the Great, which correspond in time in the history of Protestantism to the Pietist

movement and its hostility to religious art. The accidental convergence of two such different phenomena will serve as the end point
for the main track of my argument. For these events, though in
a different measure, determined the theoretical approach to
religious art by these two confessions in the eighteenth century.
However, we shall look for some lines of thought and signs of
the revival of traditional attitudes in later centuries as well, coming
up to the threshold of our time when referring to the views of
Hans Sedlmayr.

The examination of contacts between regions and centres with
such diametrically different cultures presents many difficulties.
The state of research does not even allow us to be precise about
the historical facts, not to mention wider interpretations.[1] It is
also hard to speak of any lasting dialogue between representatives
of these two Christian worlds in a situation where attempts to
establish contacts often ended in failure or where a brief stir was
followed by breaks of decades, after which it was impossible to go
back to the theological premises or initial resolutions of previous
encounters.

Despite these cautionary remarks, I feel that even in the present,
very unsatisfactory stage of research an attempt should be made
to examine relations between the Reformation and Orthodoxy.
The Orthodox world was the spiritual heir of Byzantium, having
taken over in entirety and further developed the position of the
victorious Byzantine iconodules. The image controversy that
shook the foundations of the Byzantine Church in the eighth and
ninth centuries entered into the tradition of the Eastern Church.
Both under the Turkish yoke and in the powerful world of Russian Orthodoxy, every community, even the smallest one, celebrated annually the Holy Day of Orthodoxy to commemorate
the final triumph over iconoclasm. Paradoxically, the iconoclastic
theoretical tradition also survived the Middle Ages because it was
constantly referred to in polemical writings and in rituals designed
to anathematize it.

In the centuries after the dispute ended the Orthodox doctrine
of religious art was not enriched with entirely new elements, but
various forms of the cult of icons and related ceremonies were
preserved and developed; there was also a certain sacralization of
the status and work of the painter of icons. In declining Byzantium, Hesychasm (monastic quietism) strengthened the mystical
elements of the cult of icons connected with the theory of ema-

nation and also exerted a certain influence on the Russian theology of images. Though the dispute and final break with Rome in 1054 were also indirectly connected with iconoclasm, that being one of the factors which had earlier caused the papacy to take the side of the rulers of the West, the main causes of the schism were the fight for primacy in the Church as a whole and smaller doctrinal differences – among others, the dispute over the term *filioque* in the Nicaean Creed, i.e. whether the Holy Spirit proceeds from the Father *and the Son*, and the problem of the kind of bread that should be used in the Eucharist. The Roman Church put greater emphasis on the educational function of religious images, and there was less place in its doctrine for elements of image magic. Nonetheless, none of the aspects or manifestations of the Orthodox cult of images was entirely alien to it. In this state of affairs the Eastern Church had to treat all attempts to question part or all of the cult of images as a recurrence of the old iconoclastic heresy; hence – in accordance with its own conception of tradition – it attempted to subordinate new phenomena to old formulas and opinions. Iconoclasm, or even the controlled, gradual reduction of the cult of images, was often perceived by the faithful as a specific *pars pro toto* of the entire complicated set of religious beliefs; it was the most visible sign of these beliefs, excited the imagination of believers, and could overshadow even important doctrinal similarities in other areas.

To get somewhat ahead of the story, one can say that the image question had a considerable influence on how Eastern Orthodoxy and Protestantism perceived each other for three centuries. Other questions may often have dominated in particular disputes or opinions, but in the long term none of them, as I shall try to show, was as important at the popular level as the image problem.

POINTS AND PLACES OF CONTACT

In addition to political or theological animosities or divergences, the mutual contacts between Orthodoxy and Protestantism were impeded by geography. The lands of Central and Northern Europe were separated from the Balkan and Mediterranean centres of the Eastern Church by the Ottoman empire. This empire extended to the end of the Balkan peninsula and into Hungary at precisely the time of the greatest development of the Reformation

(1526–9) and did it to a certain extent thanks to the political turmoil caused by the religious split in Germany. The way to Constantinople opened up for many Protestants, who went there as members of legations and other diplomatic missions. This obviously made possible contacts with the local patriarchate, but owing to political vicissitudes these were not lasting contacts. The areas under Turkish rule and the lands of the Polish–Lithuanian commonwealth separated the Protestants from Orthodox Russia. In time certain breaches appeared in both these barriers. For example, Protestant Transylvania (which was also inhabited by a less numerous Orthodox population) was a vassal state within the Ottoman empire bordering on Orthodox Moldavia, and the development of the situation in the eastern lands of the Polish commonwealth in the second half of the sixteenth century led to lively contacts between Catholicism and the Reformation. After 1640, however, these places became less propitious for contacts.

The only places of more lasting contact were the Baltic lands Livonia and Estonia, where the culturally dominant German burghers very quickly accepted the Reformation in its Lutheran version. These lands bordered directly on Orthodox lands. The contacts established earlier in the Hanseatic period with Novgorod and Pskov facilitated cultural exchange, which developed in an interesting way in the immediate pre-Reformation period (1490–1510). Later, however, these relations were broken off; this, as we shall see, was largely the fault of political circumstances combined with Protestant iconoclasm, and these lands, which even under Swedish or Polish rule were in an indirect way the Russian window to the world, did not maintain very close relations with the Orthodox world. The model of Baltic urban civilization based on Western European patterns was too different from the civilization of Russia, especially after the fall of the mercantile oligarchic republics of Pskov and Novgorod. A few centuries later, after the incorporation of these lands into the Russian empire, a cultural symbiosis proved again to be impossible. On the contrary, the relative tolerance of the tsarist authorities towards the Baltic Germans paradoxically led to the increase of anti-Slavic sentiments in the latter and a feeling of superiority that was visible especially in the area of culture.[2] Hence the few mixtures of the two civilizations were not very creative, and sometimes they were even grotesque, like the model of Russian bureaucracy that came from these lands. This somewhat sad pattern was confirmed by the fact that in the nineteenth century an entire galaxy of great German Lutheran theologians, who through the working of some remarkable *genius loci* had come from the Baltic regions and subsequently were active in the great theological centres of Germany (e.g. Erlangen), were chiefly responsible for the image of Russian Orthodoxy as a primitive, semi-pagan, and moreover iconodule 'lower form' of religion.

So much for the geographic and historical factors that were mainly responsible for shaping Orthodox–Protestant relations. We shall devote most of our attention to the contacts of Russian Orthodoxy with the Reformation, if only because these contacts were more frequent and less incidental.

The birth of the Reformation found the Eastern Churches in the period of their deepest decline. The paralysis caused by the fall of Byzantium and the deplorable political and spiritual situation of the patriarchate in Constantinople prevented any wider religious activity. Before the news reached it of the iconoclasm of the Reformation, the Greek Church had to contend with the everyday oppression of the Ottomans, for it was right after 1500 that confiscation of the property of the Orthodox Church reached its zenith. In this situation and in the face of the ban or limitations imposed by the Ottomans on the construction and repair of Orthodox churches, when on account of the frequent confiscations and changes of location the churches lost much of the concept of sacrality, the sacrality of icons that were transported to other buildings from the churches requisitioned by the Ottomans shone with an even brighter light. The patriarchate had at its disposal the entire iconodulic tradition, but, owing to restrictions on cult and church ceremonies, the image miracles and rites, which were so numerous in Russia, played a lesser role in its arguments. Muslim aniconism was an additional element reinforcing the iconodulism of the Greek Church. The only goal of this Church was survival, and spiritual immobility seemed best suited to serve this goal. Besides this, the late Byzantine period had not (with the exception of the not very dangerous Bogomilism) brought any iconoclastic movements towards which the Church would have to take up a position.

In the pre-Reformation period there was little knowledge in Europe of the Eastern Church. This was not changed even by the fall of Byzantium (1453) or by the negotiations connected with the Union of Florence (1438) more than a dozen years earlier.

The Greek scholars who came to the West were primarily expected to transmit the classical texts that had been saved and not to disseminate information about the religious culture of Byzantium. The fall of Constantinople was regarded as a punishment for the 'inconstancy' of the Greeks and for their equivocal stance in questions of religious policy. The theologians of the late Middle Ages were also hardly at all interested in Eastern theology.

In the period of Byzantium's fall an event took place which was to have an almost paradigmatic significance as regards the role the image question played for Orthodox–Protestant relations. In 1451 the moderate Hussite utraquists sent a delegation to Constantinople. Talks with representatives of the Greek Church – motivated by the acute political situation – brought a certain convergence of positions, but an eventual agreement (which in the situation of that time would have been without practical meaning) came to nought over the question of the cult of images and relics.[3]

THEOLOGIANS, TRAVELLERS AND ICONOCLASTS

In his youth Luther had not devoted any attention at all to the problems of Eastern Christianity. It was not until the Leipzig Debate with Johannes Eck in 1519 that he was faced with this problem. The argument of the existence of the Eastern Church served Luther to confute and deny the claims of the Pope to represent the entire Christian community.[4] From this time on Luther sometimes mentioned the Greek Church, but always in juxtaposition with the Roman Church. He did take a position on the Byzantine iconoclastic dispute, however. Luther's very brief pronouncement – analysed in Chapter 1 – enables us to see his remarkable theological insight, which sometimes had the hallmarks of genius. He approached the image dispute from the side of 'Christian freedom', seeing in the struggle between Pope and emperor an assault on the innate rights of a Christian. 'Both were in error', he stated with expressive terseness, 'because both wanted to limit the area of "Christian freedom".' Without going more deeply into the history and theological context of the dispute, which he apprehended as the fight of Rome with the Eastern empire, he regarded this dispute as an example of the harmful and needless conflicts tearing Christianity asunder. On the other hand, he did not refer to the position of the Eastern Church. In the main the views of Eastern theologians were unknown to him. In 1538 in the treatise *On Councils and Churches* Luther sharply – though in a very general way – condemned the views of the 'Greeks'.[5] Absorbed by the religious struggle going on in Germany, he took no steps to establish contacts with the patriarchate in Constantinople; his ecumenicism, which was very relative, was primarily theoretical.

On the other hand, whether because of the lack of concrete information or for tactical reasons, a group of theologians gathered around Melanchthon in the 1540s and 1550s was inclined to minimize the differences between the Orthodox Church and the Reformation. In any case, up to 1555, which closes the first turbulent period of the Reformation, the contacts between the first generation of Lutheran reformers and the Orthodox Church were very superficial. To be sure, the reformers suspected the Greeks of various 'superstitious practices', but they were not very sure of the position of the Eastern Church on the question of works, salvation and justification through faith, and in the Eucharistic controversy. The reformers surmised that on the cult of saints and monasticism the Orthodox Church held a position similar to that of the 'papists', but they did not know to what extent these beliefs were an integral part of the Orthodox religious system. We need not add that in this period Protestants were not aware of the emotions which their real or imagined iconoclasm aroused in the Orthodox.

However, we have accounts concerning the position of the first and second generation of Calvinist theologians. Calvin himself stated emphatically in the *Institutes of the Christian Religion*: 'Hence the stupid excuse of the Greeks turns out to be false: for they think that they have done everything necessary if they do not represent God in works of sculpture – but in works of painting they take more liberties than all other nations.'[6] One of the crucial elements of the Orthodox cult of images was taken up in the Calvinist *Bremen Confession*. There is a statement in this document – apparently negating the efforts of the Eastern Church to achieve a canonic and unchanging form of icons – that the images of Christ and the saints are so diverse that one cannot speak of historical truth.[7] We see here the outline of the different path that the art of Western Europe was to take up to the nineteenth century.

At the turning-point between the first and the second epoch of contacts between Orthodoxy and Protestantism an episode of the Reformation took place in Moldavia which shows as if through a lens almost the entire core of these relations. I have in mind the brief rule in Moldavia of Jacob Heraclides, who had the title of 'Despot' and who attempted to introduce the Reformation into this Orthodox country.[8] Heraclides himself, who came from one of the Greek islands, had been rewarded for his service in the imperial army with high rank and confirmation of his title of nobility. He obtained the right to bear the title of 'Palatine', but despite this he had to leave the imperial service in 1555 because since about 1550 he had been an active Protestant and was strongly influenced by Melanchthon. In 1557 Heraclides spent several months in Vilna, where he met with Lithuanian Calvinists gathered around Jan Łaski. This meeting turned out to be of tremendous importance for the future of the Greek exile. Without breaking off contacts with the Lutherans, Heraclides to all intents and purposes passed over to the Calvinist camp and accepted the Calvinist conception of religious cult. As a result of complicated and risky political manoeuvres, in 1561 he obtained the ducal throne in Moldavia. In the fight for power the support of Calvinists (mostly Polish) turned out to be decisive. In the course of his short reign they also constituted the real ruling group and enjoyed the complete confidence of the duke.

From the very outset Heraclides wanted to Protestantize Moldavia. For this unscrupulous and cynical ruler, however, the Reformation was an end in itself and not merely an instrument serving to strengthen his power. Regard for religious beliefs, and not political pragmatism, was to cause the failure of Heraclides' reign in Moldavia and thus also of his attempt to introduce the Reformation in that country. As regards his endeavour to introduce the Reformation there, one can see many analogies with the course of events in Western Europe. However, largely under the influence of his Polish and German advisers, Heraclides concluded that tactics of slow, gradual change would be an offence against the principles of the Christian religion. The process of change, which in Western Europe as a rule lasted no less than a decade and had a broad, popular basis, was greatly condensed here and was, moreover, carried through solely from above. The power elite carrying out these changes was also an ethnically alien group. After hardly more than a year or so of tolerance and apparent acceptance of the Orthodox faith, Heraclides began to agitate against the existing practice of religious cult. He stopped attending Orthodox religious services and simultaneously introduced Protestant services at court, these being limited to the sermons of the duke or his pastors. At the same time he put pressure on the Moldavian nobility to convert to the 'true faith'. For this purpose he held many public disputes – rather one-sided, of course – in which he chided the representatives of Orthodoxy by saying that their cult was full of 'superstition' and 'stupid ceremonies'. He called the Greek, mystical form of religious services 'idolatry', and made it clear that he would not rest until he had rooted out their 'inane sacred rites'.

Confiscations soon began of monastic treasures in order to replenish the empty ducal coffers. However, in conducting these operations, which can be compared with the actions of the Reformation in the west and north of Europe, the despot gave them more the nature of a struggle over symbols. For example, he confiscated several highly valuable and especially venerated monastery crosses and had them melted down, and from the metal he minted silver and gold coins with his own image.[9] This constituted symbolic blasphemous provocation of the worst kind; it was not surprising that the people refused to accept this money.

It is necessary to make a digression here. Heraclides' action contained simultaneously several elements of the image dispute – confiscation of the objects of the visual cult, the problem of images on coins and, connected with it, the legitimacy of the cult of the monarch's portrait (indeed, even the permissibility of the portrait at all), and the relation of these matters to the question of the legitimacy of religious art. At the very outset of the iconoclastic dispute the problem of images on coins began to crop up. Traditionally, the toleration of images on coins while simultaneously combatting church images was one of the charges the iconodules made against the iconoclasts. In the sixteenth century this theme intertwined with the charge levelled against the Calvinists of promoting portrait painting and of having an idolatrous attitude towards their own likenesses. Rarely, however, was this process demonstrated so clearly as in the actions of the Moldavian despot.

The confiscation of church treasures embraced not only crucifixes but also reliquaries and the costly covers of icons. In the last case, Heraclides stopped on the threshold of iconoclasm in the strict sense of the word. The removal of icons would be the next logical step. In the understanding of Orthodox believers, the despot had already committed an iconoclastic act, since stripping the images of their gold and silver covers was a blow at the very sacrality of the icons. The populace was greatly incensed, and soon after this an armed uprising broke out under the leadership of Tomza, the later hospodar Stefan IX.

In the second half of 1563 the rule of the despot came to an end, and on 8 November he was executed at Suchava by his opponents. The death of the duke was certainly consistent with a certain general model of political conduct in the Danubian states. Yet in the cruelty displayed in settling accounts not only with the duke but with his entire group there appeared something of the public grief of the Moldavians over religious desecration. From the outcome of this attempt to introduce the Reformation in an Orthodox area 'from above' the Protestants learned no lessons concerning tolerance in ritualistic matters, especially in the question of images. Lasicki, a Polish Calvinist living in Lithuania, whose views on Russian iconodulism will be examined below, seems to have known the despot personally and was well informed about his fate.[10] Despite this, he did not change his iconoclastic views one iota, even in the face of the emerging danger of a Catholic–Orthodox union, in a situation when concessions in the question of ceremonies might really have changed the attitude of the Orthodox masses towards the Reformation. So it is quite correct to state that the Protestants learned no lessons from the Moldavian catastrophe.[11]

The Moldavian episode and the sending to Constantinople of a Greek translation of the Augsburg Confession a few years earlier (1559) brought to a close the first phase of the relations of the 'founding fathers' of the new faith with the patriarchate and with the Orthodox Church in the Balkans as a whole. The patriarchate received the text of the Augsburg Confession at the end of 1559. The author of the Greek translation of the Confession was probably Melanchthon himself; he wanted to lay an objective foundation for future Protestant–Orthodox theological discussions.[12] A scrutiny of the translation clearly shows that – especially in the passages on liturgical problems – Melanchthon and his collaborators made efforts to find more dignified formulas, closer to the Greek mentality. This somewhat changed the tone and meaning of the dry Latin text of the Confession, which did not seem to set much store by liturgy. These changes were supposed to suggest to the Greeks that the Protestants were not opponents of liturgy (the problem of images does not appear in the Confession). The patriarchate in Constantinople delayed answering for fifteen years. Owing to the death of Melanchthon in 1560, the matter went no further until 1574. Only then did a group of theologians from the University of Tübingen address a letter to the patriarch Jeremiah, requesting an answer to the theological conceptions and points presented in the Augsburg Confession.[13] In 1576 the answer came to Tübingen. The patriarch responded point by point. The negotiations between the Tübingen centre and the patriarchate, and their significance for the image question will be dealt with later but now – getting somewhat ahead of chronological order – let us summarize the most important points of the position of the patriarchate, for in sum they constitute an outline of the main theological differences between the two confessions – differences which were also to exert an influence on the image dispute.

In response to the fourth point of the Augsburg Confession the patriarch Jeremiah emphasized the importance of good works for salvation. This is the first basic controversy in the approach to the Confession. In the seventh point, while generally accepting the possibility of differences in the liturgy, the patriarch straightaway questioned the Protestant reduction of the sacraments. However, not until the fifteenth point did he launch a frontal assault on the stance of the Protestants on liturgical questions. The Greek theologians charged the Lutherans with a pragmatic approach to ceremony: namely, treating liturgy only as an element of stabilization and order in the Church. They were particularly resentful of the negation of the spiritual value of ceremonies and of their role in salvation. Taking into account this fundamental approach, the fact that the Lutherans reduced the ceremonies and judged them according to the criterion of whether they provoked offence or not (i.e. were unacceptable or acceptable) played a lesser role, but the patriarch questioned even this. In the form of a commentary on the relevant passages of the text of the Confession, Jeremiah's letter also took up the problem of the adoration of Mary and the saints. The differences on this matter were so great that Jeremiah made no attempt at all to play them down. In the opinion of the patriarch, in many cases intercession to Mary and the saints is the only possible means of reaching the majesty of God. These theological problems were indirectly connected with the image dispute.

Generally speaking, as regards the problems of dogmatic

theology, the Orthodox Church in the sixteenth century was closer to Protestantism than to Catholicism, but in all problems of practical theology, above all in problems of cult, it was much closer to Catholicism. What is more, owing to the pronounced ambivalence of the Orthodox theology of that time, eventual convergences with the Reformation on the issue of predestination or the role of Scripture in the life of a Christian were rendered less important by confrontations over differences in cult.

Let me quote another brief description of the differences between Protestantism and Eastern Orthodoxy, written in 1569 (hence in the same period) by the well-known Lutheran scholar David Chytraeus in his work on the Eastern Church:

> in the question of the Holy Trinity and the doctrine of the two natures as well as the Lord's Supper they agree completely with us. But on the question of salvation through faith, the necessity of good deeds, and the effects of redemption carried out by Christ they hold with the papists, and they defend the adoration of and appeal to the holy images with great obstinacy.[14]

Chytreaus' book, *Oration on the State of the Church of this Time in Greece, Asia, Bohemia [etc.]*, which is a compendium of information related to him by Greek scholars and theologians during his stay in Austria, brings not only the first concise listing of the differences between the two confessions, but also the first concrete description and evaluation of Eastern iconodulism. On the basis of a description of Athens, Chytraeus cites the idolatrous practices performed by the Greeks before the image of Mary (*idolatriae invocationis*); from an analysis of the gestures of the faithful and the liturgical ritual he drew the conclusion that 'they adore not the saints in heaven, but their images in an idolatrous way'.[15] This is a Lutheran analysis: idolatrous practices show the inappropriateness of iconography.

As regards the attitude of the Greek Church towards the iconoclasm of the Reformation in this first period of contacts, it is difficult to find any concrete facts. The first, albeit not very comprehensive, information does not come until the 1540s. The Greek Nicandrous Nucias, who was then travelling around Germany, left a description of his trip in which he stated tersely about the Protestants: 'they observe Sunday, but they reject icons and images of the saints'.[16] However, most of the news about events in Europe reached the Greek Church, Mount Athos and the patriarchates in the form of distant and muffled echoes; the iconoclastic movements in the Netherlands and Germany were probably unknown here. Only Orthodox Russia knew Protestant iconoclasm, first and foremost from the Baltic coast. On the other hand, some information might have reached Constantinople from Hungary and Transylvania, which were leaning towards Calvinism, and above all from Moldavia. Although out of fear of provoking the Ottoman authorities the patriarchate did not speak out against Heraclides, there is certain evidence that the actions of the Protestants in the Balkans irritated it. These actions were also one of the reasons why Melanchthon's initiative did not bring immediate results.

Hence in the early period Greek Christianity already began to identify the Reformation with iconoclasm, though by sending the Augsburg Confession as the basis of a future theological discussion the Lutherans avoided this sensitive question. They wanted to negotiate in Constantinople, and though in the first period their ecumenical tendencies unquestionably had an anti-Catholic basis, their desire to reach an understanding and readiness to compromise were doubtless sincere. They were unaware of the traditionalism of the policy of the patriarchate.

In the years before the negotiations between Tübingen – the leading Protestant centre – and the patriarchate and during the negotiations themselves, ever more Protestants made journeys to the Ottoman lands, which a dozen or so years later (and sometimes after even longer) yielded a rich crop of printed travel accounts, some of which were of great cognitive value. Notwithstanding the fact that these accounts were written by Protestant theologians or laymen well informed about theological matters, it seems more appropriate to make a separate presentation of travel literature – obviously from the angle of the image question – since the literary genre itself suggests that the authors were more interested in cultural than in strictly theological questions. Owing to a certain uniformity of approach with the descriptions of Stephan Gerlach and Salomon Schweigger, the account written sixty years later by Adam Olearius will also be discussed, even though it describes the Russian cult of images, which was richer than the Greek. The texts of English travellers occupy a separate place. All the authors cited here were educated persons and aware of the cultural consequences of Lutheran theology. The first two were staying in Constantinople during the exchange of letters between Tübingen and the patriarchate. Each of them in turn was chaplain to the imperial legation, and both of them were also go-betweens as regards the correspondence. Hence they were well informed about the state of negotiations and the theological problems of the two confessions.

In his lengthy diary Stephan Gerlach (resident in Istanbul in 1571–8)[17] mentions the cult of images several times. He did not hide his decidedly negative attitude towards image worship, and regarded all forms of ceremonies performed before images as idolatry.

Chytraeus, in his *Oration on the State of the Church*, gave a second-hand description of a ceremony; Gerlach provided first-hand descriptions of events witnessed by Protestant travellers. In the travel sources there were many remarks about iconographic problems. For example, Gerlach several times emphasized the dominance of Marian images, which in his opinion occupied the place due to Christ. However, he noted the fact that in his presence a protonotary of the Greek Church kissed first the image of Christ and then the image of Mary.[18] The reverse order – which will be discussed shortly – would force an essentially different theological evaluation of these images.

In consistency with the Protestant approach to images, Gerlach categorically refused to worship an icon depicting the Annunciation ('The protonotary implored me in all possible ways that I also bow the same way as the Greeks, for otherwise the Greeks would think that I had contempt for it. But I did not want to').[19] Gerlach also engaged in disputes with the Greeks on the cult of images, rebutting their arguments in a rather obsessive manner. For example, he called the Edessa image of Christ, as well as the one allegedly painted by St Luke, 'fairy-tales'. In a typically Lutheran way, he compared the cult of images to the cult of saints, categorically denying the efficacy of intercession and allowing it only as an example of faith. He even stated his belief that one day, under the influence of the Lutherans, the Greeks would renounce idolatry:

> Theodosius the protonotary has just brought me an image of Mary painted by the hand of a skilled artist. It represents Mary, and on her right Theodosius. . . . When I began to speak to him about the connection between this image and

the appeal to the saints, the protonotary said that they have these images only as a remembrance (*zum Gedächtnis*). Which neither he nor his father had ever said before, but apparently thanks to our writings they are beginning to open their eyes.[20]

In effect, if we give credence to Gerlach's account, this would mean that the protonotary had come over to Lutheran positions, for the designation of the function of religious art *zum Gedächtnis* was part of the classical definition as laid down by Luther in 1525. However, this was an isolated response of an Orthodox Greek, and it was probably said out of politeness; as Gerlach's diary shows, its author was later unable to convince anyone on this matter.

Gerlach's successor in Constantinople, Salomon Schweigger, was much more negatively inclined towards Orthodoxy. His description of the church in Phanar is a good example of an observation containing elements of theological evaluation:

In the churches they do not have images made of stone or wood, as in ours, but only painted with oil paints (as that image of Christ, his mother, the holy apostles . . .). In a prominent place was depicted the Mother of Christ in the [natural] size of a woman down to the waist; she is holding her child, Christ, in her arms. All those who enter this church worship this image with numerous bows and kisses, but the Virgin Mary is kissed first and only then the Infant Jesus. In these images one does not see any art; they are painted clumsily.[21]

How important this practice of the cult was for Schweigger can be seen from the fact that he repeated this information in even stronger emotional tones: 'Poor Jesus is being kissed after his mother.' For Schweigger and for all Protestants, this fact was a negation of the 'primacy of Christ' in favour of the Marian cult, which had no justification in the Bible. Schweigger did not question the legitimacy of the image of the Virgin and Child outright, but in accordance with the classical Lutheran assumption suggested that this was an idolatrous icon[22] because it stimulated the faithful to actions inconsistent with the basic tenets of doctrine. Irrespective of this, he did not like the hieraticality of the Byzantine images. This bias could have arisen both from the point of view of a person who had contact with the art of the Renaissance (though in Northern Europe such knowledge in Lutheran circles was not great) and from awareness of the fact that this kind of style was integrally fused with devotional content alien to Lutheranism.

The accounts of the English travellers Richard Chancellor (1553), Anthony Jenkinson (1557) and George Turberville (1568–9) contained extremely sharp attacks on the cult of images in Russia. The Englishmen emphasized the cult of domestic icons, first and foremost the 'horrible excesse of idolatry': that is, the practices of common devotion (bows, kissing, burning candles). They also rejected the cult of St Nicholas.[23]

This side of the Orthodox cult of images completely fascinated pastor Adam Olearius of Schleswig, who in the 1630s made two journeys through Russia on his way to Persia.[24] He did not take up the traditional theme of the image dispute, but was content with presenting the Russian tradition and rites connected with the cult of icons (which was much richer than that of the Greeks). His descriptions – not so much critical as full of constant wonderment – make us aware of the enormous cultural gulf between the two confessions.[25] Olearius described various, in his opinion faked, miracles connected with icons, and superstitious practices resulting from the faith in their miraculous powers. He emphasized the fact that the local Protestants were not allowed to possess any icons and described various Russian practices aiming at resanctifying icons 'defiled' by the mere presence of the Protestants. The peculiar status of the Russian domestic icon was incomprehensible to him, as was the fact that no foreign painter was allowed to paint icons: 'as if something of the artist's religion might be transmitted to the picture'. This last exclamation is understandable in the light of the realities of artistic life in Germany, where Protestant painters (such as Sandrart) worked in Italy and painted Catholic subjects on commission. His surprise about this prohibition manifested a modern conception of artistic creation which in this context made its earliest appearance in Protestantism.

Olearius abhors the icons and the rituals and beliefs connected with them. He ends his account with a very vivid description of the disposal by the Russians of old worn-out icons by leaving them to the forces of nature (e.g. soaking them in water), a practice smacking of magical thinking. An illustration in his book shows the Russians taking an oath before a domestic icon – an epitome of idolatry.

In Olearius' book the description of Russian customs and superstitions connected with the cult of icons played a special role as a kind of introduction to the 'Oriental Journey' and consequently is intertwined with descriptions of various, chiefly Persian, 'oddities'.

Olearius would not have been a Protestant if he had not entertained the hope that among the Orthodox he would find persons who shared the Lutheran approach to images. In Narva he met an Orthodox merchant, who – sharply condemning belief in the sacrality of icons and the magical practices of their cult – even said (like Gerlach's interlocutor) that images are 'for the remembrance of God and his saints', but who, despite this Lutheran accent, defended the keeping of domestic icons. Olearius also mentioned a statement of the protopope Ivan Neronov, who, in coming out against the abuses of the cult of icons, called for giving greater veneration to man as made in the image of God – a statement with Protestantizing overtones.[26] While noting with satisfaction these signs of a differing attitude, he was nevertheless aware that they would not overcome the iconodulic attitude of most Russians.

RELIGIOUS NEGOTIATIONS

In the history of Protestant–Orthodox relations there were two attempts to overcome theological differences through an exchange of letters between theological centres – attempts which, with some exaggeration, can be called religious negotiations. These were the negotiations conducted in the years 1574–81 by the group of Lutheran theologians affiliated with the University of Tübingen (Jakob Heerbrand, Jakob Andreae, Martin Crusius and others) and in 1716–25 by a group of Anglican theologians, the so-called Nonjurors. In both cases the adversary was the patriarchate in Constantinople; thus at the same time this is one of the chapters in Protestant–Greek relations.

These negotiations obviously had no chance of success for very different reasons. One of the most important was the fact that the Protestant centres did not represent all the Protestant confessions (especially the Nonjurors, who were really an Anglican sect). On the other hand, the patriarchate, which was under constant

Ottoman pressure, had little freedom of movement. I shall pass over most of the discrepancies of a theological nature discussed by the two sides. However, from the course of the negotiations one can clearly see that the image question, which at the outset was omitted or purposely not exhibited prominently, began to grow ever more important. From the beginning a close connection existed with the problem of the theological validity of the cult of saints. Nonetheless, as regards its role in the liturgy the image question was effectively camouflaged by the rather diffuse concept of 'ceremony' – as there existed a loose agreement that ceremonies could differ. However, as in the case of the Eucharist the essence of the matter – the role of religious art in the process of salvation – could not be put off indefinitely. On this issue there was less chance of reaching a compromise.

The starting-point of the negotiations of 1574–81[27] on the image question was the passage in section 24 of the Augsburg Confession ('it is a notorious calumny to allege that all of the ceremonies, all of the former provisions have been abolished in our church'). Thus the first letter of Patriarch Jeremiah II to Tübingen (sent in 1576) did not take up the question of images. Rather, the patriarch devoted much attention to the cult of saints. In their first response of 1576, when discussing the invocation of saints, the Tübingen theologians mentioned in passing the problem of images, in the form of a positive reference to the views of the well-known patristic opponent of religious art, Bishop Epiphanius of Cyprus: 'Let those things be destroyed which have penetrated the hearts of the deceived. Let the allurement of the idol be taken from our eyes – Epiphanius has in mind here first and foremost images that are worshipped',[28] concluded the Tübingen theologians. Epiphanius was a classic reference of the iconoclasts; the patriarch felt thus provoked to take up in great detail the question of images, and this in close connection with the cult of saints. In his second letter the patriarch forcefully reiterates that the cult of images is legitimate and belongs to that part of the traditions of the Church that is inviolable. The saints and their icons are to be venerated relatively (with *schesis* or *douleia*), not absolutely (with *latreia*), since worship is due to God alone.[29] An ever-recurring *leitmotiv* of the patriarch's argument is reference to the views of St Basil that veneration passes to the prototype. The cult of images is not idolatrous, since the faithful adore not matter but the divinity represented in the image. Jeremiah appended to this thought of

St John the Damascene further long quotations from his anti-iconoclastic works. However, the patriarch refers continually to images of saints – only once mentioning images of Christ – and thus eschews the Incarnational argument.

Where he attempted to link Christology with the problem of reference – which was very important in the anti-Lutheran context – he fell into rather dubious theological constructions that constituted fallacious reminiscences of anti-Arian polemics ('Thus he who does not honour the Son ... does not honour the Father, just as he who does not venerate images does not venerate the thing to which the image refers').[30] The Lutheran theologians in their response had no difficulty in refuting this contention by pointing out that God and the Son are one essence, which cannot apply to the images and the prototype. The patriarch also quoted at length the mystical image theory of Dionysius the Areopagite, thus weakening the cohesiveness of his argument. Weaknesses appear both in his Christological and in his exegetical elements. In Jeremiah's formulation the story of the brazen serpent is seen only in the light of prefiguration of Christ:[31] it is a very narrow interpretation which leaves aside the problem of abuse. Though theoretically the patriarch admitted the possibility of abuse in the cult of images, in practice this category does not appear at all. On the other hand his response in defence of the concept of church tradition, pointing to the pitfalls of unavoidable subjectivity when choosing only particular elements of the cult, was unquestionably pertinent to the needs of the dispute.

The Lutheran theologians now had no choice: in their second response (in a letter of 1580)[32] they attacked the very concept of a relative cult and the usage of St Basil's formula ('One cannot defend the cult of images with the excuse that one is venerating not matter but what the image stands for'). The cult of images goes against the testimony of Scripture. Despite the fact that they allowed the existence of images of saints ('we will allow the martyrdom of the saints to be depicted as an example of their perseverance in the faith'), they categorically negated the cult of their images as well as the theological basis of the cult of the saints. Only Christ could be a mediator, and the virtues of the saints – here comes Luther's classic formulation – cannot be imitated. The Tübingen theologians, like all Protestants, also rejected the distinction between relative and absolute veneration (worship) because of the inadmissibility of any cult of images. This does not preclude honouring buildings or some works of art; however, to invoke or venerate them is not to be allowed. All observed practices of worship testify that the cult of images comes to stand deceitfully between man and God. Thus in a clever, though not explicitly stated argument the notion of *coram imagine* was opposed to the famous Lutheran formula of *coram Deo*.

In this persistent, though sometimes camouflaged reference to the main assumptions of the doctrine, especially the immediacy of the man–God relation, we can see the unquestioned force of the Lutheran argument, despite ostensible willingness to compromise on ceremonial matters. God does not want elements of sacrality to be transmitted to humanity through the cult of images. That is why in this discourse the Protestants rarely referred to the concept of 'superstition', for it expressed a somewhat different aspect of the relationship man–image. Basing themselves on the same assumption, the Tübingen theologians rejected also the ancillary argument of the patriarch that the homage paid to portraits of famous people and rulers should imply the relative veneration of the icons. As they stated, the former was only a kind of civil honour and cannot be compared with the aims – as stated by the Eastern Church – of the cult of images. The refutation of this charge of the iconodules is unquestionably made with some consistency, but this strand of the polemics is a reflection more of the dispute with Catholic than with Orthodox iconodulism.

On the other hand, the pronouncement of the Tübingen theologians on the subject of the spiritual fathers of the cult of icons did have direct reference to Eastern iconodulism. It is no accident that St John Damascene was the main target of the attacks; moreover, the Protestants time and again quoted the most important passages from the classic opponent of images, Epiphanius. They also questioned the infallibility of the General Councils (aiming at the Second Nicaean Council) by stating that they had already made many erroneous decisions. However, this part of the Lutheran polemics limited itself to summary judgements given without wider argument. Nonetheless, the entire early Christian theoretical heritage of iconodulism was undermined.

By putting such great emphasis on the problem of the cult and adoration of religious images – which was quite understandable from the point of view of the main principles of Lutheranism – the Lutherans weakened their position in the negotiations, for this naturally obscured the fact that they were against the strict aniconism of Calvin and against aniconism in general. That is why their assurances of toleration of images of the saints (though rather of a historical and not devotional nature – which was not explicitly stated) could not have made much of an impression on the patriarch, just as their condemnation of iconoclasm did not.

In this situation the third and last exchange of letters (1581), which was a sort of two-sided summation and listing of the differences that it had been impossible to overcome, brought a brief but extremely intransigent pronouncement in the image dispute: Patriarch Jeremiah accused the Lutherans of Judaizing. This was a traditional charge in the image dispute and was often used in Protestant polemics.[33] Jeremiah in this case put greater emphasis on its historical and less on its Old Testament aspect, but in any case this was one of the heaviest accusations – in fact the heaviest in the whole dispute – putting an end to all hopes of reaching even a tentative agreement on some limited points. The somewhat shocked Lutherans responded in their third and final letter (1581) with a categorical denial of the charge of Judaizing,[34] but without mentioning the image controversy: they seem belatedly to have realized their mistake in opening this Pandora's box at all.

In the second Protestant–Eastern Orthodox negotiations, undertaken 150 years later (1715–25/7), the participants were the patriarchates in Constantinople and Jerusalem and an offshoot of the Anglican Church, the so-called 'Nonjuring' bishops, and that is why it seems proper to place these negotiations in the context of Protestant–Greek relations, though a certain role was played here, for political reasons, by Peter the Great, who supported with all his might a Protestant–Orthodox reconciliation.[35] These negotiations were characterized by a greater readiness for compromise on the Protestant side, and consequently it was possible to eliminate some of the controversial questions. Remaining still open were the problems of the authority of the first seven General Councils, the epiclesis, the Marian cult and the cult of saints and . . . the cult of images. On the last question the positions of both sides stiffened during the course of negotiation (more on the Eastern Orthodox side) and at the end they were further apart than ever before. The Nonjurors accepted the existence of images in church, which in their eyes was a tremendous concession ('And for a further Declaration of our Sentiment upon this article, we willingly acknowledge, that the use of Images in Churches is not only lawful, but may be serviceable for representing the History of the Saints, for refreshing the memory and warming the Devotion of the People').[36] This was really a Lutheran position, if taken literally, even with some slight Catholic accents as regards the by then uncommon pictures of saints or expressions like 'warming the Devotion of the People'. It certainly went against Anglican practice. The Nonjurors could not go further, however; they rejected the cult of images by pointing to its absence in apostolic times – for by then Christianity was already perfect; it is not a religion of cumulative practice. Image worship 'gives scandal to Jews and Muhammadans'. They opposed the decisions of the Frankfurt synod, as noted in the *Libri Carolini*, to the decision of the Nicaean Council on image veneration; moreover, in an internal position paper prepared for the negotiations they went so far as to state that in some parts of Western Europe the cult of images began as late as the beginning of the thirteenth century. The Nonjurors – like the Tübingen theologians – gave short shrift to the main defensive arguments of Eastern Orthodoxy (various degrees of veneration): 'The Distinction in Worship between Latria, Dulia and Hyperdulia is what we do not understand.'[37] The Nonjurors also linked the cult of saints and the image theory in an interesting way: 'since we cannot be convinced of any liberty for invoking the saints and paying religious worship to them; we conceive the argument lies rather stronger against giving relative worship or religious respect to their images. For, since the Prototype cannot be thus addressed or regarded, 'tis still more difficult to imagine the bare representation of such a being can claim any such honour.'[38] There followed a further quotation from Epiphanius, who thus assumed in the Protestant–Eastern Orthodox image controversy a role beyond his real theological and historical importance.

The Eastern Orthodox opposed this with arguments taken from the resolutions of the Second Nicaean Council, from St Basil's theory of the prototype and, of course, from the writings of the Damascene. The relative character of the cult of icons was emphasized, but also their narrative character ('For a picture is a kind of silent history, as history is a speaking picture');[39] this was perhaps a terminological concession to Protestant thinking. They also stated that the Lutherans had images of Sts Peter and Paul in their churches. Referring to the argument of giving scandal to Jews and Muslims, they claimed somewhat facetiously that Muslims 'have no objection ... when they see us paying relative worship to images, and mentally referring that worship not to wood and figure but to the prototype'. But then came actions which made agreement impossible. The Eastern patriarchs sent to the Nonjurors – for unconditional acceptance as the basis for further contacts – the text of the so-called Confession of Dositheos,[40] which originated in 1672 under the negative influence of the shock caused by two previous Orthodox confessions: the philo-Calvinist confession of Cyril Lucaris (1629) and the confession of Peter Mohyla (1640), which showed some Latin influence. The Confession of Dositheos, leaving aside its anti-Protestant undertone, went very far on the image problem, accepting icons of God the Father; for the Nonjurors this was not acceptable at all.

The negotiations soon broke off for mainly political reasons, the Eastern Orthodox side having realized that the Nonjurors were nothing more than a rapidly diminishing Anglican sect which represented hardly anybody in the Protestant world. The course of the discussions, however, clearly shows the intractability of the image question.

These Protestant–Orthodox negotiations were conducted only with the Greek Church. Contacts with Russian Orthodoxy took the more transitory form of public disputes. The exchange of letters between Tübingen and Constantinople really put an end to this brief early period of lively contacts. In the next century the contacts of Protestants with the Greek Church showed no real historical continuity: they remained – with one exception – isolated incidents of little importance.

A CALVINIST PATRIARCH

The exception was the case of Patriarch Cyril Lucaris, called the Calvinist patriarch (d. 1638), an eminent theologian with clearly philo-Protestant leanings, who in 1620 assumed the office of patriarch in Constantinople. The case of Lucaris has a fascinating political background, and to a certain extent the state of affairs to which it owes its renown reflects the European situation of the first period of the Thirty Years' War. Cyril's support and mainstay in the fight with the majority of the Orthodox clergy arrayed against him was the English and Dutch embassies; on the other hand he was opposed by the French and Habsburg embassies and by a few Jesuits operating out of them; all the Christian intrigues had the aim of gaining the favour of the Ottomans.

Here we obviously cannot relate the successive stages of the complicated political struggle that ended in Cyril's downfall and death at the hands of Ottoman assassins.[41] On doctrinal matters Cyril attempted to break away from the disinclination of the Orthodox Church for a clear and precise formulation of its religious principles. He was attracted by the logical and tough intellectualism of Calvinism. He wanted to break with the apophatism and hazy Christology of the Eastern Church, which in his eyes were suitable nourishment for mysticism.[42] At the same time his brief stay in Poland during the setting-up of the Union of Brest had made him deeply mistrustful of Catholicism.

In 1629 he published his own confession of faith[43] in Calvinist Holland, which was unusual in so far as the Eastern Orthodox avoided systematic theological documents of this kind. Nearly every one of the eighteen points of this confession showed leanings of one kind or another towards Protestant theology, but – with the exception of two points – Lucaris did not cross the boundary beyond which his views would have been regarded as apostate. Putting greater emphasis on predestination, denying the existence of purgatory, understanding the sacraments as not automatically efficacious and limiting their number to two – all this, with its unquestionably Western undertones, did not go beyond the field of manoeuvre which the ambivalence of their religion gave to Eastern theologians. On two points Cyril went further, however. Denying transubstantiation and recognizing the material presence of Christ in the sacrament of the Eucharist only when it was dispensed, he took a very anti-Catholic stance, but at the same time he limited the role of the Holy Spirit, which was already a departure from the assumptions of Orthodoxy. It is debatable, however, whether this was a radical break with Orthodoxy; even if Lucaris' approach smacked of heresy to educated theologians, for the broad masses of the clergy this question was too abstract to arouse their indignation (by marked contrast to Protestant Europe). In my opinion, however, not without importance is the fact that for Cyril also, who had come out of a different theological tradition, the acceptance of Calvinist theology, and through this a different understanding of the symbolism of the Eucharist, was linked with the rejection of religious art. It was on these two points that he moved the furthest away from Orthodoxy. Thus the philo-Calvinist view of Lucaris appeared most clearly in the image question. He was aware of the importance of the problem and did not reveal his views on the cult of images until 1633 in another edition of the confession, to which were attached four annexes, the fourth of which condemned the cult of images.[44]

Lucaris' line of argument is characteristic. He started from a rigorist Scripturalism, asserting that the Bible rejects and condemns the cult of images. This is not surprising for a theologian who had the Bible translated into modern Greek and did everything possible to promote the reading of Scripture and biblical studies. However, he argued, since painting is a noble art, one can create images representing Christ and the saints as long as no worship at all is shown to them. Thus Lucaris questioned all, even relative, veneration (*douleia*) and thus directly opposed the resolutions of the Nicaean Council. Though this was still a Lutheran point of view enriched by a rather rarely encountered argument in support of art (as a rule put forward by Lutheran artists), it is an entirely non-theological argument clearly crammed by force into the existing theological system, an argument in which the critical elements are not entirely balanced. For on the image question Lucaris leaned towards strict Calvinism.

This is clearly apparent from a private letter which Lucaris sent to the Italian Protestant Antonio Marc de Dominis in 1618[45] – that is, before he became patriarch. In this letter Lucaris stated that the cult of images as it is practised in the East is a terrible sore on the body of Christianity, though at the same time he saw no way to remedy this. He also noted, self-critically, that he himself was helped by the sight of a crucifix during prayer. At the same time he wrote that 'unadored images in and of themselves do not lead to anything bad'. The last statement can be regarded as a typical tactical stipulation, but the first part of the statement should be taken as more important.

In fact, Lucaris' views on the cult of images stirred up a storm among the vast majority of the clergy and the faithful. His few supporters tried to defend him by asserting that the confession was a falsification prepared by the Catholic camp, but this was an improvised defence which had no chance of success because the Jesuits residing in the Ottoman capital disseminated the authentic text of the confession among the faithful in an effort to discredit Lucaris once and for all. He was soon removed from office at the instigation of his enemies and expelled from the capital. For a short time he managed to return to the patriarchal throne, but in 1638 he was stripped of his office a second time and shortly thereafter murdered by Ottoman assassins. After his death all the theological novelties that had been introduced by Cyril were completely struck out of official documents, and his few supporters went to the Calvinist countries of Western Europe.[46]

Lucaris' pronouncements against the cult of images were obviously only words; what is more, they were for the most part intended more for the public opinion of Protestant Western Europe than for the Greeks. They were not iconoclastic in the strict sense of the word, though Lucaris' theological views were unquestionably evolving ever closer to strict Calvinism. However, in no imaginable historical situation would Lucaris have been able to put his views into practice. Even the elimination of the ceremonial aura around the icons was not possible, if only because in the situation of the Greeks of that time icons were an extremely important element in the fight to preserve the remnants of national life: the religious sacrality here was integrally intertwined with national sacrality. With time, negative opinions began to predominate in the Orthodox opinion of Lucaris. He began to be regarded as an iconoclast and as a political agent of Western Protestant states. Protestant historiography has placed him, in apologetic terms, in the ranks of the great martyrs of the Reformation, among whom was also the iconoclast Heraclides of Moldavia.

If we omit the episodes of the so-called second Protestant–Orthodox negotiations described above, the events of 1620–38 are the final chord in our presentation of the image question in relations between the Protestant world and the Greek Church. The latter, and with it the Eastern patriarchates in Antioch and Jerusalem, had neither the political means nor the theological and intellectual resources to carry on a debate with the Reformation. What is more, there did not exist any important political or dogmatic reasons for establishing closer contacts between the two Churches. Consequently, these relations were the result of the rather fortuitous sojourns of Protestant travellers and diplomats to the Bosphorus and in the lands of the Levant and the Balkans.

ICONOCLASTIC HERESIES IN MEDIEVAL RUSSIA

The situation in the second great centre of Orthodox Christianity, Russian Muscovy, was somewhat different as regards relations with Protestantism; this was due to the different 500-year history of the Russian Church. The Russian Orthodox Church, of course, accepted the entire Byzantine theology of images and the tradition of the iconoclastic dispute, though many important theoretical writings seem not to have reached Russia. In the Middle Ages the ritualistic cult of icons developed here even more than in Byzantium, with a peculiar stress on miracles; the status and activities of the painter of icons were sacralized, and a local iconography of Russian saints came into being. To a greater extent than in Byzantium the cult of icons became coupled with emerging patriotism and was used in the struggle against the Golden Horde.

Let me emphasize once again how important for the Russian consciousness was the tale about the circumstances of the acceptance of Christianity by Russia – as narrated in the famous *Tale of Past Years*. According to this story, Grand Duke Vladimir made the decision to accept the Eastern rite precisely on account of the splendour and vividness of its liturgy. In the consciousness of the Russian Orthodox, this tale was the counterpart of the Western ideal projection of apostolic Christianity: that is, a state to which the situation of the Church was always referred. As we know, one of the basic controversies of the image dispute concerned the reported aniconism of the apostolic Church; despite the fact that this myth could not aspire to the rank of patristic literature, nevertheless it shows the peculiar position of the Russian cult of images, which in the general consciousness had been an integral part of the religion from the very outset and not a later accretion.

The heretical movements within the Russian Orthodox Church were of great importance for our problem.[47] In opposition to official iconodulism they created a long iconoclastic tradition, or a somewhat less extreme tradition of cultural reductionism, which for nearly two centuries was an alternative to the cult of images of the official Church. On Russian soil they anticipated some of the problems of theology and the attitude towards the cult which appeared in the radical Reformation. Even following the final suppression of these movements after 1550, the iconoclastic tradition revived from time to time in the world of Russian

Orthodoxy. The existence of a native iconoclastic tradition gave rise to the highly interesting phenomenon of the overlapping and accumulation, in the eyes of the Orthodox, of internal with external heresy: i.e. Russian with Protestant iconoclasm, with which the Russians had come into contact on the fringes of their country – on the frontiers with the Baltic, Polish–Lithuanian and Ukrainian lands. That is why I shall devote no less attention to the image dispute in the territories that were not part of the tsarist state and shall examine them in close connection with Russia, despite the fact that at that time these lands were hardly (and in the case of the Baltic coast not at all) connected with Russia either culturally or politically.

In the middle of the fourteenth century the Strigolniki heresy broke out in Russia, chiefly in the cities in the north of the country, which gave this movement a proto-Reformation character (though this suggestion should not be taken too literally) somewhat similar to Western movements. In many of its manifestations it was still a medieval heresy, feeding on the dualistic assumptions of Bogomilism. The Strigolniki came out against the monasteries and the upper clergy. It is debatable whether they openly came out against the cult of icons[48] (though their theoretical rejection of the notion of the earthly Church should logically have led to the rejection of the visual cult); what is important, however, is the fact that iconoclastic tendencies were ascribed to this heresy in the later tradition of the Orthodox Church. However, such a tendency was openly displayed by the so-called 'heresy of Marcian', which arose as a specific epiphenomenon of the Strigolniki heresy in Rostov around 1380. The heretic Marcian,[49] whose views and activities are known from the *Life of St James Rostovsky*, a hagiographic description of the activities of the opponent of the heresiarch, came out against images of the saints and Christ, in the latter case making use of antitrinitarian arguments. After 1400 the Strigolniki and the heretical movements sympathizing with them disappeared as a result of persecutions.

Around 1480 there appeared, once again chiefly in the north, in Novgorod and Pskov, the heresy of the so-called Judaizers (*zidovstvujuscie*). One of the first propagators of this movement was allegedly the semi-mythical Jew Skharia (Zechariah). It seems, however, that the Jews played a minimal or an entirely imagined role in this movement.[50] The name itself, however, largely comes from the strict Scripturalism and adherence to Old Testament ceremonies ascribed to the supporters of this trend, which included observing the sabbath and hostility to religious images. Owing to the quasi-Nicodemite nature of this movement, information about the Judaizers is very uncertain and the interpretations of scholars highly divergent. What we know about their hostility to images may not fully portray the complexity of their religious beliefs, since isolated cases of iconoclasm were the only overt actions showing themselves through the skin – to put it figuratively – of their frequent practice of Nicodemism.

Thus we are still a long way from getting any clear picture and knowledge of the doctrine of the Judaizing heretics of 1480–1500 – that 'conglomerate of various trends', as Erich Donnert aptly called it. According to the view predominant today, they were divided into the more radical Novgorod–Pskov wing (lower clergy, artisans, some merchants) and the Moscow wing (parts of the upper clergy, scholars, some high officials). For a certain time (up to 1502/3) the latter enjoyed the support of Tsar Ivan III and a part of his court.

Uncompromising hostility to images appeared more in the north, while the Moscow centre was more interested in a programme of moderate church reform. George Vernadsky and J. Wieczynski retain the distinction between the Novgorod–Pskov and Moscow centres, but they propose a different division. According to them, the Judaizers were divided into three doctrinal groups: real Judaizers, the so-called antitrinitarian group, and the Moscow circle, the most moderate. The first group would consist of Judaizers whose only clearly authenticated doctrinal element was a hostility to images. The other postulates supposedly led in the direction of strict adherence to Old Testament ceremonial legislation.

The history and state of research on the Judaizers was negatively influenced by the fact that scholars of the Russian movement for too long attempted to winnow out the concrete influence of some Russian Jewish circles and failed to relate the concept of 'Judaizing' to similar phenomena in Western Europe. For example, neither A. I. Klibanov, who justifies the demand to observe the sabbath on social grounds, nor Wieczynski understands that Judaizing constitutes an ahistorical model and cannot be explained solely by a suddenly arisen predilection for the Judaic faith. The crucial element here was that most of the Judaizers renounced circumcision. In any case, hostility to images appeared in most of the movements which strove to observe the injunctions of the Old Testament. (as a rule they had no connections with Jewish communities in medieval and pre-Reformation Europe).

The second splinter group distinguished by Vernadsky and Wieczynski is the group of 'rational antitrinitarians'; they also were active in Novgorod and Pskov. The only convergence with the first group was their rejection of religious images (with the exception of the image of Christ). They also rejected the cult of saints and Mary and called for a radical change in Eastern monasticism. Had it not been for the negation of the divinity of Christ, this would have been a Lutheran programme, for it took a very similar stance on the image problem.

There remains the third group. It seems that in the Moscow group the image problem did not play such an important role. It appears that their programme was more political in nature, while religiously it was quite moderate (fighting against simony).

Both the concept of 'Judaizing' and the clearly 'pro-Western' leanings of the second, antitrinitarian group raise questions about the nature of analogies with Western proto-Reformation movements. As regards Judaizing, the drawing of historical parallels is unnecessary, since the similarities, especially in the image question, are deeply rooted in the basic structures of Christian thinking and are an unavoidable consequence of Old Testament law. Some scholars (Wieczynski, Onasch) have suggested – especially in relation to the Novgorod antitrinitarians – the possibility of inspiration from the Hussites and Wycliffites through the contact point of the Baltic coast. However, such contacts cannot explain either the more extreme forms of spiritualistic ceremonialism or the antitrinitarian elements, unless one assumes that in Russia Western impulses underwent a process of radicalization. The attempt itself also gives rise to certain doubts. We do know of individual contacts. For example, in 1414 Jerome of Prague spent some time in Pskov, but the more than half-century interval makes any eventual influence highly unlikely. Hussitism did exist on the Baltic coast, but both politically and doctrinally it was a weak epiphenomenon of the great Czech movement – so many doubts remain.[51]

In 1486–8 several iconoclastic incidents took place in Novgorod and Pskov. According to the accusations levelled against the Judaizers by their opponents in the 1490 Moscow synod, they

did insult the image of Christ and that of the Most Pure

[Mary], some of them insulted the crucifix, others delivered vilifying speeches against many sacred icons. Some of them had split up holy icons and burned them ... some of them have smashed the icons and the cross against the earth and defiled it with dirt.[52]

Moreover, the subdeacon Alexeiko urinated drunkenly on icons and turned them upside-down (a typical iconoclast inversion rite). The Moscow synod condemned the Judaizers and sent many of them to prison. The repressive measures taken against the radical circles of the northern cities caused this movement to die out before the end of the century. After 1500 repressive measures were taken also against the Moscow circle, where there was no iconoclasm.

For about forty years the iconoclastic movement in Russia vanished more or less completely, but the alarmed Russian Church (especially Joseph of Volokolamsk) continued its polemic with the iconoclasts, preserving a remarkable continuity on this issue. Thus the iconoclastic aspect of this movement weighed very heavily on its reception and was connected with charges of following the 'Jewish Decalogue'.

Soon after the first wave of Judaizing heresies died out, the Russian Orthodox Church was torn apart by the dispute between the so-called Nilovites – supporters of the famous hermit Nil Sorskii, who came out with the slogan of 'the poor Church' – and their opponents, defenders of large landed estates and ecclesiastical luxury, who gathered around the great metropolitan Joseph of Volokolamsk (the so-called Josephites). Despite their criticisms of ecclesiastical luxury, the Nilovites did not oppose the cult of icons or images.

Nil Sorskii himself wrote treatises against the Judaizers and the iconoclasts. The treatise against the iconoclasts was later used by the Russian Orthodox Church against the Reformation. Here is a very important moment that shows certain wider patterns, for it turns out that there are certain convergences between the heretic or protest movement of Eastern and of Western Europe. In practice the motto 'the poor Church' hardly resulted in automatic negation of the validity of religious art – by contrast, for example, with the slogan of a fight against the 'visible Church' ('brick Church') or rigorous adherence to the Ten Commandments of the Bible. This pattern also holds for Russia, where the Nilovites, who did not break completely with the Church, did not take up the iconoclastic tradition.

The Josephites achieved final victory in this internal church controversy around 1530. Before long, however, as though in consistency with the principle that life does not endure the lack of opposition, a new recurrence of the Judaizing heresy appeared in central Russia in the 1540s, this time more closely affiliated with poor monks and peasant circles. The leaders were Matvei Bashkin and Feodosii Kosoi.[53] They held very radical social views, which put them close to Müntzer, and at the same time they represented a Russian offshoot of antitrinitarianism. Their opponents called it a Jewish monotheism negating the divinity of Christ.

The antitrinitarian Christology, rejection of the church tradition and the cult of saints, and rigorism in the interpretation of the Decalogue alone would have sufficed completely to negate the theological basis of the cult of images and their validity. However, Kosoi also wanted to return to an apostolic age, when people did not pray to 'idols'. To the gaudy churches he opposed 'simple' ones or 'modest homes' in which Christians live and pray. Like the myth of the cave, this is an old Christian commonplace serving the concept of the 'poor Church'. In these 'modest homes' – whose very utilitarianism was inconsistent with Orthodox theology – there were obviously not supposed to be objects or decorations serving 'the worship of idols'. Kosoi also came out strongly against the cult of the cross and against images of St Nicholas. Bashkin denied the Real Presence and strongly attacked the cult of images and the saints – thus establishing an indigenous Russian tradition paralleling the schema of negation of the Real Presence/negation of images later to be taken up by the unhappy Foma Ivanov. Kosoi and his supporters allegedly committed some iconoclastic acts in Russia.

At the beginning of the 1550s Kosoi and his group of Russian Judaizers escaped to the freer atmosphere of Polish Lithuania; Matviei Bashkin was denounced by his confessor and duly imprisoned. In Lithuania the Russian Judaizers (only Bashkin seems to have had earlier contacts with Lithuanian Protestants) now came into contact with the semi-Judaizing tendencies of the Polish antitrinitarians, the hostility to images serving as a convenient bond. It suffices to mention the almost identical understanding of the commonplace of the 'poor Church' in the Polish Arian Kolodynski's *Letter of the Polovtsian Smera*. In the lands of the Polish commonwealth Kosoi allegedly committed a famous iconoclastic act in Vitebsk in 1552. This episode, as well as the later activity of his supporter Foma, who became a Calvinist pastor in Polotsk (I shall refer to it in detail later), intertwines the subject-matter of heresy in the Eastern Church with the nascent Reformation in the lands of the Polish commonwealth. For the Orthodox Church, which in the period 1350–1550 wrestled almost incessantly with various iconoclastic heresies, this merging, superficial as it was, of foreign and native iconoclastic traditions was evidence enough that there was some model of heresy in which the attitude towards images played the major role. The Russian theologian Zinovei Otenskii knew about Luther only that he was an iconoclast.[54]

The development of the Reformation in Western, Central and Northern Europe and its influence on the peripheries of the tsarist state – not only in the lands of the Polish commonwealth – caused an overlapping and accumulation of external and internal iconoclasm; from then on the Russian iconoclasts were inspired time and again by actions of this kind committed by Protestants. On the other hand, owing to the fact that the native skein of iconoclasm was broken off after 1550, it became easier for the Russian Orthodox Church to discredit individual local iconoclasts as supporters of heretical 'foreign' novelties.

RUSSIA AND THE REFORMATION

From this turning-point of 1552 – the collapse of the second Judaizing movement – we have to go back thirty years to trace the reception of the Reformation movement of Western Europe by the Russian Orthodox Church. In this largely independent subject the image problem played a very important role.

The first news about the Reformation reached Russia in 1518 (in a letter of Emperor Maximilian I to the tsar), but obviously this could not contain much important information about the barely emergent religious movement. However, the next period of contacts, which began several years later, was to play a crucial role for the mutual relations of the Reformation and Orthodoxy. The events took place chiefly in the Baltic areas. These lands rapidly accepted the Reformation (1524–35/40) in its Lutheran version. In spite of this, the process of conversion to Lutheranism in many cities was accompanied by short but violent explosions of iconoclasm. Iconoclastic disturbances touched this relatively homogeneous cultural area in two clear waves: 1524/5 in Elbing, Stralsund, Braniewo (Braunsberg), Riga, Stockholm and Dorpat and, 1529/30 in Copenhagen and Malmö.

The first wave of iconoclasm embraced the eastern regions of this area, where Livonia bordered directly on Russian territories. In Dorpat there was a numerous Russian artisan-merchant colony with its own Orthodox church of St Nicholas. In 1525 the Dorpat burghers, incited by the radical preacher and later Anabaptist Melchior Hofmann, not only demolished the furnishings of the town churches but also smashed the icons in the small church of St Nicholas. The latter event obviously might have been caused not only by doctrinal reasons but also by local ethnic antagonisms, but that does not change the complexion of the matter (on the contrary, it makes it even worse from the Russian point of view). Hence from the very outset the Lutheran Reformation stood before the Russians as an iconoclastic movement.

Though for the moment limiting itself to diplomatic interventions, the Russian reaction was obviously very vociferous. Tsar Vasilii III allegedly threatened the German burghers: 'I am not like the pope and the emperor, who are unable to protect their churches.'[55] This would indicate that some news about the events in Germany had already reached Russia.

The second wave of Baltic iconoclasm of 1529–30, which also was connected with the Lutheran Reformation, embraced the western part of the Baltic coast, but its echoes unquestionably reached Russia, the Baltic coast (long before Russia gained access to the sea) being the main channel of information. This confirmed the identification of Lutheranism with iconoclasm and made the Orthodox disinclined to distinguish the simplified Lutheran cult from Calvinist iconoclasm. The fact that some of the surviving images were returned to the churches (though for patronage in furnishing the churches one would have to wait until the second half of the sixteenth century) was of little importance for Orthodox opinion, especially since Orthodox churches were still being devastated. Even the Protestant Livonian chronicler Balthasar Rüssow had to confirm the complaints of the Russians: 'the Russian churches were transformed into houses of all kinds of filth, and images of the Saviour, apostles or martyrs were burned or desecrated'.[56] Let us conclude this list of iconoclastic acts committed by the Baltic Protestants with an incident in Russia itself, in

Novgorod, where in 1557 a servant accompanying the Swedish legation set fire to icons in an inn. The importance which the Orthodox attached to this deed can be seen from the fact that the Swedish diplomats were forced to hand over this servant to the local authorities.

A year later (in 1558) the army of Ivan the Terrible attacked Livonia, and a long war began. The devastation caused by the Russian forces and the persecutions of the local Protestants were justified in official tsarist propaganda by their iconoclastic past. This obviously was merely a pretext, but in fact it was precisely towards the residents of Dorpat that the Russians were the most pitiless – perhaps there was a grain of truth in this attempt to justify aggression. This war gave rise to many anti-iconoclastic legends. For a long time thereafter tsarist propaganda labelled all opponents of Russia iconoclasts, which apparently was the most catchy of all slogans.

In one of the propaganda statements of the patriarchate Ivan the Terrible's war was justified by the fact that 'the godless Crimean Khan Devlet Girey with all of his mamelukes and Latinists [sic!], the Lithuanian King Sigismund August and the loathsome Germans had succumbed to many various heresies, above all fallacy of Luther, destroying holy churches and desecrating venerable images'.[57] This passage of 1567 from the Moscow patriarch Philip clearly shows the importance of anti-iconoclastic slogans in Russia itself. In the Russian political-propagandist polemic this strand would continue right up to the nineteenth century. The successive invaders attacking 'holy Russia' were presented as iconoclasts even when – as the Polish army occupying Moscow in 1610 – they scrupulously adhered to the iconodulic attitude. (A Polish soldier who destroyed an icon was sentenced to death by his own superiors and burned at the stake as a heretic.) This is a fascinating item both for the history of Russian national consciousness and for its anti-Western xenophobic currents. The 'political career' of this motif was unquestionably grounded, however, in authentic experiences and indignation connected with the iconoclasm of the Reformation.

Though the letter of the Moscow patriarch quoted above was the first official reaction of the Russian Orthodox Church to the events of the Reformation, its first echoes had already appeared in the theological writings of Russian Orthodoxy in the 1530s. Characteristically, perhaps the first comment on the Reformation referred directly to the iconoclastic movement of Marcian and the Judaizers. The aforementioned treatise of Nil Sorskii, *A Speech on the Worship of Holy Icons written against the Heretics* (attributed by some scholars to Maxim the Greek), attacking the iconoclastic tendencies of the Judaizers was written between 1515 and 1530.[58] In this treatise, despite condemning the 'luxury of the Church', Nil Sorskii presented an apologia for religious art that was directed chiefly against the Judaizers. In any case, while writing this rather conventional (apart from accents of the 'poor Church') defence of icons Nil Sorskii still did not know anything concrete about the Reformation, and there is no mention of its hostility to images in his treatise. An unknown copyist who copied the text several years later (*c.* 1540) changed the title to *Against the Lutherans* to enhance its popularity, but the text remained unchanged. This offhand, uncritical identification of Russian iconoclastic movements with the new West European phenomenon is the best evidence of the force of the traditional thinking of the Russian Orthodox church, which immediately put new phenomena in old schemata. In the case both of Russian heretical movements and of early Protestantism iconoclasm played the role of the main discriminant.

The identification of the Reformation with old heresies was not only a defensive act on the part of Orthodoxy. This was confirmed, though to a very limited extent, by the actions of the heretics themselves, who often also accepted the 'struggle over the sign' as a form of struggle against the official Church. Especially significant seems to be the episode that we know from Andrzej Węgierski's account in his *Slavonia Reformata* of fifty years later (1609).

In 1552 three Judaizers – Artiemii, Foma and the already-mentioned Feodosii Kosoi – arrived in Vitebsk in their flight from Ivan the Terrible's police. They had heard about the beginning of the Reformation in the Grand Duchy of Lithuania, and it also seemed to them that they would find more freedom of action in the Polish commonwealth. In Vitebsk they immediately took up the fight against 'idolatry'.[59] They made the rounds of the homes of the local Orthodox faithful and attempted to persuade them to remove the icons from the churches and from private homes. With the help of fanatical believers the local Orthodox clergy managed to expel them from the city. Several years later, one of them, Foma, became the pastor of a small Protestant community which

was just beginning to form in Polotsk. We know too little about
the views of Foma himself and about the community in Polotsk
to be able to present the evolution of religious views which
brought about the fusion of Judaizing elements with Protestant
thought, but will probably commit no error if we assume that
hostility to visual cult was the main link between these hetero-
geneous currents from two very dissimilar regions. The community in Polotsk was apparently established by Calvinists. In
the winter of 1563 Russian forces took Polotsk. On the orders of
the tsar, Foma was seized and drowned in holes cut out in the
ice of the frozen river together with the whole Calvinist and
Jewish community. As we see, Ivan suspected here the collabor-
ation of the Judaizers and Calvinists with the, so to say, 'authentic'
Jews, probably seeing in iconophobia their common bond. He was
wrong, however, in attributing to all Russian exiles iconoclastic
tendencies. Most of the emigrés who left their country either for
political (Prince Kurbskii) or religious (some of the Niloviers)
reasons and had settled in the mostly Orthodox lands of the
Polish–Lithuanian commonwealth moved about in local Eastern
Orthodox circles and actively opposed Protestant propaganda.[60]
These emigrés preserved and upheld the iconodulic attitude,
especially towards the supporters of the Reformation.

Hence this episode on the eastern confines of the Polish commonwealth had very close links with the Russian situation. In the
1540s and 1550s many German and English Protestants (merchants, artisans, physicians) came to Russia. The tsarist government granted them certain privileges, including the right to follow
their own religious practices. In 1557 an attempt was even made
to hold a public religious dispute between the envoys of the
Swedish King and the Moscow patriarch (they spoke of 'fasting
and icons'), but owing to language difficulties it yielded no result.
In this period the police apparatus managed to stamp out the
Judaizing heresy once and for all. Though the anti-Judaizing polemic around the image problem continued, it was being simultaneously used for anti-Protestant purposes.

Around 1560 Parfiemii Iurodivyi of Suzdal wrote the treatise
Letter to a Stranger against the Lutherans.[61] Parfiemii's polemic
is directed mainly against the Russian Judaizers; even where he
comes out explicitly against the Lutherans, he mostly ascribes
Judaizing views to them. In a more concrete way he argues with
Lutheran Christology, with the rejection by the Protestants of the

cult of Mary, which in particular roused the indignation of the Orthodoxy.

At times Parfiemii's polemic recalls the words of Luther against Karlstadt in *Against the Heavenly Prophets,* since both of them accuse their iconoclastic opponents of Judaizing. The Law of Moses is no longer binding on Christians, and Moses himself allowed images (cherubs on the Ark of the Covenant). Parfiemii states that the Lutherans, who hold that icons and idols (graven images) are the same, combine under one concept the image of Christ and Apollo, the likeness of the Mother of God and the pagan goddess Diana. Icons come from apostolic times, especially the image of Christ from Edessa 'not created by human hand' and the painting of the Mother of God by the evangelist Luke which is now in Moscow. For the Russian faithful this latter argument was of tremendous importance and also served in the official mythology of the 'Third Rome'. Icons stimulate noble feelings and help the work of salvation, and they have attested their validity – now comes the classic Russian Orthodox argument – with numerous miracles.

Without real knowledge of the doctrine of Lutheranism, Parfiemii's polemic has no closer reference to its subject-matter. The exception here is the quite correct, perhaps intuitive, statement that the negative attitude of Protestants towards the cult of saints impoverishes their liturgy. Taking up the issue of Epiphanius' aversion to religious art, Parfiemii questions this argument often used by the Protestants, stating that the cult of icons never ceased in Cyprus. For the Orthodox polemic this is a characteristic theme, a historic argument put forward against the erroneous efforts of the opponents of iconoclasm, for the very historic existence of the cult of icons seemed to prove its legitimacy. St Basil's teaching about the image as the antitype of the supernatural reality also closes this chapter.

Parfiemii's treatise was to have an unusual history. In 1570 a public dispute took place in Moscow between a member of the Polish legation, Jan Rokita, who was a senior of the radically Protestant Czech Brethren, and Tsar Ivan the Terrible. At the end of the dispute (about which more will be said below) the tsar handed Rokita a treatise allegedly written by himself and explaining the main principles of the Orthodox faith. Not until 1951 did it emerge[62] that this was a copy of Parfiemii's treatise (with some minor changes). And so what had been considered a theological dialogue between Rokita and Ivan was really one between Parfiemii and Rokita in which the discussants did not address each other's arguments. However, there exists a Protestant reply to Parfiemii's charges. For the treatise, which was regarded as the work of Ivan the Terrible and a reply to Rokita, was translated into Latin and commented upon by the Polish Calvinist Jan Lasicki in 1582, hence about twenty years after it had been written. Lasicki was quite familiar with Orthodoxy from the eastern lands of the Polish commonwealth, but this did not change the fact that he took a very hostile position on the cult of icons.

Lasicki's polemic[63] was very malicious and had a strong political undertone. He tried primarily to show the negative role of the Moscow Church, charging it with numerous falsehoods and falsifications. He made less mention of the Greek sources of iconodulism. Lasicki put forward a classic type of biblical argument, sedulously citing passages of the Old and New Testaments prohibiting images. This introduced nothing new into the Orthodox–Protestant polemic, and nor did Lasicki's main thesis, which can be summed up in the expressive formula 'images are like unto idols'. On the other hand Lasicki's remarks about miracles, which in his opinion were the defining characteristics of the idols in antiquity, have a specifically anti-Orthodox edge. Citing ancient authors (e.g. Cicero) Lasicki tried to show that the alleged power to perform miracles automatically, as it were, qualifies an image for the category of idolatrous object. For Lasicki one of the arguments that icons are in fact idols or graven images was the Russian practice of the cult.

In the logical order of things the Polish Calvinist also referred to the writings of Calvin. Nor did Lasicki in his anti-Orthodox polemic spare other opponents. He criticized the Lutherans indirectly, but on the image question he saw a fundamental convergence between Moscow and Rome. In his comment on the religious images which the papal legate, the famous Possevino, was to bring to Moscow in 1581 one can sense an understandable fear on the part of the Protestant of a coordinated action of the two great Churches, especially in the eastern lands of the Polish–Lithuanian commonwealth. Parfiemii had also noted that on the image question the Roman Church was closer to Orthodoxy than to the Reformation.

The chapter 'Lasicki against images' can hardly be called a profound theological analysis of the image problem. Lasicki perhaps lacked not so much theological education as greater familiarity with theological discourse; time and again typical historical interests take first place in his treatise. What is more, he thought that he was writing a commentary on the work of Ivan the Terrible himself, and he was doing this at the very time of the climax of the Polish–Russian war. This accounts for the sharpness of some of the anti-Russian statements and also for his sensitivity to any changes in Catholic–Orthodox relations that might threaten the Protestant cause. Despite this, Łasicki was not inclined to make any compromises in relation either to Russian iconodulism or to Catholic visualness. We can take as a symbol of this the fact that in almost the same breath he attacks Russian Marian images and the famous image of the Black Madonna in Polish Czestochowa. Hence the Protestants began with a serious disadvantage in the religious struggle to win over the Orthodox masses which was soon to take place in the eastern lands of the Polish–Lithuanian commonwealth.

During Ivan the Terrible's reign many Protestants from the northern countries settled in Russia, and they were granted greater privileges than the few Catholics. Despite this, the tsar was extremely sensitive to the cult of images. The necessity of respecting holy icons time and again comes up as the leitmotiv of many of his pronouncements. Not all these pronouncements were motivated by political and propaganda reasons, though as a rule they had a political context. In the famous public correspondence with Prince Kurbskii, who had escaped to Lithuania, the tsar accused his former trusted adviser of entering into contact there with those 'who have ceased to worship holy icons, have violated all the divine commandments, have destroyed holy churches, have defiled holy vessels and images and trampled them as once the Isaurian [Leo III], the Soundrel [Constantine V] and the Armenian [Leo V] had done'.[64] Several years later, in a talk with his Polish supporters, who had put forward the tsar's candidacy in the first free election (1573) to the Polish throne, Ivan the Terrible stated that his opponents in Poland were 'supporters of the teaching of Luther, who destroy holy images – it is they who do not want to have me for their lord and ruler'.[65] In both cases the tsar erred or wanted to err. To the end of his life Prince Kurbskii obstinately defended the dogmas of Orthodoxy in an unfavourable Catholic–Protestant environment, and in the period of the first interregnum many Lithuanian Calvinists supported the candidacy of Ivan or his son Fiodor to the Polish throne. The fact that the tsar had a real obsession with the image question appeared most clearly in the aforementioned famous dispute with Jan Rokita, which took place in the spring of 1570 in Moscow.[66]

The initiator of this dispute was the tsar himself. He called upon Rokita to explain the principles of the Protestant faith, at the same time extending him full immunity (the Russian court of that time did not honour diplomatic immunity very strictly). Despite this, it is hard to say whether the accounts that we have of Rokita's pronouncement – all of them are Protestant sources – were not calculated for internal Protestant use, for it is hard to believe that Rokita would have had the nerve to make such sharp and sometimes outrageous remarks about the Orthodox faith before the Russian court and Ivan the Terrible, known for his unpredictable acts. Regardless of this, Rokita's treatise gives us the views of a certain group of Protestants on the subject of religious art and the position of Russian Orthodoxy on the image question.

The tsar began the dispute by stating that through the bizarre words of 'your teachers – Luther and Hus' ancient heresies had revived that had been condemned many times by church councils. In his opinion, the Protestants had never proved the validity of their faith with the help of miracles. These first comments of the tsar were already closely linked with the image problem, but first the tsar raised other issues. Then came the question of images: 'Added to all of this', the tsar charged the Protestants, 'you are enemies of our beloved saints in heaven . . . you revile and abuse them, you destroy their churches, their altars'. Immediately after this the tsar said to Rokita:

> consequently you not only fail to worship holy images, but you throw them out of your churches and homes, though all of the nooks and crannies of your homes ought to be filled with images of the saints. Which ought to be regarded as an even greater sin, since in this way you show contempt for God himself and oppose him. Who as punishment for your godlessness afflicted you with irreconcilable sects and divisions.

After this anti-iconoclastic diatribe, the tsar asked Rokita ten questions, one of which concerned the image problem.

Rokita spoke next. His pronouncement was a curious mixture

of Lutheran and Calvinist elements and weak echoes of radical theology. With the exception of the chapter on the Church and the passage on the cult of images, however, very moderate Lutheran elements dominated. Rokita took an extremely uncompromising stance on all manifestations of visual cult. In conformity with typical Protestant rationalism, Rokita rejected all image miracles, since Protestants 'do not need miraculous signs in order to strengthen their faith'. Rokita also rejected the cult of the saints; his arguments on this question were a sort of introduction to the basic problem of the entire treatise – the image question. 'That is why [just as we teach that one should not appeal to the saints] we also teach that one should neither pray to nor worship images, since they do not feel and do not hear.'

Rokita in his approach to the image problem appreciated the weight which it had for the Orthodox side. He put special emphasis on condemning and combatting the semi-magical practices connected with the cult of icons; several times he emphasized 'they do not see and do not hear'. Another ever-present motif is the 'corporeality' of these objects of the cult. This singular demystification of corporeality, which Luther himself sometimes used, was opposed to the Orthodox sacralization of objects – hierophantism. Heading off the charges of the opposing side, Rokita stated that the cult as practised by the Orthodox does not allow one to assume that 'they know the distinction between the image and the material', but it shows that the Orthodox pray to 'inanimate idols'. This line of thought appears most clearly in Rokita's statement that he would rather allow a deification of the living – a kind of euhemerism, as it were – as something less reprehensible than the adoration of dead idols. 'You abominable and clumsy images, you sway man to seek help in wood and stones.' In the face of the practices of the Russian iconodules Rokita himself constantly refers to the biblical opposition – which, as Karl H. Bernhardt showed, played an important role in the image dispute – of dead matter and the 'principle of life'.[67] Rokita's point of view is obviously only antithetical on the surface; in fact it totally denies the role of art as a means of transmitting religious meanings.

Though it is hard to say that it is on a high level, Rokita's critique of the cult of icons arouses interest on account of the multiplicity of its points of views and references. In the fight with Orthodox iconodulism Rokita refers to two concepts formulated by Luther (and made more strict by Calvin): namely, to the doctrine of 'the hidden God' and to 'faith from hearing'. Rokita uses them in a simplified way: 'How can one seek the unattainable God in a sculpted image?', he asks. He thus somehow failed to notice the fact that the Russians did not allow statues as an element of the interior decoration of churches – a circumstance which was emphasized by all Protestant travellers and criticized mildly by Catholics.

Rokita was a maximalist in his attitude towards the image question. Despite the fact that he was aware of the role which icons played in Russian homes, he stated: 'it is necessary to remove the idolatrous images and statue-idols not only from churches, but also completely to throw them out of towns and homes'. Without question this was an extreme position, which did not even leave the loophole that Calvinism provided for works of religious art in homes. Yet it must be said that Protestants of all tendencies were hostile towards 'domestic icons', as is clear from the travel account of Olearius. Rokita touched also on the traditional problem of the existence or non-existence of images in the days of the first Christians, and of course he came out in favour of the thesis of their non-existence in apostolic times.

The dispute between the tsar and Jan Rokita clearly shows what passions and emotions – not only of a theological kind – the image problem aroused at that time. While the tsar was obsessed with defending the icons, a strident enmity towards images dominates among Rokita's theological views. The moderate tone in which he discussed other theological problems changed here. Nor did he continue his own earlier adiaphorist construction on the question of fasting, which he connected in a logical and clear way with the concept of a 'free ceremony', showing its relative nature.

In his response to Rokita's pronouncement the tsar allegedly said that the speech of his adversary pleased him and that it ought to be printed. Then the tsar handed him as his own work a copy of Parfiemii's treatise. Rokita was happy that 'we had been able to reject the old religion'. The description of the tsar's reaction as transmitted and commented on by the Lutheran chronist Paul Oderborn is certainly a product of fantasy, for in reality Rokita's views and the whole episode played no role in the further course of Protestant–Orthodox relations. The conciliatory tone of the tsar's response – if we can give any credence to the sources – might have been influenced by diplomatic considerations.

Hence in the history of the Protestant–Russian Orthodox dialogue the 1560s were the high-water mark, for soon after this there was a break-in, or rather a weakening of, these relations. In Russia the emerging political crisis, which would last until 1613, and invasions of foreign armies – all this linked the problem of images (understood as the defence of icons) to the political-propagandist issues of the time.

Meanwhile, from 1555–60 onwards the eastern lands of the Polish commonwealth became the scene of the next iconomachy, though it was of a different nature. Leaving aside the few Judaizers who attempted to bring their hostility to images to the eastern lands, it was the progress of the Reformation in these lands that made the image question a major issue.

ENCOUNTERS IN THE POLISH–LITHUANIAN COMMONWEALTH

A large majority of the population inhabiting the eastern lands of the Polish commonwealth were followers of the Orthodox faith. In the sixteenth century the Orthodox Church was going through a severe crisis, especially as regards theological centres and the higher clergy. However, despite the increasing pressure of the Catholic Church, the main, peasant core of Orthodoxy remained intact.

The Reformation introduced a new element into this equation.[68] For decades it so weakened the Catholic Church that its pressure on the 'Ruthenians' (today's Ukrainians) ceased almost entirely, but later Rome resumed the offensive with renewed energy. As we shall see, the Reformation aroused not lesser but perhaps even greater concerns on the part of the Orthodox masses than the attacks of the 'Latinists'. In Lithuania some of the magnates (e.g. the Radziwills) and part of the middle gentry went over to Calvinism, while in the Ukraine – especially after 1565 – Anabaptism and Polish antitrinitarianism spread, and the Czech Brethren were also active. All these currents, down to the most moderate Calvinists, held a negative position on religious art. We know little about the relations between the various factions of the Reformation and the Orthodox, especially as regards the occupation of churches and eventual iconoclastic incidents. One can generally say that where Catholicism was stronger or just as strong as Orthodoxy the main attack of the Reformation was directed against it. For example, in the district of Przemyśl the occupation of churches and throwing images out of them was limited to Catholic churches. In his treatise on the Union of Brest, the famous Catholic preacher Piotr Skarga gave the number of 650 Orthodox churches plundered by the Protestants in the province of Nowogródek alone, which was unquestionably an exaggerated figure. In many cases radical groups of dissenters did not take over churches (limiting themselves to closing them), for they did not need a special building for their simplified services. The Reformation of all shades quite rightly regarded Catholicism as the more dangerous opponent. Most of the polemical literature in the eastern lands was directed against Catholicism, and after 1570 often against the Jesuits in particular.

The Reformation conversion and propaganda campaign directed towards the Orthodox was not conducted with great energy – despite the appearance of publications in Ukrainian – and it did not yield any great results.

What weighted most heavily, however, was the rejection of the liturgy and the cult of Marian images, of the saints and of images in general. If we leave out small groups of rich patricians in Lvov and Kiev and a group of magnates and gentry which was shrinking on account of Polonization, Orthodoxy was a peasants' creed. The same factors as had deterred the peasants in central Poland from accepting Calvinism were working against the Reformation in the eastern territories. Hence the efforts of the Reformation in the eastern lands were doomed in advance to failure (which one cannot say about the Reformation in Poland), and the concern they aroused among the Orthodox was disproportionate to the real danger. From the struggle of three confessions (taking the Reformation as a whole), a fight that reached its apogee in 1595–9, Roman Catholicism emerged victorious. It was obviously helped in this by an alliance with political authority, but also to a large extent by its willingness to make certain concessions in the liturgy (e.g. retaining the iconostasis).

The Protestant propaganda directed at the Orthodox began in the 1560s. In 1562 Szymon Budny, later an antitrinitarian, published a Calvinist catechism in 'Ruthenian' in Nieświez 'for the simple Ruthenian people and for Christian Ruthenian children'. Other books by Budny followed, and in time he became the best-known Reformation writer among the Orthodox. Budny's catechism contained a condemnation of images,[69] which put him on the index of iconoclasts drawn up later by the Orthodox clergy. The most original Reformation treatise addressed to the Orthodox is, however, unquestionably the so-called *Letter of the Polovtsian Ivan Smera to Grand Duke St Vladimir*. According the contemporary Arian writers, it was supposedly found around 1570 in the Ruthenian Orthodox Church of the Saviour near Stary Sambor (district of Przemyśl) by the Ruthenian deacon Andrew Kolodyński; it was reportedly written 'on copper tablets with iron letters in Old Slavonic'. At that time numerous copies and translations into Polish were circulating around the Ukraine, distributed by the local Arians. Kolodyński himself, probably the author of this mythologizing account, was an Arian.

Here we shall follow the excellent summary of Lewicki, who perfectly stresses the main elements of the tale:

> The fictitious author of the so-called letter, the court physician and rhetor of Duke Vladimir, was supposedly sent to Greece in 980 to acquaint himself with the faith of the Christians there. After long and difficult travels through the European and Asian possessions of the Greek emperor, the Polovtsian Smera arrived in Alexandria, where he encountered some more perfect kind of Christians, who differed in their faith and customs from other Greeks. Captivated by their teaching and life, our envoy accepted their faith; however, having learned that Vladimir had become converted to the Greek faith, Smera decided not to return to Russia. And it was then that he allegedly wrote this letter in which he described the habits and customs of these perfect Christians in inviting colours. Under this figure the author of this letter wanted to present the contemporary Arians. They were upright, God-fearing people, theologians and called by other nations the holy nation, God's people, the new Israel. These angels of God above all love peace and quiet; in their houses of prayer there are no idols, only benches and tables – here they gather for prayer and to hear teaching before sunrise and after sunset, sometimes at the third and ninth hours of the day.[70]

There follows a short account of the main points of the Arian faith and a description of the persecutions of these true Christians, who are coerced by the Greeks to attend their splendid churches and worship idols. The true Christians are thus forced to gather in forest clearings, catacombs and hills. However, the letter ends on a chiliastic note – among the Slavs, scholars of the Scriptures will arise who will pave the way for the reign of truth, and the Greek persecutors and their idols will become the laughing-stock of other nations. Smera's letter ends with an appeal to Vladimir not to accept the Greek (and, some copies added, Roman) customs and faith.

The Letter of the Polovtsian Smera is unquestionably the most interesting example of Reformation propaganda calculated to win over the Orthodox of the Ukraine and Lithuania. In a clever way the author of this mythologizing account referred to the famous *Tale of Past Years*, which tells about the acceptance of Christianity by Kievan Russia. As we know, according to this famous mythical account it was the pomp of the Byzantine liturgy and the grandeur of the cult, hence its extreme pictorialness, that inclined the Russians to accept Christianity at the hands of the Byzantines. Thus Smera's letter had the aim of creating with hindsight the illusion of the existence of still another alternative (in addition to the rather unattractively described religions of the Germans, Khazars and Bulgarians). This alternative was, supposedly, the possibility of accepting the pure, obviously aniconic, form of Christianity of apostolic times. Two motifs intertwine here: the first five hundred happy years of Christianity, and the commonplace connected with this of a Christianity 'of the caves'. In the sixteenth century the latter in turn intertwined with the motif of the 'Church in the wilderness'.

The author of *The Letter of the Polovtsian Smera* wanted to treat the times of St Vladimir as the Russian counterpart of apostolic times; he wanted to show aniconism as the natural, innate state of the Christian Church. Considering the wide dissemination and specific role of the legend of the *Tale of Past Years* in the mind of the Orthodox both in Russia and in the Ukraine and Lithuania, Smera's letter was an attempt to question – on the canvas of this mythical tale – the decision made by Duke Vladimir; though the author of the letter did not say why the duke chose the Greek religion, but limited himself to raising doubts about the correctness of the choice.

The role of the discussions on 'whether images existed in the original Church' for the entire field of the image dispute in sixteenth-century Europe has already been mentioned several times. This subject also continually recurred in Orthodox–Protestant relations and was one of the most important issues, used

with equal readiness by both sides. However, through the consistency with which the author used this motif and attempted to make
it real in a historical context, Smera's letter leaves all previous and
all future attempts far behind. All the same, despite the skill of
its mythologizing, it obviously had no chance of reaching the
broad Orthodox masses. It unquestionably came from humanistic
circles affiliated with Arianism (we know almost nothing about
its supposed author, Kolodyński). Several critical remarks about
Catholicism show, however, that not for a moment had the Arians
forgotten the Catholic danger.

In the eastern lands of the Polish commonwealth these theoretical pronouncements on the cult of images in Orthodoxy were
accompanied by various iconoclastic acts; also, in a more or less
ostentatious way, Orthodox churches were often closed. They
were rarely used as Protestant churches, but more often ruined
or turned into farm buildings. For example, the Arian noble
Strzemeski turned one of the Orthodox churches in Zydaczow
into a pigsty, and since this happened in the time of the triumphant
Counter-Reformation, in 1644 he was condemned as a blasphemer
for this deed. The court records often tell of such typical symbolic
acts as running icons through with sabres or the even more
common destruction of crucifixes. Even the Arians in the service
of Orthodox magnates did not hesitate to destroy Orthodox
churches and 'do mischief to images'. In many cases the iconoclastic acts of the Arians were associated with the well-known heresy
of the Judaizers, despite the fact that during this time theologians
had already emphasized the Western origin of this heresy. In
1585 the Orthodox gentry in the district of Halicz charged the
metropolitan of Kiev with tolerating the iconoclasm of the Judaizers 'and also the hacking-up of holy crosses, collecting bells for
the sake of the Jews. And your honour even gives open letters to
the Jews opposed to the Church, to aid and abet them'.[71] These
supposed Jews – obviously a synonym for the Judaizers – are
none other than the first Arians who appeared in these territories
and whose iconoclastic inclinations found their main outlet in the
destruction of roadside crucifixes. The letter quoted brings one of
the last reflexes of the traditional identification of Judaizing with
iconoclasm. The fact that the anger of the broad Orthodox masses
was directed against more or less imaginary 'Judaizers' – hence
against home-bred iconoclasts – was transitory and in the long

146

run could not protect the Reformation against the negative effects of its actions and stance on the image question.

The Protestant actions evoked a powerful reaction from the Orthodox side. Individual leaders of the Orthodox camp accused one another of being too tolerant of the actions of the Reformation – and the anti-Protestant religious polemic heated up. The treatises written in the Ukraine towards the end of the sixteenth century – which have not been adequately studied up to now – were of great importance for defining the dogmatic position of Orthodoxy in relation to Protestantism. What is more, they circulated in numerous copies around Russia during the crisis and helped to shape the theological attitude of the Russian Orthodox Church. They were used until mid-century in official Russian polemic.

In 1588 the Orthodox clergyman Vasil Ostrogsky wrote the theological treatise *On the One Orthodox Church*, which was mainly directed against the 'Latinists'. The treatise's sixth and final chapter, which in itself is more important than its placing would indicate, contains a polemic with the Reformation on the eastern fringes of the Polish commonwealth. The internal division of the chapter is significant.[72] It has two sub-chapters: 'On churches or houses of prayer' and the much longer 'On images or icons'. In the passage on Orthodox churches Ostrogsky attempts to show that an Orthodox church as a temple of God is something infinitely higher than, and beyond comparison with, the 'ordinary houses' in which the Protestants conduct their false services and in which they live after their conclusion. Hence the strongest argument against the conception of Protestant churches is their utility, the very fact that they can be used for other purposes besides worship. This line of argument would persist in the Orthodox view of Protestant churches as an axiomatic criterion, though often in its most primitive version as an argument about dogs strolling in Protestant churches.

More important is the sub-chapter on church images. Ostrogsky clearly states that, owing to the position of Protestants on the image question, those Orthodox Ruthenians do wrong who seek in them allies in the fight with Catholics. It is the actions of the heretics that make the author take up his pen 'to shut the mouth of those who speak falsehood': that is, who incite others not to venerate icons:

In venerating holy icons, in bending down before them and

kissing them . . . we do not adore the icons themselves, we do not put our hope in them, as the enemies of Christ accuse us of doing, but we direct our thoughts to the archetype. And when we come into church we see the saints of the Lord as though they were living.[73]

Despite the fact that they do not have souls and are dead, icons serve as vessels (the line of thinking here shows analogies to the doctrine of enoikism) for the miraculous divine power. To illustrate this idea Ostrogsky uses a beautiful metaphor about a blooming tree. In his arguments we can detect the desire for a certain very modest limitation of the cult of icons which already foreshadows the seventeenth-century rejection of the notion of 'gods' as a pagan relic in Orthodox terminology. However, this relativization did not weaken the polemical force of Ostrogsky's arguments. The remaining passages of the chapter belong to traditional polemics, the author using passages from the Old and New Testaments (some of the arguments were taken from Nil Sorskii's treatise). Another fragment refers directly to the notion of the sacrality of the Orthodox church and combines in one whole the arguments of the two sub-chapters by stating that an Orthodox church without images would be indistinguishable from an ordinary home. In a somewhat exaggerated way, this statement expresses one of the main features of Orthodox thinking of that time: images were given the main symbolic role, more important than the external form of the building. In that position we might discern the direct influence of the image controversy. The Orthodox church building as a national religious-symbolic form, a symbol of civilization and of 'holy Russia', seems a product of later times – perhaps even the nineteenth century.

More than ten years later (in 1602) the Ruthenian theologian Zachary Kopistenski published a treatise directed entirely against the Protestants, whose second part bore the title 'On images, on the cross, on the worship of God and the worship and prayers to the saints'. This part comprised twelve chapters, six of which – the first three on icons, and the next three on the cross – were directly devoted to the image problem. Two later editions explicitly characterized the aim of the book as a fight with the 'iconoclastic protestants'. Rejecting the allegation of the heretics that icons and the crucifix were a human invention, Kopistenski states that in the New Testament Christ, through the apostles, passed on to the world his image and cross as symbols of his passion.

However, the most interesting passage of the treatise is connected with the history of iconoclasm, which the Orthodox author identifies with the history of heresy. For iconoclasm – by contrast to veneration of icons – is a human work. It began with Arius, the author states, and this starting-point simultaneously illustrates the weight of the Christological controversy both for the outcome of the image dispute and for larger theological interpretations of its history. The next iconoclasts, according to the author of the treatise, were Julian the Apostate, Philip, Leo III and Leo IV but

in 1430 iconoclasm arose in Germany and England from Wiflak [sic, for Wyclif] and Jan Huss, who was burned in Constance. Then in 1517 came Martin Luther, whose teachings the Germans follow to this day. Soon after this Martin's pupil Calvin raised his head and reversed the teaching of his master; the so-called evangelists use Calvin's teaching. Later there appeared Calvin's friend, an even worse iconoclast named Michael Servetus, who had studied in the Lutheran school of a certain Faler [Farel]; he began to propagate an even worse teaching than the one [professed by] the unchaste Calvin; many peoples accepted this wicked doctrine. Calvin, revenging himself on his former friend for such a crime, brought about the burning of Servetus at the stake in Geneva. After Servetus had been burned, his followers, iconoclasts, appeared: Blandrat, Alstatus, Socinius, Davidovitch [F. David], and other ministers from Transylvania. At that time Budny appeared in Lithuania, and Czechowic in Lublin. These iconoclasts even differ greatly among themselves on many matters. Thus Czechowic with his close supporters thrust Budny from him and put a curse on him, while Budny called Czechowic the Lublin pope and refused to accept his decrees. . . . When Servetus was still alive another great iconoclast appeared, Valentin Entilis [V. Gentilis], who spread his iconoclastic heresy all over Switzerland, France and other countries. When he returned to Switzerland for the second time, he was seized and burned at the stake in Berne, eleven years after Servetus.[74]

This passage ends with the statement that it is impossible to name all the iconoclasts continuing the wicked teaching of Luther,

Calvin and Zwingli, for they have been active right up to our times.

In all Orthodox writings this list is perhaps the most extreme example of a real obsession with iconoclasm, an obsession whose effect was the tendency to present it as a linear historical sequence. This brief history of heresy, in which the emphasis was put mainly on the degree of intensity of iconoclasm and which passed over all other theological problems, brings out the conspicuous role that the image question played in Orthodox thinking. There is no sense in going into the errors of particular assumptions, since in the light of the general approach they are obvious. All the heresi-archs mentioned in the treatise – with the obvious exceptions of Luther, Huss and Wyclif – were iconophobic; in some of them this hostility was expressed openly, while in others it came from the general assumptions of their Christology. For example, the conflict between Servetus and Calvin concerned various problems, without reference to the image question at all. In later histori-ography in Western Europe there are no examples of a similar approach to the conflict. The obsession with iconoclasm thus transcends the bounds of ordinary polemic.

With hindsight we know that Protestantism could not be an alternative to Catholicism in these territories – not to mention the vain hope of its becoming the dominant religion. The reformers obviously would not have been aware of this. They dreamed of the day when – as Rokita once expressed it – 'the torch of the new faith will illuminate the eastern darkness'. However, both on questions of the main articles of faith and on 'ceremonial matters' dear to the Orthodox, the reformers lacked any flexibility. This was a remarkable sort of feedback: in the encounters with Eastern iconodulism the image problem also began to assume in the minds of the reformers an importance which even the most extreme iconoclasts would not ascribe to it in the abstract. Hence as a rule the views of the Calvinists, antitrinitarians and Arians on the image question were uncompromising. Only once did the Prot-estants seem ready to make concessions. On the other hand, numerous iconoclastic acts, which were taken up and amplified by the propaganda of the Counter-Reformation, made the Refor-mation odious in the eyes of the Orthodox.

Despite this, it is difficult to say with absolute certainty what influence the image question had on the historical process of that time. Irrespective of the impact of the Reformation, the pressure of Catholicism, which was helped by the government apparatus, and the political weakness of Orthodoxy alone sufficed to bring about the Catholic–Orthodox Union of Brest (1596). The Catholic camp – which on the image question was not separated from Orthodoxy by fundamental theoretical differences on the validity of religious art, but had much in common with it – was willing to make great concessions in all liturgical matters, despite the fact that it did not regard all the elements of Eastern religious art as necessary (especially the iconostasis). The Catholic Church would not withdraw from some of the concessions until the synod in Zamość in 1720.

In the last years of the sixteenth century efforts were made to forge a special Protestant–Orthodox alliance. The initiative for this alliance, which came much too late, was taken by the more moderate Protestant circles (represented by, among others, the Lutheran Erazm Gliczner), though representatives of the Calvinists and Czech Brethren participated in the preparations for the meeting.[75] The synod of the non-Catholics of the Polish commonwealth was convened in 1599 in Vilna. In the preparatory memorandum specifying the position of the Protestant side, drafted by a group of Reformation theologians and disseminated by the voivode of Smolensk, Jan Abramowicz, much attention was devoted to the image question. One can regard as a significant concession on the part of the Protestants the fact that the memorandum – though it unequivocally rejected the cult of images – nevertheless allowed the possibility of tolerating it for a certain time if the Orthodox insisted that they could not do without it.[76] However, in the opinion of the authors of the memorandum, the Orthodox priests ought incessantly to explain its harmfulness to the faithful. No boundary was drawn between the cult and the complete abolition of icons – an omission which seems to have been intended. On account of the resistance of the Orthodox, who were unwilling to engage in any more substantive talks on fundamental theology, the Vilna synod resulted in only a very limited theological understanding (the so-called Eighteen Points) and a more important promise to wage a common fight against the attacks of the Counter-Reformation. The image question was not mentioned in these eighteen points.

In political–religious practice the Vilna synod was to remain an interesting episode, but it lacked more important consequences. The shock caused by the Union of Brest did not push the

Orthodox into the arms of the Protestants; the gulf between them was already too great and was skilfully exploited by Catholic propaganda.

Though the quotation below comes from a somewhat later time (1632), it clearly illustrates the main thrust of the Catholic attack around 1600. The famous preacher Fabian Birkowski appealed to the Orthodox, saying that if they continued their contacts with the Protestants, then 'while before you were only schismatics, now you will also be Calvinists: that is, vile heretics. Then the images will vanish from your churches, for the wicked Calvin does not like them, and the holy sacraments also will vanish'.[77] The only alternative was to join the union with Rome.

After 1596 Protestantism in the eastern lands of Poland–Lithuania entered a period of decline. Though this phase lasted longer than in central Poland – many centres of the Reformation survived until the second half of the seventeenth century – it was a survival that lacked any dynamism and was made possible only by the weakness of the central authority in the borderlands. Iconoclastic incidents took place up to the 1640s and even later, sometimes punished but more often not. Most of them, however, were due to the lawlessness of the gentry than to the conscious action of the Reformation. The failure of the Reformation in the eastern lands of the Polish commonwealth cannot be explained – as in the case of Moldavia – by the different cultural background of the reformers, for many of them, such as Budny, Łasicki or the later well-known Arian family Niemirycz, came from these parts and were familiar with the peasant religion and with the religious practices of these lands. What had a negative effect here was the tendency of the new confession to reduce ceremonies – a reductionism so severe that it made the few Lutherans, who paradoxically were in fact culturally alien, the only reformers who had theoretically a limited chance of influencing the Orthodox.

RUSSIA IN THE SEVENTEENTH CENTURY

After the reign of Ivan the Terrible, there was an almost thirty-year interlude in the theological polemic between Russian Orthodoxy and Protestantism. The Time of Troubles and the events associated with the False Dimitri, coupled with the invasion of Lutheran Swedish and Catholic Polish forces as well as iconoclastic incidents perpetrated by mercenary German regiments (which several times changed their masters), strengthened the xenophobia of the Orthodox believers and the cult of icons.

With the stabilization of the internal situation after 1620 there came a new period of contacts between the two confessions. The accounts of Western travellers present a rather uniform picture of Russia, in which the cult of images played a cardinal role. Simultaneously Moscow fashioned a stereotypical set of information about Protestantism, which from then on appeared in theological treatises without greater changes. This period was to last for an entire century (1620–1720) and ended with the religious reforms of Peter the Great. While the first half of the century, apart from the account of Olearius, did not bring much new, from the 1660s onwards one can sense a clear intensification of contacts.

The 'institutionalization' of these contacts, as it were, did not occur until the end of the seventeenth century. The University of Halle played the role of the main link with Russia. Though the Pietists from Halle concentrated on dissemination of the Scriptures and catechisms, avoiding ceremonial matters, nevertheless the old schemes (Biblicism, iconoclasm) as well as the Pietists' real aversion to religious art did not create a promising starting-base for these contacts and aroused serious concerns among the Orthodox traditionalists. Many Protestants settled in the so-called Sloboda, a suburb of Moscow, which had been specially set apart for the members of this faith. The Protestant church erected there was a thorn in the side of the Orthodox clergy. This fact partially explains the continuance of the anti-Protestant polemic in a situation when the direct threat from the Reformation, both in Russia and in the neighbouring Poland–Lithuania, had already passed.

The internal conflict within the Russian Orthodox Church connected with the so-called reforms of Patriarch Nikon (after 1642) also concerned questions of liturgy, including that of a correct iconography and form of the icons.[78] Both sides used tropes and commonplaces from the repertoire of the image controversy[79] and Nikon in particular was accused of iconoclasm. When Nikon ordered the withdrawal of some 'faulty' icons in 1654 a panic broke out in Moscow which reminds us of some stages of Reformation iconoclasm (e.g. in Stralsund in 1525).[80] People began frantically to reclaim their small, private icons from the churches, fearing that they might be destroyed. The struggle with the Old Believers (Raskolniki), who opposed the reforms of Nikon, waned in intensity at the end of the seventeenth century, when Peter the Great came to the throne. The problem of liturgical change and the abolition or restriction of the cult of images then came back on to the agenda – to be sure, less as part of a programme of the young ruler and more in the form of fears on the part of conservative church circles.

Let us return to the beginning of the century. In 1623, Ivan Nasedka, a well-known Orthodox polemicist, copied the aforementioned 1602 treatise of Kopistenski, providing it with some new commentaries and adding a short treatise on 'Danish customs', and published the whole of it as a 'Treatise against the Lutherans'. In 1621 Nasedka had visited Denmark with a Russian legation and had seen with his own eyes the effects of restricting the image cult (but not iconoclasm, since Denmark remained a Lutheran country). Nasedka described with outrage the 'bare' Danish churches, which displayed no 'decorum' appropriate to a sacred place.[81]

Despite the fact that he was probably aware of the fact that Denmark was a Lutheran and not a Calvinist country, Nasedka made no distinction between these two denominations as regards their attitude – obviously worthy of condemnation – towards sacred objects. Apart from the absence of images and decorated altars – a relative absence, let us emphasize – the main source of offence for Nasedka was the liberty accorded to people (and dogs) to move freely about the church. That this was really so is attested not only by travellers' accounts but also by Dutch paintings of church interiors by such artists as Pieter Saenredam and Pieter Neeffs. The last motif, the casual attitude towards a sacred place, which appears in Nasedka with particular intensity, was incessantly repeated by all the Orthodox polemicists; as in a lens, it seemed to focus the entire, desacralizing attitude of the Protestants to their own houses of worship. What was irritating to the Orthodox was the Protestant criterion of utility and the resulting disrespect for elements of traditional symbolism. They could not understand the abandonment by the Reformation of the immanent sacrality of a church for a temporal sacrality, created by the presence of a worshipping congregation.

In the 1640s two long theological treatises appeared in Moscow – the so-called *Book of Cyril* (1644) and the *Book on the Faith* (1648).[82] The two books had a similar structure, and in both chapter 10 was devoted to polemic against Protestant iconoclasm.

Both of them were compilations from other sources, mostly from the 1602 Ukrainian treatise of Kopistenski, especially from the chapter on images.

In the *Book of Cyril* – despite the charge that the Protestants listen only to Scripture and ignore church traditions – a broad attempt was made to engage in scriptural-exegetical polemics, but the vast majority of the examples cited were not aptly chosen. The Eastern Orthodox had no tradition of biblical argument, and in this case this had an especially negative effect on the level of theological argument. The polemic against the Protestants was conducted according to a set pattern: 'the iconomachs say; we reply', and it did not introduce any new elements. Here we have a typical line of argument for which the starting-point was the miracles performed by icons (a difference of emphasis appears in comparison to the Greek church), a reference to the writings of Dionysius the Areopagite and of course to the image theory of the Damascene. One interesting new argument appears in the *Book of Cyril*. In answering the charges of the 'iconomachs' reproaching the Orthodox with idolatrous adoration of images (*latreia*), the Eastern Orthodox reverse the situation by asking the Protestants: 'Why then do you not give at least normal veneration (*douleia*) to the images, as a corrective to our 'idolatrous' worshipful veneration (*hyperdouleia*) or adoration (*latreia*)?' As a a theological argument it did not amount to much, being more a clever polemical ruse.

The reign of Peter the Great (1682–1725) ends the traditional line of criticism addressed by Russian Orthodoxy against Protestantism. A nebulous feeling of some future danger from the young ruler pushed the conservative Orthodox religious hierarchy to an intensive anti-Protestant polemic: the occidental, philo-Protestant leanings of Peter were an open secret. They originated in the ruler's voyages to England and Holland, whence Peter brought not only belief in the superiority of the northern countries over both Russian civilization and southern Catholicism, but also a specific awareness of the necessity of making all kinds of changes in Russia itself.

It is hard to say how loyal a son of the Orthodox Church Peter was. Throughout his life, gestures of sincere religiosity were intertwined with crass, if implicit blasphemies which erased the boundary between the sacred and the profane. With a high degree of probability, one can surmise that Peter was an opponent of the cult of icons. During his youth, in talk with an Anglican bishop (1698), he allegedly declared himself an absolute opponent of religious art. Hence his early reforms, first and foremost the famous cutting-off of beards, appeared to Orthodox circles as the prelude to a final attack on the ceremonies of the Orthodox Church. As we know, Peter followed another path.[83] He imposed on the Orthodox Church a specific Russian model of the Protestant state-dominated synodal system (abolishing the position of the patriarch and replacing it with the Holy Synod), thus choosing a path more suited to the interests of central authority. As a skilful politician – if only from the experiences gathered from the reforms of Nikon – he knew that combining political-administrative reforms with a battle over images might cause civil disorder of incalculable effect. Hence one of the greatest ironies in the history of the Russian Orthodox Church is the fact that the philo-Protestantism of Peter revealed itself from the least expected side. So some of his actions in the realm of the cult of icons, about which more will be said below, might appear designed to deceive.

From the Protestants and their few Russian allies the Russian hierarchy and clergy expected namely nothing less than another version of iconoclasm, and their anti-Reformation polemics thus had the aim of serving the defence of images and the cult of icons. As always in a period of danger, an ever-stronger emphasis was put on the miraculous properties of icons. In the anti-Protestant passages of his treatise *The Clear Looking-Glass* (c. 1700), the well-known writer Ivan Pososhkov[84] gives a number of examples of how Protestants met with deserved punishment for disrespect to icons (a carriage of Protestants which overtook an icon being carried in a procession fell apart and the travellers were killed). Pososhkov's controversialist strategies were skilful. The only proof of the falseness of the cult of icons cannot be the physical destruction of images by Protestant iconoclasts, but something like a spiritual iconoclastic miracle. Hence he challenges the Protestants: 'go ye into a holy church, shout with all of your Lutheran force . . . scream against the holy icons for them to fall on the ground and turn to dust'.[85] The legitimacy of the Orthodox Church is based on ever new icon miracles. Pososhkov also found extremely harsh words for Luther, 'the heretic of heretics', who with his hostility towards liturgy and images was worse than the Scythians. With his peculiar wry humour, he finally stated that Luther's only positive aspect was the fact that at least he did not multiply the number of heresies with some new doctrine but took up such an old heresy as iconoclasm.

The epoch of Peter I deepened the crisis of Orthodox theology, which, under the double pressure of Catholic and of Protestant theology, gradually lost its own features. In his polemic with Protestantism in the pages of his voluminous theological treatise *The Rock of Faith* (*c.* 1714); the metropolitan Stefan Javorsky,[86] a contemporary of Pososhkov and antagonist of the tsar but also a passive instrument in his hands, used classical patterns of Jesuit discourse in defence of images.

Arguments stemming from popular Jesuit controversialist tactics intertwine with more substantive arguments. For example, in the context of discussion on abuses of the cult of icons he put forward the classic Lutheran argument that some people may be tempted to adore heavenly bodies; yet while a sword can be an instrument of crime or wine its cause, we do not deny the right of these things to exist. Javorsky's reversal of the Eucharistic argument will be discussed in Chapter 5.

Javorsky rejects the assertion about the aniconism of the first 500 years of Christianity – even if this really was so in some places, it would only signify that not all churches were equally developed. God reveals himself to people – Javorsky claims – not in his essence but in a visible form. The spiritual worship shown to God does not clash with the material form. Finally, Javorsky states with satisfaction that iconoclasm came into being not in the East but in the West.

Javorsky was the leader of the 'pro-Latin' faction of the Orthodox clergy. Peter I consistently supported the group hostile to the metropolitan gathered around the eminent theologian Feofan Prokopovich, archbishop of Pskov. From Javorsky's correspondence with the tsar and his office, one can clearly see that the 'anti-iconoclastic' passages of *The Rock of Faith* were a stumbling-block for Peter and his advisers. Though the tsar did not deny the necessity of conducting a polemic against Protestant iconoclasm (which was a tactical concession), he continually demanded that Javorsky change and modify the anti-Protestant polemical passages – first and foremost those which concerned the cult of images. As a result, *The Rock of Faith* was not published until 1727, a few years after the death of the two protagonists in the dispute. The anti-Protestant passages then gave rise to a polemic from the Lutheran side in which a lot of attention was devoted to the image question. However, the main Lutheran polemicist, Johannes Buddeus,[87] was at least ready to acknowledge that the Eastern Orthodox gave only a relative veneration to images. He also stressed the positive fact that the Eastern churches do not tolerate statues – suggesting that these are most liable to provoke idolatrous abuse. Zwingli would have supported that view.

Both Javorsky and Peter the Great himself were involved in the case of the Moscow heretic Dimitri Tveritinov.[88] Javorsky demanded the severest punishment for him; the tsar protected Tveritinov for a certain time and then later softened his punishment. Tveritinov, a physician who lived in Moscow during Peter's reign, spoke out against the cult of images. This free-thinking Muscovite conducted agitation among his patients, primarily but not solely combating faith in 'icon miracles'. In his home only a single icon – which belonged to his still iconodulic wife – could be found, but two tablets with inscriptions were prominently displayed. The first contained pronouncements by Tveritinov himself, the second the first two Commandments. Tveritinov also propagated his views among students, and among icon painters. One of them, a certain Kudrin subsequently overthrew an icon of St Nicholas – the choice seems very characteristic – and trampled on it. It is possible that Tveritinov wrote a longer treatise against veneration of icons. He and several of his followers were arrested in 1714 on charges of atheism and impiety. After prolonged interrogation and imprisonment Tveritinov finally succumbed and recanted his views: he obviously was not a fanatic. His fight against the cult of icons combines various elements which make this episode all the more fascinating: first, there were Tveritinov's contacts with the Moscow Protestants and his knowledge of Lutheran catechisms, then his possession of the 1562 iconophobic catechism of Szymon Budny written in Ruthenian, as mentioned above (an astounding case of Russian iconoclastic tradition). At the same time one can sense a certain kind of Enlightenment rationalism before its time, perhaps connected with Tveritinov's profession. This attitude was directed not so much against the images themselves as against the ideas and superstitions connected with the cult of icons. Tveritinov was probably not very familiar with Western Calvinism and its liturgical objects: more astonishing, therefore, is his tablet with the two Commandments, which amounted to a declaration against any icon painting and against the status of the Russian house icon. A tablet containing the Ten Commandments was however, often the sole decoration in Calvinist churches in the West (thus the importance of the ban on images became somewhat diluted). In Russia c. 1700 this still amounted to a blasphemy – the first Protestant church with no decoration save a tablet with the Ten Commandments was opened in St Petersburg as late as 1772 (a Huguenot church).[89]

In the case of Tveritinov one can speak of undogmatic freethinking in the modern sense of the word, if only on account of his tolerance of his wife's different views, but some of his supporters, after a lapse of more than 150 years, took up the iconoclastic tradition of the Judaizers, which was based on rigorous hostility to the image. The icon painter Kudrin has already been mentioned, but worse acts were to come. The barber Foma Ivanov, a member of Tveritinov's entourage, committed an act while imprisoned with the physician in a monastery, which was positively suicidal considering the fact that the interrogation was still in progress. When his abjuration was rejected, he publicly destroyed an icon of St Alexius hanging in the church, and stated that in his opinion 'in the holy sacrament of the Eucharist the body and blood of Christ are only bad bread and wine'.[90] Here we have the classic 'iconoclastic syndrome', though the question of the Eucharist played a lesser role in the Judaizing tradition. A month later (November 1714) the unfortunate Foma was burned at the stake. In 1716 the Tveritinov case reached its conclusion. After displaying a very docile attitude, the physician was released from prison and was sentenced to several years of house arrest, which – by a perfidious decision of the tsar himself – he had to spend in the house of Javorsky.

Tveritinov was also charged in ecclesiastical circles with cooperating with the Protestants in Moscow. However, the tsarist authorities watching over the various 'heretics' (at that time the conquest of the Baltic lands had ended, as a result of which Lutheranism became the second state religion) toned down these charges, and the case did not bring the Orthodox clergy greater success. The Tveritinov case is one of those events that was influenced by two epochs, although the notion of Enlightenment rationalism can be applied to the Russia of the first half of the eighteenth century only with the greatest caution.

Despite his Protestant leanings, Peter the Great did not himself engage in open dispute with the cult of icons. However, the tsarist government did take certain steps, whose moving spirits were the tsar and Bishop Feofan Prokopovich,[91] to limit the excesses of the cult. The main concern was – as Peter himself stated – that the 'foreigners', mainly Protestants, whose opinion was important to the tsar, should have no reason to abhor superstitious Russian practices. The depositing of small icons in churches was prohibited, and a determined struggle was carried on against belief in the alleged miracles performed by icons; in some cases death sentences were even meted out to persons who claimed to have witnessed them. At the same time, and with equally brutal means, a campaign was initiated to sacralize portraits of the tsar, to which almost religious worship began to be paid. In 1720 Feofan Prokopovich launched a further attack on excesses in the cult of icons. If there were any concrete plans for expanding this campaign – which is doubtful, especially since Prokopovich did not totally reject the cult of icons itself – the death of Peter in 1725 and the hostile reaction to his reforms which then set in put an end to any such plans. Thus, to sum up, the Protestant attitude towards religious art on the part of the tsar manifested itself in forms that were not very dangerous to the cult of icons – that is, in a tolerant attitude towards heretics and some attempts to control excesses in the cult.

Weakened and undermined by a deep theological and political crisis, the Russian Orthodox Church had to coexist with Protestantism, while sectarian movements (Old Believers, and the heirs of the Nilovites), despite differences on iconography, were not hotbeds of iconophobia. However, the image problem and the hostility of Protestants to Russian religious art left an indelible mark on the historical consciousness of the Orthodox Church and on the cultural consciousness of the Russians.

With the reign of Peter the Great ended a certain chronological sequence, which started from the movements of the strigolniks and the Judaizers. However, certain problems which do not emerge clearly from a chronological treatment will be examined in the last pages of this chapter.

EAST AND WEST: A CONCLUSION

Iconographic problems played a minor role in the image dispute as conducted by the two sides. They were dealt with in close conjunction with the major question of the validity of religious art. This happened, for example, with questions about the representation of Christ, the legitimacy of representations of Mary and the saints and the role of and worship due to these intermediaries between God and man. More important, however, were observations on the devotional role of iconography as related by travellers such as Gerlach, Schweigger and Olearius. From them one can conclude that Protestants especially did not like hieratic, 'idolatrous' Marian images. The Protestants were also interested in more specific, local versions of religious iconography. Nearly all of them questioned the inordinately popular cult of St Nicholas in Russia. Paul Oderborn even suggested that images of the saint were more popular in Russia than images of Mary; he also observed that extensive rites were associated with this cult. Going further, Oderborn, whether intuitively or to exaggerate his point, also noticed that the Russians adored St Nicholas like God.[92] The observations of Oderborn and other travellers, including the Englishman Turberville,[93] recently became the subject of a very important scholarly debate on the pagan aspects of the cult of St Nicholas (Boris Uspenski vs. Gail Lenhoff).[94] Among the six charges made against the Russian Orthodox Church (three of them, characteristically, concerning the cult of icons) Michael Siricius (1661)[95] mentioned faith in images of the saints, faith in Marian images, and erecting altars to St Nicholas. He ironically called St Nicholas 'the protective deity of all Russians'. He also described how the Russians gave up the siege of Riga in 1656 when an icon of this saint was destroyed by chance during the military operations. For Siricius this is a clear example of idolatry. The story cited by Siricius, probably apocryphal, is a good example of the persistence of Protestant ideas about Russian iconodulism. On the other hand there were probably no wider commentaries from the Protestant viewpoint on the strictly theological aspects of religious iconography.

In presenting the image problem and its role in relations between Protestant or heretical movements and Russian and Ukrainian Orthodoxy in a more or less chronological order, I was guided by the relative permanence of these relations. The specific features of the Protestant–Russian debate can thus be easily grasped from the Russian side; this involved first and foremost looking at manifestations of Protestantism from the angle of iconoclasm, thus arbitrarily creating iconoclastic traditions and emphasizing the miraculous power of icons and the miracles performed by them. Much less space was devoted to scriptural argument,

which should not be surprising considering the generally iconophobic tone of most passages of Scripture and the lack of a
tradition of biblical studies in the Orthodox Church. On the other
hand, arguments on the veneration due to the saints and their
images were close to the typical Catholic arguments, but with a
stronger accent on the intermediary role of the saints, which was
understood in a way similar to the role of images in showing the
path to God, with a denial of the possibility of their direct intercession. Marian subjects were touched on only marginally, which
is surprising in view of the role of Marian iconography in Russian
art. As a rule iconographic subjects were rarely talked about in
Protestant–Russian discussions, the exception being travellers'
accounts. In these accounts one can detect a great sensitivity to
the practice of the cult as if in accordance with Luther's postulate
that a work of religious art should be evaluated according to how
it functions in religious life. This is true both for the Lutheran
travellers and, paradoxically, for the Russian traveller Nasedka,
who evaluated the approach of Protestants to their own religious
buildings in accordance with similar criteria.

Relations between the two confessions were also greatly affected
by theological differences and a different understanding of certain
concepts. In Orthodox terminology there was no concept of *adiaphora* to designate objects between the sacred and the profane;
on the other hand the notion of 'ceremony', which was used by
both sides imprecisely, had a value of its own in the Eastern
Church.

The tradition of the iconoclastic dispute also worked in various
ways. The Protestants often did not use traditional iconoclastic
arguments, but attempted to assess the resolutions of the Nicaean
Council, thereby moving the dispute from the strictly dogmatic
plane to the historical–dogmatic plane. As an example one might
mention the great Lutheran theologian Martin Chemnitz, who
clearly states that the Council should be evaluated by the yardstick
of the sensibleness of its resolutions.[96] This attitude appears in
even more extreme form in the Calvinist Innocent Gentillet.[97] In
view of their support for the councils as such, this Protestant
attitude smacked of subjectivism.

The Protestant approach to the image dispute clearly bore the
mark of modern historical thinking, in conjunction with Scripturalism. No one grasped this more clearly and more succinctly than
the Orthodox theologian the monk Jevfimii in the middle of the

seventeenth century. In a short, forceful statement he shows how much the Orthodox were irritated by the rejection of tradition as a value *per se* and by the Biblicism of the Reformation, perhaps even more by its historical approach: 'The Lutherans and the Calvinists . . . ridicule the written and unwritten tradition of the Church and speak about fasting, the worship of icons, and monastic vows: why this exists and whence it came . . . where is this written?'[98] Neither side understood the position of the other. The Protestants lacked spiritual and cultural reference for the pictorial culture of Orthodoxy, while for the Orthodox every reduction of the cult meant an assault on the sacred.

For the Orthodox, iconoclasm was a crime that could touch only the physical existence of icons. The only valid response to the cult of icons could be an iconoclastic miracle, such as the one demanded of his Reformation antagonists by Pososhkov. Like the Counter-Reformation, the Orthodox created many legends in which the injured cult object offers passive or active resistance (especially the *contrapasso* motif).[99] Hence in the logical order of things the cultural rationalism of the Protestants – if hostility to images can be regarded as rationalism – led to an increase of miraculous and mythographic elements in Orthodoxy. The Byzantine image dispute, which – especially for Russian Orthodoxy – was a constant point of reference, played a bigger role in the relations between Protestantism and Orthodoxy than in the relations between Orthodoxy and Catholicism.

It must be stated that the greatest distance between positions appeared not in theory but in the practice of the cult of images. If we leave aside the polar opposites of active iconodulism and iconoclasm, a certain observation of D. M. Tsvetayev best illustrates the great gulf between the two confessions. As the Russian scholar noted,[100] the very entry of a Protestant into a Russian home immediately became a manifestation of religious differences: Protestants, for whom the very notion of 'domestic icon' was unacceptable, the more categorically refused to bow before the images after crossing the threshold (in the seventeenth century this was a customary gesture of Russians), a refusal in which the host saw both a blasphemous act and – on the level of purely personal contact – insulting behaviour.

AFTERMATH

In the history of the Orthodox–Protestant image controversy the most interesting moments are those where ancient motifs reappear and where the tradition of certain theological viewpoints and the forms of opposition to these viewpoints last a long time. Both the iconoclast heretics – like Tveritinov – and the iconodulic official Church seemed through their actions and responses tacitly to assume that an iconoclastic tradition with a standard set of references did indeed exist. When after 1815 Russia was swept by Adventist movements, whose followers benefited from the support of the mystics gathered around Alexander I, the traditional defenders of Orthodoxy raised the alarm. In a memorial addressed to the tsar in 1824, one of them, Admiral Nicholas Shyshkov, came out against Biblicism (by which he understood both a theological trend and the dissemination in Russia of the Bible in Russian by the Protestants), arguing that it would inexorably lead to a decline of the image cult and to iconoclasm. Here the old, unthinkingly accepted identification from the history of the antiheretical struggles made itself felt.

The nineteenth century in Russia brought both a continuation of the traditional line and new events. In a certain sense even Leo Tolstoy found himself under the influence of Protestantism. The caustic remarks against the cult of icons which can be found in *Resurrection* were influenced by Protestant literature, among others the books of Zschokke.[101] Tolstoy was not a 'Westernizer', which makes even more important those passages of the novel in which Toporov (a grotesque portrait of the famous Pobedonostsev) considers the cult of the icon of the Mother of God of Kazan as 'vulgar idolatry'. The last link of the equation 'occidentalizing heresy equals Protestantism' were the Stundists, a Biblicist movement which also rejected the cult of icons. The Stundists were especially active from 1880 until 1920.[102] The iconoclastic incidents recorded by the authorities in these years were committed mostly by them but also by Baptists and other Protestant sects. In the words of a Stundist, 'The word of God enlightened us that we should not adore the holy images . . . my wife whitened our home at Easter and threw the icons out, she did not want to have anything in common with them since the house was pure and white.' Both the choice of Easter for the abolition of the domestic icons as a parable of overcoming the demons and the expression 'pure and white', reminiscent of Zwingli, testify to the fascinating long life of iconoclastic topoi and commonplaces. Another Russian sectarian related that after reading Isaiah 44 about the idols made of wood he decided to destroy his idols by burning them to gain some warmth – since this is implied by the Bible passage. Isaiah 44 had inspired Karlstadt and Hätzer and many iconoclasts who used idols in their stoves as firewood – here can be seen another long iconoclastic tradition.[103]

Worse still, some iconoclastic incidents perpetrated by the Protestant sectarians happened as late as the 1920s, when Bolshevik iconoclasm began to destroy the Russian Church. Some Protestants welcomed the fact that the first Communist attack was directed against the cult of images and relics of which their sects and churches were free. However, if they hoped for tolerance of their aniconic religion, they were to be brutally disillusioned in the 1930s.

Let us return, however, to the Russian Church. As the nineteenth century progressed, its apologetics for the use of pictorial representation in its religious forms intensified; such apologetics were congruent with the general Slavophilic current. This had obvious anti-Protestant undertones, for it was in this religion that the nationalists saw the main source of Western materialism and the mainstay of the process of secularization. A significant change took place, however. The degenerate West was charged not so much with the loss of holy symbols through some new iconoclastic act as with exchanging them for frivolous images of the *imagérie populaire* and with indifference to religious visualness. Iconoclasm, which was now identified with the forces destroying civilization, was expected from the direction of the steppes: as a new wave of attacks of Asia on holy Russia. This reversion to entirely mythical commonplaces, which replaced the mythologized experience of the anti-Reformation struggles, is characteristic of the evolution of Orthodox thought of that time. As late as the 1920s, the famous Orthodox theologian and scholar Pavel Florenski[104] wrote a treatise on the iconostasis and in the margin of this now classic work he elaborated thoughts on the lack of sacrality in Protestant art. In his opinion, the Reformation expressed itself best in graphic art, in a characteristic civilization of printing and paper, where the material itself did not have a sacral context. At the opposite pole was the icon, which united spiritualism with visual materiality. Hence the ancient controversy between the two confessions still remained open, a controversy that best expressed itself in the opposition of the hierophantic view that 'the icon is a prayer hidden in painted wood' (Zernov) to the deep conviction of the Protestants that inanimate objects cannot possess an 'inner sanctity'.

Throughout the entire nineteenth century German Protestants came out every few years with treatises and longer works devoted to the Orthodox Church in Russia (they were less interested in the Greek Church). The Russian Church became one of the favourite subjects of a Protestant interest in comparative confessional religion. Even a superficial glance at the publications of 1815–1920 shows the absolute dominance of negative stereotypes: a tendency that reached its apogee in the theological circle of the great Adolf von Harnack. In nearly every work the image problem played an important role, often functioning – which was something of a tradition – as a *pars pro toto* for the criticism of the liturgy and ceremonies of the Orthodox Church. These condemnations of the cult of images do not bring anything new to the history of our problem, though they provide interesting material for the historian of culture.

A marked change took place in the years 1890–1920. Starting with a new generation of Protestant theologians and historians (among others, Karl Holl, Karl Schwarzlose) who expressed from a nascent ecumenical point of view understanding for the eastern cult of images, the momentum accelerated and after 1910, and especially after 1920, the aesthetic qualities of the icon also began to be appreciated. Various factors contributed to this process: the demise of Protestantism as a 'high-culture religion', the influence of the artistic avant-garde and, last but not least, the Bolshevist takeover of 1917 and the almost complete annihilation of Russian religious culture that followed. The analogies with the post-1945 nostalgia for the Jewish East European *shtetl* are evident: in the moment that Russia succumbed to Bolshevism, the vestiges of its religious culture began a sentimental career of their own. An additional catalyst was the arrival in the West of many emigrant or expelled Orthodox scholars and theologians. In literally a few years the traditional Protestant attitude gave way to a new, ever more enthusiastic appreciation of the spiritual values of the cult of icons. But that is another story.

Old cultural motifs and mental associations last a long time and manifest themselves in the most unexpected circumstances. In

Sergei Eisenstein's magnificent but unfinished film *Bezhynski Meadows* (1936), which shows the transformation of a Soviet village, the scene in which the peasants commit an iconoclastic act in an Orthodox church was presented entirely in accordance with the old cultural code, the 'anti-behaviour' being portrayed as part of a ritual – a biblical ritual, we might add. Here is a description of this scene by the eminent critic Victor Shklovsky: 'Enemies hide in the church. The peasants destroy the church. A powerful peasant moves the holy gates as Samson had once moved the columns of the temple of the Philistines. A highly mythical image'.[105] Despite its revolutionary content, one can still sense here the Orthodox obsession with iconoclasm, if only because parasacral mythogenic action is required to strike at the sacred. When, in the first stormy years after the Revolution, Lenin had to check the fired-up 'proletcultists' who wanted to destroy the cultural tradition, he used a comparison with iconoclasm in a talk with Clara Zetkin· 'It seems to me that we too have our Doctor Karlstadts. We are too much iconoclasts.'[106] Obviously the name of Karlstadt had not been known before this in the Orthodox world. So this is an example of how well Lenin knew the history of revolutionary struggles, among which he included the Reformation. On the other hand, the comparison with the concept of iconoclasm shows how deeply he was rooted in the Orthodox cultural tradition.

With the new problems of art of the twentieth century – in particular the birth of abstract art, the decline of religious art and the rise of an artistic consciousness integrating the traditions of various cultures – the critics of the evolution of modern art began to think in genetic–comparative categories. Hans Sedlmayr, an apologist of the sacral element in art who from this position heatedly combated abstract art, with remarkable intuition turned to the history of the iconoclastic dispute, comparing the iconoclasts of the West and Russia. In discussing the 'striving for purity' as one of the features of abstract art, he says:

> one of the sources of this longing for purity is unques-
> tionably Calvinist purism. We can see this from the fact that
> 'pure' abstract art found especially fertile soil in Holland and
> the United States. There the Old Testament prohibition of
> images was referred to in defence of abstract art. The fact
> that abstract art sprang up in Russia on the eve of the

revolution becomes understandable in the cultural–spiritual aspect if we go back to the history of their sects.[107]

Whether Sedlmayr's anti-modernistic stance is right (in my opinion it is not) is not exactly the problem here; more important is his polemical intuition. Every historian of culture must be fascinated by the drawing of such long lines of tradition, one of which would be – according to the logic of Sedlmayr's suggestion – a line marked by the names of Kosoi, Tveritinov and Malevich.

This kind of creation of traditional lines of thought and their extension up to our century may give rise to various doubts, especially since there are many sweeping generalizations here presenting or comparing the symbolic representation of the European East and West. Despite this, the subject itself seems to call for such generalizations, especially today, when an authentic aesthetic cult of icons and growing understanding for the spiritual values of Orthodox theology coexists with the dominance of 'bare churches', with the iconophobic movement within the great denominations of the West – Protestantism but also Catholicism – and the demise of figurative religious art.

5

Symbols and commonplaces, or the conceptual background of the dispute on images

In this chapter I attempt to analyse the conceptual background of the image dispute. It is somewhat surprising that the prolific development of studies on rhetoric, commonplaces and semiotics has passed over the image dispute.

IMAGES AND THE EUCHARIST

The image dispute is linked primarily, by thousands of threads, to the Eucharistic dispute, which is so important from the point of view of fundamental theology. Let us start from the end, from the statement that as a rule the opponents of the Real Presence of Christ in the sacrament were supporters of religious aniconism. During the Reformation this pattern was very clear: the views of Luther as a supporter, though moderate, of religious art and of the Real Presence collide here directly[1] with the iconophobia of Karlstadt, Zwingli and Calvin, all of whom denied (though in different ways) the Real Presence of Christ in the Host.[2] This pattern is also confirmed in the case of the Eastern Orthodox with Protestant leanings, such as the Calvinizing patriarch Cyril Lucaris, the Judaizer Bashkin and especially the Moscow adherent of Tveritinov the barber Foma Ivanov, who, following his seizure after an iconoclastic act, stated immediately that he did not believe in icons and in the Real Presence of Christ in the Host. Also significant is the fact that Luther's faithful comrade Melanchthon differed from Luther only as regards his views on antinomianism, the image question (where he had some doubts) and the Real Presence.[3] Thus we see once again a characteristic convergence of iconophobia with a symbolic view of the Eucharist. In the case of the Wyclifites and the Hussites, the confluence of these problems was more complicated – with different starting-points and ultimately different doctrinal solutions.

The link between the image question and the Eucharist dates back to the Byzantine image dispute in the eighth and ninth centuries. During this dispute Christological arguments were used by both sides, the iconoclasts and the iconodules. The iconoclasts, who denied the possibility of representing the sacred in a religious image, leaned towards Monophysitism, a doctrine which 'overdeified' Christ, while the iconodules more strongly accented the human nature of Christ, which could be grasped and described, although they were not Nestorians (as their opponents called them).

At the iconoclastic council of 754 in Constantinople, both the iconophobic emperor Constantine V and the subsequent resolution of the council fathers declared that the Eucharist is the true image of Christ, being a *typos*, a form of 'his body'.[4] It was and is the only permissible form in which to represent the Incarnation. Moreover, Constantine V in a hitherto overlooked argument, pushed the analogy even further by declaring that through the consecration bread and wine are transformed from the realm of dissimilar 'hand-made' elements to that of those 'made without hands' (*acheiropoietos*). However, the latter term was never used in the Eucharist controversy either before or after, since it designated the so-called icons, 'not made with hands', such as the famous linen cloth upon which Christ had impressed his image while drying his face. It was said that the Saviour had sent this image to King Abgar of Edessa, where it remained until the tenth century as a fountainhead of the image cult. The persistence with which Constantine attacked even such miraculous images is astounding.

By contrast to the iconophobes of the Reformation, the Byzantine iconoclasts maintained *prima facie* a 'realist' view of the Eucharist: they believed that it truly was the body and blood of Christ. However, first fissures do appear here: for in calling the Eucharist an image the iconoclasts subjected this fundamental liturgical mystery to their general critique of images and the scrutiny of iconic relations. This process by implication could not but lower its elevated position as the central mystery of faith.

The iconodules had no difficulty in rejecting this view: as Theodore the Studite stated, the Eucharist is not an image but Christ himself. However, the iconophobes were aided in their endeavour by the imprecise terminology of image theology, especially by a misunderstanding concerning the concept of 'antitype'. It has its source in the terminology of the liturgy of St Basil and, as the following quotation from the renowned theologian Gustave Martelet shows, it was used both in the image dispute and in the Eucharistic dispute. Martelet writes:

> In his liturgy St Basil uses the term 'antitype', which opposed to the term 'type' expresses the relation of a shadow to reality. In the liturgy in question the meaning of the two terms is *de facto* almost identical; both of them seem to mean that the body of Christ is present in the sacrament, as opposed to the body in a state of glory. St John Damascene, who explains 'antitype' as a *figure* in opposition to the body, thinks that this term was specially reserved by the liturgy of St Basil for the moment preceding consecration and that in this way it permits one to evaluate the real working of the Holy Spirit in the epiclesis that comes after consecration. Thus, according to St John Damascene, the post-consecration epiclesis works to make the elements, which before this were only 'figures', to become, now in the strict sense, the reality of the body of Christ. This is a false semantic interpretation, but it reveals a theological view of the role of the Holy Spirit in the Eucharistic consecration that is entirely alien to Western thought.
>
> Though such an argument may seem very weak, nevertheless in the East it provided a response to those who at that time wanted to condemn the use of images. The iconoclasts held that the only legitimate representation of Christ is the Eucharist, about which St Basil said, as we know, that it is the antitype or figure of the body of Christ. Following St John Damascene, these purists were told that the Eucharist is not only the figure of Christ, but that it is his reality itself. In such a case, if St Basil calls the Eucharist the 'figure of Christ' he has in mind the host *before the epiclesis*, never after it.[5]

The main link between the image problem and the Eucharist is the terminology itself, especially the pair of concepts *typos/antitypos*. (In the context of my remarks the problem of epiclesis opposed to consecration, which was the main issue troubling Martelet, is not important, for in principle it does not concern the question of the Real Presence.) For the iconodules, accepting the concept of antitypes for images – that is, the reflection of the archetype – the basic issue on the theoretical plane was the rejection of the iconoclasts' charge that images must have the same *ousia*, or essence, as the archetype. Then the conclusion would suggest itself that the Eucharist can be the only image. Since in this case the notion of *eikon* would mean not an ordinary image but an image-model of its essence, the Eucharist elements would be a kind of 'dissimilar', but let me add, consubstantial image of Christ himself. Hence by a strange paradox, in the point of view of the iconoclasts, a tendency of many theologians of the patristic period and later reached its zenith – as in the father of iconodulism, St John Damascene – to apply concepts from the theology of the reality of the image (*symbolon, eikon, homoioma, typos, antitypos*) to deliberations on the real nature of the Eucharistic elements. Thus, considering the starting-point, this was not an independent Eucharistic heresy but only an epiphenomenon of the iconoclastic dispute.

The iconodulic party set in opposition to this trend the Neoplatonic distinction of image and archetype. Theodore the Studite wrote: 'Images of archetypes made from the material formed by art do not participate in the nature of the archetype, but they do show as in a mirror their similarity with the images whose reflections they are.'[6] In this context the simile of the mirror, which will recur later, should be remembered.

The lines of thinking drawn in Byzantium lasted through the entire early Middle Ages, but they underwent certain modifications. In a famous Eucharistic dispute in the West in the middle of the ninth century (Paschasius Radbertus vs. Ratramnus) an attempt was made to describe the theology of image reality. Paschasius stated:

If we go more deeply [into the Eucharistic mystery], then we correctly define it as simultaneously reality and image: hence the image or the reflection of reality is what is perceived from the outside, while the reality is what can be understood and what is believed in reference to the inner essence of this mystery. For not every image is a shadow or falsehood.[7]

In this dispute, however, the religious image was not cited as the point of comparison.

Another linkage of the image dispute with the Eucharistic question was made by the famous fourteenth-century theologian John Wyclif. Contrary to popular opinion, Wyclif was not an iconoclast; his position on the image question was quite moderate.[8] (The Lollards later showed a tendency to reject images completely, but this is another matter.) Wyclif's main purpose was to fight, like Luther, against excesses and to eliminate ostentation (*vana pompa*) from the Church (like St Bernard of Clairvaux). The Catholics located Wyclif's Eucharistic teaching in the tradition of doctrines negating the Real Presence of Christ in the Eucharist,[9] though, more strongly than the other medieval theologians of this current – not excluding Berengarius himself – he underlined the tropic, hence more than merely symbolic, nature of the sacrament:

> According to the concepts of Wyclif, the way in which the body of Christ is present in the Eucharist occupies an intermediate place between the reality professed by the Catholic Church and the purely figurative presence that we encounter, for example, in the image of the Crucified on wood or canvas or the sacrifices of the Old Testament.[10]

Wyclif focused on the concept of greater effectiveness (*efficacitas*) of the sacramental symbol. This can be clearly seen from the various terms with which he attempted to define the presence of Christ in the Host (*figuraliter, in signo, sacramentaliter, virtualiter, spiritualiter*). For Wyclif, Christ is 'in the sign, but not as if a sign' (*in signo sed non ut in signo*). Wyclif, however, criticized the so-called 'mirror analogy' – that is, the drawing of an analogy between a division of the sacrament (in the form of the Host) and a fragmented mirror still reflecting the sun's rays.[11]

Here it is necessary to explore the specific theme of the mirror image. If we refer this passage from the *Sermons* to the passages cited earlier from the writings of Theodore the Studite, it might seem that for Wyclif the comparison of the reflection in a mirror to the Host excludes its participation in the *ousia* of Christ. This would obviously be an argument in support of the symbolic conception of the Eucharist were it not for the fact that the Studite's conception of the image was unacceptable to the West.

This problem became more complicated in the views of the Hussites. The dispute on communion in both kinds (*sub utraque specie*) only marginally touched on the problem of the Real Presence of Christ in the sacrament;[12] the lines of division among the

Hussites were quite muddled, and in spite of Cook's and Vooght's studies there are still many unexplained questions. Among some Taborites after 1420 the classic syndrome unquestionably existed: that is, the denial of images and the Real Presence (by, for example, Peter Payne). However, there were still other links between the two matters. The eminent theologian and utraquist activist Jacobellus de Stribro, in his 1417 treatise on images, rejected all 'images and relics or other objects that stand in the way of the true adoration of the image of Our Lord Jesus embodied in the Eucharist'.[13] He thereby rejected (as emerges from other passages of the treatise) nearly all religious painting. Jacobellus simply believed that the image cult obscures the Eucharistic cult and for this reason should be abolished. Parallels to the Byzantine iconoclasts do appear; but such a point of view remained an isolated one.

In England in 1492, on the eve of the Reformation, the later Lollards continuing the work of John Wyclif categorically rejected the Real Presence and the cult of the Host as well as the cult of images – the boundary with complete rejection of all religious images is hard to draw. Historians of the English Reformation still entertain some doubts as to whether the late Lollards were an essential link between the English Reformation and medieval heresy. A lively debate continues on this question. Margaret Aston has recently gathered certain evidence on the revival among the first English reformers of the iconoclastic tradition of the Lollards. Despite this, she states: 'Lollard iconomachy neither caused nor enabled Reformation iconomachy. . . . No adequate method has been found to test the plausible hypothesis that there was some continuity between pre- and post-Reformation dissent. . . . At the critical point of transition, however, we can see some fusing of views.'[14] This fusion pertained also to the Eucharist–image syndrome.

And so we come to the age of the Reformation. The convergence of the two disputes takes place here on various planes: the conceptual, that of the attitudes of the leading reformers, and that of popular controversy. Starting from the last, it should be noted that at that time many terms were carried over from the image dispute to the Eucharistic controversy. The name 'idolatry' became extremely popular for the cult of the Eucharist. Towards the end of 1521 the Wittenberg iconoclast Gabriel Zwilling called the adoration of the Host idolatry (*Götzendienst*). In almost equally common use was the expression 'idol of bread' for the Host. The Polish antitrinitarian Szymon Budny said: 'Once again they bow down . . . and kneel before wooden, silver and bread idols.'[15] John Knox struck the same chord: 'the god of bread manufactured by the papists was essentially the same as the gods of wood and stone'.[16] It was on this plane that the two problems were most broadly linked, though of course in the most superficial way.

This linkage and the difficulties consequent upon it are also connected to a specific mode of thinking about the category of the image and the notion of depiction, reflection and representation.

Religious images understood as the visualization or reflection of the sacred are closely linked with these categories; it suffices to recall the etymology of the popular term icon (*eikon*). It must be said at the outset that in the present state of research even an introductory analysis of the conceptual context is scarcely possible. In the sixteenth century and at the beginning of the seventeenth there was a remarkable expansion of terms connected with the notion of image; 'convention', 'projection', 'mirror reflection', 'sympathy', 'antipathy', 'type', 'antitype', to name but a few. Other popular terms were *simulacrum* and *effigies*. Then there was the term *repraesentatio*, which, though less often used in modern times than in the Middle Ages, was to have a stong impact on Calvin's approach to the relationship of the Eucharist to the image. Finally, there were many terms revolving around the concept of symbol and sign: *signum*, *symbolum*, *veritas et figura*, *res figurata*, *pignus*, *ektypoma*. At the very end, though not least important, the concept of the sacrament must be mentioned.

The best example is to be found in Calvin. An analysis of the conceptual apparatus in the Eucharistic dispute and of its implied connections with the image dispute is only partly possible. Symptomatic of Calvin's attitude, and forming a conceptual bridge to the image question is the use of the concept *repraesentatio* (instead of 'presence') to define the reality of the Eucharist. In this case, acceptance of this word – used in the Middle Ages to designate the functions of art – is absolutely explicit; Calvin makes a clear comparison with images 'in as far as they represent the sacraments as if in a picture for viewing'.[17] On the other hand analysis of other concepts provides no comparable frame of reference. Calvin uses the terms *signum*, *figura*, *sacramentum* in a very imprecise way; to a large extent they overlap. In particular this concerns the pair of concepts *sacramentum/signum*.

The concept of *signum* (sign) played an important role in the Eucharistic controversy. Although introduced into theological deliberations by St Augustine and later developed by Bonaventura[18] and Thomas Aquinas, it did not attain any degree of precision in the theology and logic of the late Middle Ages. Lutheran theologians – Luther included – as supporters of the Real Presence of Christ in the Eucharist, generally agreed that the sacrament is a sign participating in the power (*virtus*) of the object represented.

The theme of the Eucharistic sign – examined once again in connection with the image question – found its most characteristic form in the young Melanchthon, in his *Theses on the Mass* (1521). Melanchthon calls both the crucifix and the sun signs through which the Word of God manifests itself. The sacrament is the stronger sign, for it is a sign instituted by God. Both types of sign – the crucifix image of Christ and the sacrament image of the Eucharist – belong to (and this is very important) the category of remembrance signs (*signum admonens*) In Melanchthon's approach the validity of religious art, despite a certain personal distance on his part and the numerous excesses which he had observed, was derived from its place in an arrangement which can be imagined as a semiotic pyramid, directly under the highest category of visible signs, the sacraments. On the other hand using the term *signum admonens* to designate the Eucharist has an additional context, unnoticed by Wilhelm Neuser,[19] which situates the deliberations of Melanchthon not far from the Eucharistic conceptions of Karlstadt: in 1524 a supporter of Karlstadt, the painter Hans Greiffenberger, called the Eucharistic sacrament a 'commemorative' sign (*Gedenkzeichen*).[20] Another, rarely used definition of religious images was proposed by irenic Catholics: an 'indicative sign' (*Deutzeichen*).[21]

With Luther the problem of the Eucharist and images took a special form. In *Against the Heavenly Prophets* he expanded the terms referring to the symbolic function of a work of art, coining terms like *Merkbilder* (images to capture the attention), *Spiegelbilder* (mirror images) and the formula that art serves *zum Ansehen, zum Zeugnis, zum Gedächtnis, zum Zeichen* (to gaze upon, as a witness, for commemoration, as a sign). In the same treatise he examined the Eucharistic dispute, but he neither perceived nor was aware of the connections between the two questions. By contrast to the writings of Melanchthon, there is no analogy here between definition of the functions of art as *zum Gedächtnis* and

Luther's designations of the Eucharistic sign. To be sure, for Luther the Eucharist was also a sign, but so strong a sign (*Kraftzeichen*) and of such a special kind that the theme and the sign (*Zeichen und Sache*) cannot be separated in any way. The basic difference between the Lutheran and the Calvinist understanding of the sacrament of the Eucharist on the semiotic plane consists primarily in a synecdochic understanding of the sacrament by the first reformer and the metaphorical–allegorical conception of the second. For Luther Christ is not immanently connected with any given external (*res externa*), and only in the sacrament of the Eucharist can he be 'bound'. The sacrament is a synecdoche on the principle of *pars pro toto*, and so its link with the body of Christ – by contrast to other tropes – is inseparable.[22]

Let us return for a moment to the concept of remembrance (*memoria*). In a polemic with Luther, who placed special emphasis on the ceremony of the Eucharist as an 'event', the little-known Catholic theologian Caspar Schatzgeyer (d. 1527) tried to present a new understanding of this act. In his Eucharistic theology the concept of 'a remembrance existing here and now' played a crucial role, so that he came out against Luther's separation of the sacrifice and remembrance of the sacrifice. Schatzgeyer stated:

> The sacrifice made on the altar by the Christian Church and its servant is the same sacrifice that was made on the cross, and it is not only a remembrance of this sacrifice on the cross but also its splendid and true manifestation. . . . That is why the charge made by some that an image of Hercules is not Hercules is baseless, and for this reason also the manifestation (which takes place in spirit) is really not the sacrifice made on the cross. The answer to this is that the sacrifice made now is not an image of the past sacrifice but past things renewed before the Father, as though they were taking place right now on the cross.[23]

Schatzgeyer's Eucharistic conception, which is an excellent approach to the problem of figurativeness and the relationship of the Eucharistic act itself with Christ's sacrifice on the cross (and not only of the sacrament), was not taken up by the Catholic side at that time. In fact, this was a moderate position not far from the Lutheran one.

Schatzgeyer was obviously opposed to Zwingli's reiterated views that a sacramental bond, like the Eucharist, does nothing

more than 'carry an image of a holy thing'.[24] Close to Schatzgeyer
was Erasmus, who used the Platonic concept of *methexis* to
explain in his Eucharistic theory that the image participated to a
limited degree in the essence of the prototype.[25] In the twentieth
century some strands of this were taken up in the theory of the
Eucharist elaborated by the Benedictine Odo Casel, in which the
re-enactment of the Eucharist ceremony was explained in terms
of iconic representation of the prototype.[26] But a closer analysis
would lead us too far from our theme.

Let us now return to the concept of the 'mirror image',[27] leaving
aside the earliest biblical career of the term (connected more with
the opposition shadow vs. essence of things) as well as its later
career, when it became a metaphor for realism in the fine arts.
(By way of an aside, it should be said that is was also used by
Luther in this context, hardly a dozen or so years after Leonardo,
the first to use the concept since Antiquity). The mirror image is
a very specific image; the directness of imitation – or, rather,
reflection – creates a higher degree of truthfulness than in the case
of other signs. The same thing happens with the term 'shadow',
which implies, despite its negative connotations in the context of
imitation, a certain inseparability of the archetype and the reflection; perhaps it was for this reason that the iconoclasts rather
tended to avoid this epithet which was used in other polemics.

The mirror image can be regarded as the essence of a certain
type of sign. The mirror image is in its turn connected with the
sacrament by the fact that the partition of a mirror does not
weaken its effectiveness. The Hussite Thomas of Stitne, along with
many other theologians, compared the existence of God as infinite
substance and as 'part' of this substance in the Host, which is its
material expression, to a reflection in a mirror – the face is
reflected in the entire mirror in the same way as in a fragment of
it.[28] The same form (*figura*) can be reflected simultaneously in
many mirrors. Both possibilities were cited in the Eucharistic
controversy from different positions (Wyclif, Luther, St Thomas
Aquinas).[29] For Luther this example clearly served to build up
Christ's ubiquity; its meaning in Wyclif is more complex. Unquestionably, however, the 'mirror image' is almost ideally situated in
the semantic field between the concept of image symbol and the
Eucharist as traditionally understood.

So we can say that – besides the concept of *figura*[30] – the terms
which come closest to grasping the functions of the religious image

and the Host are the manifested remembrance and the mirror image, the first because it shows the dynamic representational nature of the Eucharistic ceremony, the second because it separates the sign from its material base and gives it a semantic immediacy – in fact, as an illusion – on the basis of an analogy of form. To the extent that a religious image contains both of these features it can serve as a point of comparison for the sacrament of the Eucharist.

The great dispute over the Eucharist died out in the seventeenth century, despite the fact that the positions of the Lutherans and Calvinists had not changed. From time to time the problem of the Eucharist–image syndrome attracted the interest of polemicists, though usually in rather primitive form. It is characteristic that the Orthodox theologian Stefan Javorsky, in *The Rock of Faith* (1727),[31] in a simplified way returns to the starting-point of the debate and only reverses the argument. Javorsky states that the supporters of Calvin see in the Eucharist the image of the body and blood of Christ, and it is for this reason that they ought also to accept a painted image of Christ.

The discussion in the Eastern Church did not always use controversialist arguments of this kind. The eminent Russian semiotist Boris Uspenski recently recalled that in texts on icon theology, more precisely on sacralization of the work of the iconographer, one can find passages in which the priest is identified outright with the icon painter. What is more, these passages express the belief that the icon painter creates Christ's body with paints in the same way as the priest changes bread and wine into the body and blood of the Lord.[32]

To the extent that the dispute over the Eucharistic sacrament and the Byzantine image dispute were a dispute over incarnation and over the possibility of grasping the divinity in the image, they were also connected with the problem of docetism: that is, the belief, that the Incarnation is at best an appearance. This was noted recently by Patrick Henry, who stated that through the Byzantine image controversy the problem of docetism was posed anew with great intensity.[33] Though Henry tends to overemphasize the existence of docetism in the eighth and ninth centuries – the docetic dispute was integrally connected with Gnosticism, which at that time had been largely overcome – nevertheless there is unquestionably a certain connection between docetism and the cult of images, and this in the negative sense that recollection of the link helped the iconoclasts. For example, Karlstadt's almost complete lack of interest in the life of Christ and his Passion – seen by him only in the light of the final act of Redemption – had something in it of the Gnostic mistrust towards the real, historical Christ.

Another example can be found in the Stephanite heresy in Ethiopia in the fifteenth and sixteenth centuries. In the Stephanites one can find an almost classic iconoclastic syndrome – rejection of the cult of Mary and the cult of the cross. They were also charged with disbelief in the Real Presence of Christ in the Eucharist.[34] At the same time one can notice there a certain influence of docetism. On the other hand docetism did not appear in Calvinism or in Lutheranism (for Luther it was only a certain controversialist assumption), but it did appear in the form of weak echoes in some currents of the radical Reformation.

In the above remarks the chief interest has been in the problems of the Christological context of sacramentology: that is, in the iconic dimension of Christology. As has been mentioned, in its initial phase the Byzantine image dispute had stronger reference to the great Christological controversies (Nestorianism, Monophysitism) connected with the problems of combining or separating the natures of Christ. In these deliberations, though to a much lesser degree than in the Eucharistic dispute, the concept of image appeared as a specific means of reference and comparison. Luther was interested in this problem only as a side issue to the trinitarian discussions that were beginning. However, in a commentary on the Epistle to the Hebrews he wrote a passage that can be regarded as closing the line initiated in Byzantium, and in a certain, albeit indirect, sense as an answer to the theology of the image of Theodore the Studite. Theodore credited the icon of Christ with being a personal expression (*hypostasis*) of Christ's nature. In this passage we can also see clearly Luther's tendency to use Christological terms (nature, substance) interchangeably: 'All the images there have a different essence and nature from their archetype. But the Son is an image of the essence of the Father in the sense that the image is made from the essence of the Father.'[35] Luther's approach is a late triumph of nominalistic thinking over the remnants of Platonism.

ANTITHETICAL CONCEPTS

The image dispute was conducted on various planes: theological discourse, liturgical discourse, and popular controversy. On each of these planes, however, the substance of the dispute became overgrown with many slogan-like, antithetical concepts, which, together with a certain number of commonplaces, demarcated the field of dispute.

The most essential of them, especially those connected with fundamental theology (e.g. the Law vs. Christian freedom) have already been discussed elsewhere. However, there remains another group of interesting commonplaces and pairs of antithetical concepts less closely connected with theology that are worth examining.

Let us begin with the opposition body–soul: that is, with the basic starting-point of all spiritualistic currents. This antithesis played a special role in Zwingli's thought, and its implications for the image question have already been discussed. It was also Zwingli who in the image controversy made the transition from this pair to a narrower antithesis more connected with liturgy: namely that of content–form. It is, however, obvious that to the very essence of the concept of 'form' belongs its outwardness. Thus we have come to the opposition external–internal (*foris–intus*), an opposition with an obvious connotation, especially in theology. Images were categorized as belonging to the external domain, as *res externa*. For Luther the distinction between 'exterior idolatry' (the image cult) and the more dangerous 'interior idolatry' was the starting-point in attempts to weaken the anti-image message of the First Commandment; for Zwingli it served only as an argument for the abolition of images.

The term 'external' was obviously already an evaluative term, connoting something less important, though it could be understood in the adiaphorist sense. On the other hand, in Sebastian Franck's understanding the term 'external' definitely had a negative, anti-image connotation. 'For this reason we do not want to bring the external man into the church through images and ceremonies.'[36] Franck's external man was opposed to the 'new creature', the Reformation man, and he was also, as it were, an anthropocentric extension of the dichotomy of content and form.

The term 'internal ideas'[37] was one of the most important in the image dispute. It is closely connected with the opposition internal–external; even more noteworthy are the connections with the popular antithesis linked with the tactics of removing images (*ab Auge, ab Herz*), which will be discussed below. On closer scrutiny this concept – as we have tried to demonstrate in the case of Karlstadt – reveals extremely interesting patterns of iconoclastic thought. Obviously the subject-matter implied by this concept was largely shaped by the ambivalence of the concept of 'image.'

Here one should refer to the classic study by Frances Yates, *The Art of Memory*.[38] Yates clearly demonstrated that the opponents (such as the famous Ramus or the Anglican Pastor William Perkins) of the old, traditional art of memory (mnemonics), which had made use of images and figurative ideas, were also vehement enemies of religious art. Perkins' tract *A Warning against the Idolatrie of the Last Times* (1603), condemned those who

> used images and other ceremonies to procure the presence of angels and celestiall powers that by them they might attaine to the knowledge of God . . . for we may not binde the presence of God. . . . Now God hath not bound himself by any word to be present at images.[39]

So far this is a typical Calvinist discourse, as it is when Perkins extends the ban on images to include internal images: 'So soone as the minde frames unto it selfe any forme of God (as when he is popishly conceived to be like an old man in heaven in a throne with a sceptre in hand) an idol is set up in the minde . . . [40] A thing faigned in the mind by imagination is an idol.'[41] But Perkins extends his anti-image stance to cover traditional mnemonic art. Logical dissection has greater value for the memory than the art of using images and 'umbrages' (i.e. shadows). All ideas of the latter are completely false, since only an aniconic logical dissection contains the logical capacity for remembering.

Yates concluded from this that the exceptional success that Ramism, as a rather superficial pedagogical method, enjoyed in the Protestant countries, especially in England, was certainly partially due to the fact that it expressed a certain kind of internal iconoclasm, corresponding to its external manifestations. One cannot accept the interesting suggestion of Yates as relevant to all aspects of the art of memory. Without going more deeply into the complicated problems of sixteenth-century mnemonics, it should however be noted that Giordano Bruno also wrote a mnemonic treatise whose leading principle was the extreme opposite of Ramism: namely, Aristotle's dictum 'to think means to consider with the help of images'. Starting from a somewhat different doctrinal position close to pantheism, Bruno was an opponent of images and sculptures in the Calvinist fashion, though he criticized the cult of saints and relics even more strongly.[42] It appears that, independently of doctrinal formulations, national characteristics played a certain role here, since the Italians, even if they found themselves in the camp of the Protestants, lacked the 'fear of images' that was so common north of the Alps.

In reflecting on the various categories of images, I have stated that an examination of the semantic field of the concept of image and its synonyms (or terms close to it) in the sixteenth century is impossible at the present stage of research. Sometimes the distinctions between particular terms were intentionally erased by asserting that all the possible categories of an image fell under the concept of 'idol'. This was done, for example, by Ludwig Hätzer, and it is interesting that even Zwingli took over this assertion (though it was rather inconsistent with his position on the image question). To quote Hätzer:

> One must also know that the word *idolon*, which in Latin means *simulacrum* (likeness), in German means *bildnus* (picture) or *glychnus* (allegory or story). That is why in those places in the Scriptures where idols are prohibited this applies not only to idols but also to pictures and allegories. So the papists are wrong when they say that only an idol (*Abgott*) is the equivalent of an idol – no, *bild* or *glychnus* also means the same.[43]

As regards the concept of image, the Calvinists invoked an even stronger theological foundation. We read, for example, in the Second Helvetic Confession of 1566:

> An image, as Lactantius states, Book 2, chapter 18, has its name from delusion. However, the object of delusion is of necessity something false, and it can never be called true because it pretends to be true by means of its external appearance and imitation. So if all imitation is not the thing itself but only play, then there is nothing of religion in images. Hence let us fashion a better, higher and more spiritual notion of Christ than when we look at him by means

of paint and images, which differ from the truth as far as is possible.[44]

Here we encounter a dualism already known from the Eucharistic controversy: image or sign vs. the thing itself (*res ipsa*) and the rejection of the illusion-creating functions of art resulting from the definition of image. Lactantius, to whom the author of the Confession refers, had a big impact on the image dispute, both as regards the definition of image and as the father of the idea that the cult of images derives from pagan cults. In this sense, as Willy Rordorf has recently shown, he exerted an important influence on the views of the young Bullinger.[45]

The Calvinist condemnation of the image as a category (which is one of the trends of thought about art in general) had further resonances in a negative attitude towards aesthetic illusion, an attitude whose Platonic roots are obvious. This kind of approach appeared quite rarely in the image dispute and was used perhaps only once as the main argument. In his poem *True Crucifixe* (1629) the Scottish Puritan Sir William Mure based his main accusation against religious art on the total inadequacy of artistic illusion and artistic devices. Mure accents the themes of artificiality ('artificiall crucifixe') and deceitful illusion ('cows'ning poore people by deceitfull slight, of paynter's arte affording false delight') as opposed to the requirements and position of the Sacred. For the Catholic idol is 'the Semblance of a thing but faind to bee, which no subsistance hath essentially'.[46]

Disputes on the natural order for removing images also took on the character of a fight about topoi – whether the images ought to be first removed from the eye or from the heart as well. Karlstadt argued 'out of the eye, out of the heart' (*ab Auge, ab Herz*). Luther criticized him for removing only the visible idols and leaving the more dangerous internal idols in the heart. Let us turn our attention once more to the 'internal–external' opposition, which, together with the 'body–spirit' dichotomy, delineates the semantic field of the 'heart–eye' pair. Martin Bucer, who for a certain time espoused a mediating position in the image dispute, emphasized that 'idols ought to be removed first from the heart, and then from the eye';[47] this was, however, connected with criticism of the readiness of the Lutherans to remove images only rhetorically. The heart–eye pair, based on the scholastic theory of knowledge,[48] turned up almost monotonously in every Lutheran–

Calvinist polemic. For Lutherans, reversing the order of removing idols (first from the heart, then from the eye) was obviously a tactical measure to a certain extent. In 1611 an uncompromising opponent of religous art, the Calvinist preacher Abraham Sculte-tus, summed up nearly a century of controversy by stating that in more than a hundred years the Lutherans had not even removed the idols from the heart.[49]

The eye, as the organ of sight, gave rise to various mental associations. It was the symbol of the dangers inherent in visual cognition, understood as something superficial. The supporters of Wyclif, referring to the image dispute, said that what nourishes the sight poisons the soul.[50] On a lower, more pragmatic plane Protestants believed that the visual beholding of images can be an impediment to faith from hearing. In a more specific form this belief appeared in the well-known Lutheran Flacius Illyricus, who allowed, willy-nilly, the existence of images in church, as long as they were located far away from the pulpit.[51]

The image dispute was also associated with the topoi of apostolic simplicity and the aniconism of the first Christians. As regards the image question, the topos of apostolic simplicity cannot be fitted into the famous schema of Boas and Lovejoy ('soft' vs. 'hard' primitivism) precisely because 'hard primitivism' in this case has an entirely positive connotation. According to the vision of primitive Christianity conceived in the circles of the radical Reformation, ceremonies and adornments (including images) had no part in the life and cult of the first Christians. They lived either in caves, in inaccessible places or in 'simple homes'.[52] The churches of the first Christians were located in caves, or were modest, even barn-like wooden houses. The 'barn-church' is a separate theme (Scheunenkirche), which was used as a rhetorical ploy even by Luther, and was often used in a negative sense by the Counter-Reformation polemicists.[53]

A polemic based on commonplaces rarely explains concepts and problems. A first-rate example here might be the idea of the cave-church. For a cave, like all dark abysses, also has negative connotations. Thus some Reformation polemicists spoke meta-phorically of the Roman caves as seats of the 'godless papacy',[54] thus obviously weakening the meaning of the commonplace; in their turn Catholic polemicists, referring directly to the common-place of the cave, described the pictorial interiors of the Christian catacombs, thereby giving the lie to the reformers' assertions about early aniconicity. Describing a newly discovered Roman catacomb in 1578, an unknown Catholic reflects, in direct reference to Reformation iconoclasm, the godliness of the first Christians, who 'took refuge from persecution in the caves, where they painted pious images and adored them'.[55]

When referring to the simple beginnings of Christianity, the iconophobes monotonously presented one simple assertion: that there were no religious images at that time. They thus defined them as later 'additions'; English Puritans even spoke metaphorically of a special 'varnish on true religion'.[56] The removal of images therefore functioned in the realm of what scholars of literature now call a 'great metaphor', as a metaphor of the purification of the Christian soul; more popular approaches referred to a similar example, the expulsion of the money-changers from the Temple. Between the metaphorical and the literal context of the concept one can obviously place Zwingli's term 'beautifully white' (hübsch wyss)[57] or other similar terms used by the reformers to describe the condition of churches after the removal of images. A reference to the positive connotation of lucidity is obvious, although it was not much emphasized by the reformers: at that time the medieval tradition of claritas as a principal aesthetic value was already much weakened. The Protestants spoke of the brightness of their churches, their opponents of their bare walls ('as empty as a Lutheran church').

So images were associated by their opponents with the decline of the Church, with an exceptional corruption and a departure from the simplicity of the first Christians. Among the opponents of images, opinions were divided on when this decline had begun. The most prevalent view was that the first five hundred years of Christianity were undefiled (consensus quinquesaecularis).[58] In other sources this turning-point was shifted to the age of Constantine: 'let us promise ourselves in a virtuous Christian word, to retain only whatever existed in these first three hundred years. Look and you will see the result, that images will disappear from our churches.'[59] The Lutherans, in turn, complained: 'they do not want to heed this, that since apostolic times all of this [i.e. images] has existed in the Church of God without scandal'.[60]

The notion of 'the visible Church' – or, in a more literal version, 'the brick Church' – played a certain role in the history of the image controversy. First and foremost its use marks a boundary between the radical Reformation and Lutheranism and Calvinism.

Despite many rhetorical condemnations, neither Karlstadt, Zwingli nor Calvin entirely questioned its validity.[61] That is why one could not say that all supporters of the notion of the 'visible Church' espoused an iconodulic position. Thus, in practice this concept does not delimit the antagonistic positions in the image controversy as does the Eucharistic controversy.

Epiphanius, bishop of Cyprus, a patristic opponent of religious art, had already juxtaposed 'dead images' to the magnificent 'living God'.[62] The cult of images was compared to prayers to the dead. Idols are dead, do not see, cannot hear, do not react to aggression or verbal abuse (compare the challenges of the iconoclasts quoted in Chapter 3). Luther himself also referred to this opposition. A logical scrutiny of the paired concepts living–dead suggests further questions, especially in view of a possible subcutaneous animistic element in the image dispute. If idols are really 'dead', is it then worth devoting so much attention to them? Paracelsus used to say, referring to another topos, that 'living idols' are more dangerous than images or statues.[63] However, Ambrosius Blarer found here an unsurpassed rhetorical answer: 'dead images' ought nonetheless to be shunned, for even 'dead flies can poison good food'.[64] With Blarer's phrase the tendency to play off antithetical metaphors as disputational stratagems reached its zenith.

Also connected with the concept of 'deadness' was a distinctive strand of contempt for created matter (better expressed in the German term *Stoffverspottung*). This term denotes a tendency to emphasize the mere materiality of a cultic object in a negatively demystifying sense: that idols are made of ordinary, lifeless wood, stone, paint or glass. Carlyle relates that John Knox, while on the galleys in Catholic captivity, was given an image of the Mother of God to worship: ' "Mother? Mother of God?" said Knox when the turn came to him: "This is no Mother of God: this is a pented bredd [painted board] – a piece of wood, I tell you, with paint on it! She is fitter for swimming, I think, than for being worshipped," added Knox and flung the thing into the river.'[65]

Rejection of the material work of art as a means of transmitting the sacred reached its apogee in the vitriolic comments on the process of making sculptures from wood. Both Karlstadt and the Swiss Anabaptist Ludwig Hätzer, whom he influenced, used a biblical passage (Isaiah 44:16–18) to deprecate the materiality of idols:

He [the sculptor] cuts down cedars, takes a holm or an
oak.... With a part of their wood he warms himself, or
makes a fire for baking bread; but with another part he
makes a god which he adores.... Half of it he burns in the
fire, and on its embers he roasts his meat and eats it...
from what remains he makes a god, his idol.[66]

Karlstadt and Hätzer's argument, which Calvin also took up in
his *Institutes*, can serve as a paradigm of the controversialist figures
of speech of that time. It has already been mentioned that this
passage served as an incentive for an iconoclastic act committed
by a Russian Stundist as late as 1900.

Lifelessness is a feature of the work of human hands. So from
the living–dead opposition was derived another pair of antithetic
concepts, human work–divine work. Images and sculptures are
only miserable competitors with God's work: namely, man (as
imago Dei) or the forms of nature. God must be worshipped in
his 'true and living works', says Martin Bucer,[67] in the 'living
images', as the iconoclast Duke Frederick III of the Palatinate
proclaimed. We find similar thoughts in Calvin and in a clearly
pantheistic context in Giordano Bruno. According to Theodore
Beza, the works of human hands cannot be 'more beautiful and
true to life than those which God himself has painted and illustrated with his hand ... plants, herbs and flowers are more alive
and real than all the images that priests have in their churches'.[68]

In the polemics referring to *adiaphora* there also appeared a
group of metaphors connected with the child: toy, cane and knife
as symbols of transience, of temporary support but also of danger.
In his early deliberations Luther himself had included religious
images among 'childish things' (*puerilia*). This classification,
though not entirely negative, certainly implied that when the faithful were more grown-up images could be rejected (this was a kind
of pedagogical utopia that was juxtaposed to the utopia of simple,
aniconic beginnings). A contiguous term to *puerilia* was the designation of images and sculptures as a toy or a temporary support
(a cane). The child then became in turn a symbol of the 'simple
folk' for whom images are intended in the famous utterance of
Gregory the Great. The opponents of images did not, of course,
accept this line of argument. Karlstadt expressed this most forcefully: from his point of view images were like a knife with which
a child plays, unconscious of the danger; it must obviously be

taken away from him at once.[69] An iconoclast in Reutlingen demanded immediate action lest the 'child hurt himself with the knife'.[70] Sebastian Franck, the Reformation mystic, who took a somewhat more moderate iconophobic position, criticized iconoclasm and argued differently:

> God has allowed external signs. He himself gave them, just as he gave a doll to the Church in its youth. . . . This happened because the Church in its childhood was not able to do without these things as a kind of supporting cane. But now, when the child is strong enough, it can cast away the cane without fear of angering the Father.[71]

The metaphor of the knife transposed the dispute from the commonplace of childhood and growing up to the problem of art as a tool. Luther had emphasized that the abuse of wine does not abrogate the right to drink this noble beverage. Dürer himself took up the above metaphor in defence of art: 'No Christian will be attracted to an idolatrous faith by a painting or figure, just as a pious man will not allow himself to be induced to murder just because he carries a weapon at his side.'[72] And once again a distinctive metaphorical circle was closed.

DEFINITIONS OF ART AND IDOLATRY

This work would not be complete if certain tendencies in the interpretation of the status and nomenclature of art that appeared on the fringes of the image dispute were omitted. As was emphasized in the discussion of Calvin's views, the great historical flowering of secular art and patronage in the Protestant countries was not accompanied by any wide-ranging theoretical discussion. Nor was any concept of secular art elaborated. Calvin's remark that art can represent 'everything that one can see', or Luther's terms *Merkbilder*, *Spiegelbilder* ('images to capture the attention', 'mirror-images') were too general to provide the broad outlines for a new field of art. It must be emphasized that towards the end of the sixteenth century the term 'civil' images appeared. It unquestionably came from the term 'civil cult' (*cultus civilis*), which was one of the main concepts of Lutheran orthodoxy.[73] After 1620 the term 'civil' images was used primarily by Calvinists and Anglicans and obviously referred to entirely secular representations.

In his poetic treatise, *True Crucifixe*, Sir William Mure wrote: 'Let civil images for civil use have their place, we challenge only the abuse.'[74] In this very interesting approach, Mure included in the 'civil' sphere all images that take their beginnings from imitation or the imagination of the artist. This concept seemingly did not acquire wide popularity.[75] It was the same with the tripartite division of the uses of art: *usus superstitiosus, typicus, politicus*.[76] The first two categories – devotional and typological images – were rejected. On the other hand, *usus politicus* referred to portraits and 'histories' and functioned as just another name for secular art. In 1602 the Lutheran theologian Polycarp Leyser proposed a similar tripartite division: *superstitiosae, typicae* and *historicae imagines*, of which he allowed only the third category.[77] The concept *usus politicus*, significantly, came from Luther's analysis of the legal validity of the Old Testament.

Finally, let us take a look at some of the central polemical concepts that have appeared so frequently in our remarks on the image dispute – idols and graven images, *Götze*, idolatry, *Abgötterei*, *adiaphora* and 'intermediate things'. The most popular was the term 'idol' or *idole* (in English and French respectively), derived of course from Latin, and *Götze* in German. None of them had a precisely defined field of meaning. The German term gained perhaps the greatest popularity. Though the word itself goes back to at least 1376, it was Luther in 1520 who gave it its modern meaning ('false God', 'idol').[78] The term *Ölgötze* (literally 'oil idol', i.e. painted idol), which referred to painting or polychrome sculpture, also became very popular. The phrase 'wie ein Ölgötze stehen' ('stand immovably like a painted idol') has lasted to this day as a German idiom. From the outset *Götze* was more popular than its theological counterpart, *Abgott*. Though meaning almost the same thing (referring also to false gods in general) *Abgott* was less used in the sixteenth century, and when it was used it was in a more philosophical–theological context. To give some idea of the diversity of terms, I should like to cite yet another one, namely, *Beygott* (literally 'added idol', 'side idol'), which was used in some Catholic circles critical of the cult of images.[79]

Equally rich in variants was the term *idolatria* (or *idololatria*). Perhaps the most inventive were among the vocabulary of the English Puritans (among others 'idolatria', 'idolatrousness', 'idolomania', 'idolservice', 'idolgadding', 'idolpleasure').[80] Few of these words have survived into modern times, and the same thing can be said for the German *Götzendienst* (*abgöttisch* has survived, however).

The term *adiaphora*[81] dominated in its Greek version in all countries with the exception of Germany. For a long time the word *Mitteldinge*, which means 'intermediate things', was popular here. We meet also such terms as 'neutral', 'indifferent', or 'free' things (e.g. in Luther). In some cases, *adiaphora* were identified with 'ceremonial things'. And here the previously analysed relativizing concept of 'outwardness' – connected, of course, with the theological opposition *foris–intus* – played a certain role: one might think of such curious formulations as 'outer neutral things'.[82]

THE FATE OF ART

Finally, a separate problem worth looking at is the position of art as an institutional system at various levels of the image dispute, a dispute which put the theme of 'art in danger' on the agenda. It will be the task of future research to determine the influence of the image dispute and iconoclasm on shaping the modern concept of art and on the metaphors of its rise and decline. The problem is that Vasari, with his classic formulation of the biological cycle of art, was not very much influenced by northern iconoclasm. Moreover, although people in the sixteenth century were more or less aware of some kind of notion of the end of the Middle Ages, they did not associate this with the decline of a 'great culture'. For obvious reasons, Huizinga's point of view was alien to them. Despite this, they very soon became aware that the Reformation meant the end of the previous forms of organization of the fine arts. The earliest signs of the crisis were provided by artists themselves. Some of them became iconoclasts, others, like Dürer, took up the defence of art, but most of them, impoverished by the disappearance of church patronage, in desperation sought other means of livelihood. This was pointed out with grotesque exaggeration by the Nuremberg artist Hans Greiffenberger, who oscillated between Lutheranism and Zwinglianism: 'Painters, woodcarvers . . . say: since the saints no longer matter, then we shall paint harlots and scoundrels, if this will bring money.'[83] Nearly a century had to pass before a new model of artistic life could develop north of the Alps, and during this time the aware-

ness of danger was constant.[84] This question appears in a characteristic way in Dürer, who stressed the fact that painting – which
requires great skill – is a gift of God. This thesis survived in
polemics up to the seventeenth century. As the main argument
justifying the existence of religious art it was even used by the
Calvinist-inclined patriarch Lucaris, though without great conviction. As I have already tried to show, he used it to skirt other
issues of a more fundamental nature. However, this argument
could be only a weak response to the harsh formulation 'here the
arts do freeze' coined by the pessimistic Erasmus, who in 1526
initiated a discussion on the responsibility of Protestantism for
the decline of art in Germany. In his *Kunstbüchlin* (1538) the
Lutheran artist Heinrich Vogtherr the Elder stated that the events
in Germany 'have considerably reduced all the fine and free arts'.
Towards the end of the sixteenth century in Saxony[85] there was
a clear awareness that the Protestants would have to take art under
their patronage in order to rebuff charges of an asceticism hostile
to art. One can also say that on the eve of the Thirty Years'
War considerable financial support was given to the arts in some
Protestant territories. The vehement reaction of many Lutheran
circles to the Calvinist iconoclasm in Prague (1619/20) was not
only due to awareness of the political harmfulness of this act but
also indicated a conscious defence of culture.

A separate problem, somewhat on the margin of this subject,
is the question whether painting is able to express the complexity
of religious truth (sculpture was regarded more unequivocally),
and whether superb artistic form or the magnificence of the
materials used are not obstacles to the reception of a religious
work of art. Somewhat connected with this was the problem *ut
pictura poesis*.

In order to understand the reasons for the deep Protestant
mistrust of images, let us recall once more some of the more
extreme iconodulic pronouncements from the eve of the Reformation. Jakob Ziegler, a Bavarian humanist who in 1510–12
debated with the Czech Brethren, uttered an apology for images
in church. His main point was that the image is a better and
more explicit means of communication than writing, not excluding
Scripture. The emphasis which the Protestants put on 'faith from
hearing' now becomes understandable against the background of
Ziegler's pronouncement. During prayer, Ziegler notes, there is
the danger that the thoughts of the believer may become scattered.

However, if he sees an image, his thoughts will be directed to a particular goal. If the image contains unworthy content, Ziegler maintains, then the body of the believer will be seized by convulsions. Images are more effective than Scripture. Ziegler gives an extreme version of St Augustine's thought, that it suffices to look at an image but a text must be understood: Scripture is understandable only to educated people, but images (an echo of Gregory the Great) can be understood by all. The image is a purer means of communication than the Bible.[86]

To this position the Lutherans opposed the belief that, while painting has the right to exist, it is not as versatile a means of communicating complicated religious truths as words. Luther strongly emphasized that the basic truths of faith are complicated and 'spiritual matters' (geistliche Sachen) which cannot be grasped through images. For the reformer spiritual matters were a problem of a higher order, where human thought came into contact with the inscrutable, fundamental mysteries of faith. According to an account of Caspar Peucer, Albrecht Dürer allegedly took a similar position on the Eucharistic question, stating that it could not be expressed by means of an image.[87] Looked at in the context of Raphael's Disputa created ten years earlier, which also dealt with the mystery of the Eucharist, this statement was the harbinger of a new era.

The Lutherans emphasized that a work of art ought to be orderly (ordentlich), iconographically correct and rather simple. Luther spoke of simple (einfältig) painting. Among the three styles of ancient painting – genus grande, mediocre, humilis – Melanchthon preferred genus humilis, the simple style.[88]

It is significant that even the Catholics were generally agreed that artistically refined (künstliche) images are unsuited for the propagation of religious truths. The Catholic Church, unlike the Protestants, did not acknowledge the problem of luxury and its inappropriateness; on the other hand, anticipating the resolutions of the Council of Trent, it expressed the view that images ought to speak in a forceful and simple language. In 1524 Hugo von Hohenlandenberg, bishop of Konstanz, came out against over-elaborate (überkünstliche) images, which focus the attention of believers on the artistic and not the theological merits of a work of art. Hieronymus Emser said the same thing:

the greater the art (künstlich) with which an image is made,

the more it concentrates the attention of the viewer on looking at the art, while he ought to shift his attention from the
images to the dear saints [depicted on them]. It would be
better if we followed the old customs and had more simple
images in the churches.[89]

So there is no doubt that in principle both confessions agreed that
'mysteries do not fight' (*mysteria streiten nicht*): allegories could
not be a weapon in religious dispute and in teaching the faith.

Thus from the theoretical side the fate of Mannerism as an
artistic style which preferred allegories and a complicated iconography was sealed. Both sides seemed to be agreed not to use
images with manneristic formulas in the religious polemic. The
visual forms of the Renaissance were on the whole alien to the
Protestants. Thus until the advent of the Baroque, there was no
concrete affiliation of a religious confession with an artistic style;
however, a direct cause–effect relationship is not discernible. The
point is that the morphological development of art has a logic and
dynamic of its own, and theoretical or dogmatic pronouncements
can change very little, with the obvious exception of the avant-
garde. That is why it seems impossible to link the Reformation
as a cultural form with the great concepts of style among which
it grew up – late Gothic, Renaissance, Mannerism and early
Baroque. On the other hand, the Reformation image dispute had
far-reaching effects on iconography, on the birth of new genres
and, last but not least, on the rise of secular art. It was thanks to
this dispute that art came to be perceived as a separate category,
and that, after a certain hiatus, attention began to be paid to the
problems of patronage and of the artistic process itself. Since that
time art has been viewed in social consciousness as an expression
of the culture of great political, ideological and religious systems.
It is a strange paradox that this process took place through an
awareness of a crisis of art, of its fragility and the peril of iconoclasm – an awareness which since that time, save in the optimistic
nineteenth century, has never permanently left us.

Appendix
Protestant and Muslim aniconism: attempts at comparison

The charge of 'Judaizing' – implying an affinity to Jewish religious aniconism – belonged, as we have seen, to the standard topoi of the image controversy. Less well known is the fact that iconoclastic Protestants were often compared with the second great monotheist aniconic religion: that is, Muhammadanism. These comparisons form a fascinating, kaleidoscopic image of Catholic, Lutheran, Calvinist and, last but not least, Ottoman self-assertions and perceptions. In his diary reporting the events of his stay in Constantinople, the Lutheran Stephan Gerlach – whose observations were discussed in Chapter 4 – stated tersely: 'The Lutherans are more liked by the Ottomans than the papists, since they condemn the adoration of images, and thus they [the Ottomans] think that they might much more easily become Ottoman than the Italians.'[1] Of course, it was the Catholics who most insisted on comparing Protestant iconoclasts to the Ottomans. The English expatriate Jesuit William Rainolds (Reginald) in his famous treatise *Calvinoturcismus* (1597) harped with great intensity on the aniconic similarities between Muslim and Anglican practice.[2]

Whereas the Lutheran Gerlach reported this aniconic convergence without any comment, other Lutherans used this argument to establish a distinction between the moderate Lutheran practice and the 'iconoclastic folly' of the rival Calvinists. Around 1600 the debate must have been particularly intense, some German Lutherans ostensibly preferring an alliance with Rome to joining forces with Geneva and Heidelberg. The famous case of the Calvinist Adam Neuser, who converted to Islam, seemed to lend credibility to the Calvinist–Ottoman syndrome. The Saxon Lutheran Gabriel Kaldemarckt in 1587, saw the Lutherans in a middle position between the 'papist and idolatrous heathens' and 'the

195

Ottomans and the sectarians' who do not tolerate images.[3] The Lutheran theologian Simon Geddicus declared in 1597 that 'accursed Calvinism' paves the way, by means of iconoclasm, for the Ottoman Alcoran.[4]

The Calvinists in their turn were not much inclined to dwell on this analogy. One of the few exceptions was the Anglican writer Paul Rycaut, who in 1678 stated boldly[5] that the only positive aspect of Muslim religion was its enmity to religious art. There also exists a very long tradition of reports – though sometimes no doubt fictitious[6] – about the Turks' benevolent treatment of Calvinists or Protestants in general solely by virtue of their real or presumed aniconism. It ends with a bemused entry in Voltaire's *Dictionnaire philosophique*:

A nobleman from the entourage of Prince Ragotski [Rakoczy] assured me that once when he entered a café in Constantinople the lady of the establishment ordered her waiters not to serve him anything because she thought him an idolator. The nobleman, being however a Protestant, gave her his word that he adored neither the Host nor images. 'If that is so,' said the lady, 'come to me every day and you will be served free of charge.'[7]

Notes

1 Martin Luther: cultic abuse, religious art and Christian freedom

1 G. Benn, *Briefe an F. W. Oelze 1932–1945*, Wiesbaden 1977, p. 88.
2 On the different contexts of *weltlich*, see F. Lau, *'Äusserlich Ordnung' und 'weltlich Ding' in Luthers Theologie*, Göttingen 1933.
3 All quotations from Luther are – unless otherwise indicated – from the Weimar edition of his collected works: *D. Martin Luthers Werke. Kritische Gesamtausgabe*, vols 1–60, Weimar 1883–1980 (referred to here as *Luthers Werke*).
4 See, e.g., Erwin Iserloh, 'Bildfeindlichkeit des Nominalismus und Bildersturm im 16. Jh.', in *Bild-Wort-Symbol in der Theologie*, ed. W. Heinen, Würzburg 1969, pp. 119–39.
5 *Luthers Werke*, vol. 56, p. 453.
6 Quoted after J. Ficker, *Luthers Vorlesung über den Hebräerbrief 1517/18*, Leipzig 1929, vol. II, p. 23.
7 Speaking of the 'First Commandment' or, when quoting Calvinist sources, the 'Second Commandment', I refer of course always to the same part of the Decalogue (Exodus 20:2 ff.; Deuteronomy 5:6) as to whose numeration an important disagreement existed – see the excellent analysis in M. Stirm, *Die Bilderfrage in der Reformation*, Gütersloh 1977, pp. 17–22, 139, 161, 229.
8 *Luthers Werke*, vol. 1 pp. 399–401, 404.
9 ibid., p. 235.
10 ibid., p. 598.
11 ibid., vol. 6, pp. 43–5.
12 ibid., p. 211.
13 ibid., vol. 7, p. 37.
14 See also H. Pohlmann, *Hat Luther Paulus entdeckt?*, Berlin 1959.
15 A good analysis of Melanchthon's vacillation is in W. Maurer, *Der junge Melanchthon*, Göttingen 1967, vol. II, p. 210.
16 The best account is in U. Bubenheimer, 'Scandalum et ius divinum. Theologische und rechtstheologische Probleme der ersten reformatorischen Innovationen in Wittenberg 1521/22', *Zeitschrift der Savigny-Stiftung für Rechtsgeschichte, Kanonistische Abteilung*, 59, 1973,

pp. 263–342. See also H. Barge, *Aktenstücke zur Wittenberger Bewegung 1521, Anfang 1522*, Leipzig 1912.

17 See the analysis in Chapter 2.

18 H. Barge, *Andreas Bodenstein von Karlstadt*, Leipzig 1905, vol. I, p. 434.

19 G. R. Williams, *The Radical Reformation*, Philadelphia 1962.

20 The chapter 'On images' is edited in *Luthers Werke*, vol. 10, III, pp. 26–36. On the various editions, see J. Benzing, *Lutherbibliographie*, Baden-Baden 1966, vol. I, nos 1320–6.

21 *Luthers Werke*, vol. 10, III, p. 26.

22 ibid., p. 35.

23 ibid., p. 31.

24 ibid., vol. 51, p. 496.

25 See also G. Ruhbach, 'Luthers Stellung zur alten Kirche', *Wort und Dienst*, 10, 1969, pp. 68–84.

26 A good analysis of the concept is in G. Stählin, *Skandalon*, Gütersloh 1930.

27 *Luthers Werke*, vol. 10, III, p. 29.

28 Helmar Junghans, 'Freiheit und Ordnung bei Luther während der Wittenberger Bewegung und bei den Visitationen', *Theologische Literaturzeitung*, 97, 1972, cols 95–103.

29 The term was popularized in H. Barge, *Frühprotestantisches Gemeindechristentum in Wittenberg und Orlamünde*, Leipzig 1909.

30 K. H. Bernhardt, *Gott und Bild. Ein Beitrag zur Begründung und Deutung des Bilderverbotes im Alten Testament*, Berlin 1956; Ch. Dohmen, *Das Bilderverbot. Seine Entstehung und Entwicklung im Alten Testament*, Königstein 1985.

31 *Luthers Werke*, vol. 10, III, pp. 27–8.

32 ibid., p. 29; Andreas Bodenstein von Karlstadt, *Von Abtuhung der Bilder*, ed. H. Lietzmann, Bonn 1911, p. 11.

33 *Die Wahrheit muss ans Licht, Dialoge aus der Zeit der Reformation*, ed. R. Bentzinger, Leipzig 1982, p. 250 (the whole treatise on pp. 223–60).

34 *Luthers Werke*, vol. 24, p. 553.

35 H. Emser, *Das man der heyligen Bilder yn den Kirchen nit abthon noch unehren soll*, Dresden 1522 – see H. Smolinsky, 'Reformation und Bildersturm. Hieronymus Emsers Schrift gegen Karlstadt über die Bilderverehrung', in *Reformatio Ecclesiae. Festgabe für Erwin Iserloh*, ed. R. Bäumer, Paderborn 1980, pp. 427–40.

36 J. Eck, *De non tollendis Christi et Sanctorum Imaginibus*, Ingolstadt 1522 – see E. Iserloh, 'Die Verteidigung der Bilder durch Johannes Eck zu Beginn des reformatorischen Bildersturmes', in *Aus Reformation und Gegenreformation. Festschrift für Theodor Freudenberger* (Würzburger Diözesangeschichtsblätter 35/36), Würzburg 1974, pp. 75–87.

37 Barge, *Karlstadt*, vol. I, p. 455.

38 See, in a vast bibliography, H. Gerdes, *Luthers Streit mit den Schwärmern um das rechte Verständnis des Gesetzes Mose*, Göttingen 1955 (especially as concerns the problem of Judaizing); H. Loewen, *Luther*

and the Radicals: Another Look at Some Aspects of the Struggle between Luther and the Radical Reformation, Waterloo 1974; B. Lohse, 'Luther und der Radikalismus', *Lutherjahrbuch*, 44, 1977, pp. 1–27.

39 *Luthers Werke*, vol. 24, p. 10.
40 ibid., vol. 18, p. 81.
41 ibid., vol. 15, pp. 210–21.
42 ibid., p. 219.
43 A somewhat biased but very vivid account of the meeting in Orlamünde is provided by the so-called *Acta Ienensia*, in *Luthers Werke*, vol. 15, pp. 343–7.
44 The treatise is edited in *Luthers Werke*, vol. 18, pp. 62–125.
45 ibid., p. 67.
46 ibid., p. 68.
47 ibid., p. 71.
48 *Karlstadts Schriften aus den Jahren 1523–25*, ed. E. Hertzsch, vol. I, Halle 1956, pp. 73–97.
49 G. Leff, 'Wycliffe and the Augustinian tradition', *Medievalia et Humanistica: Studies in Medieval and Renaissance Culture*, 2, 1970, p. 29.
50 *Luthers Werke*, vol. 18, p. 83.
51 ibid.
52 ibid., vol. 10, II, p. 458.
53 W. Köhler, *Zwingli und Luther. Ihr Streit über das Abendmahl nach ihren politischen und religiösen Beziehungen*, vol. 2, Gütersloh 1953.
54 Elisabeth Anton, *Studien zur Wand- und Deckenmalerei des 16. und 17. Jh. in protestantischen Kirchen Norddeutschlands*, diss. Munich 1977, pp. 20 ff.
55 *Luthers Werke*, vol. 41, p. 432.
56 See the precise analysis in Dieter Koepplin, 'Kommet zu mir alle. Das tröstliche Bild des Gekreuzigten nach dem Verständnis Luthers', in *Martin Luther und die Reformation in Deutschland*, ed. K. Löcher, Nuremberg 1987, pp. 153–99.
57 *Luthers Werke*, vol. 43, II, p. 512.
58 H. C. von Haebler, *Das Bild in der evangelischen Kirche*, Berlin 1957, pp. 50–1, analyses this scheme.
59 The most recent publication on this subject is F. Ohly, *Gesetz und Evangelium. Zur Typologie bei Luther und Lucas Cranach. Zum Blutstrahl der Gnade in der Kunst*, Münster 1985.
60 This concerns especially the controversial theses of Jean Wirth, 'Le dogme en image: Luther et l'iconographie', *Revue de l'art*, 52, 1981, pp. 9–23, where Wirth tries to separate the theme into two parts, reflecting different stages of Luther's antinomian stance.
61 L. Pinomaa, *Die Heiligen bei Luther*, Helsinki 1977; M. Lienhard, 'La Sainteté et les saints chez Luther', *La vie spirituelle*, 69, 1989, pp. 521–32.
62 Paul Kalkoff, *Ablass und Reliquienverehrung in der Schlosskirche zu Wittenberg unter Friedrich dem Weisen*, Gotha 1907.
63 H. Düfel, 'Luther und die Marienbilder seiner Zeit', *Kirche und*

Kunst, 1961, no. 3, pp. 21–4, no. 4, pp. 29–31; 1962, no. 1, pp. 2–9. See also H. M. Stamm, 'Die "Humilitas" Mariens als Ansatzpunkt der Marientheologie und Marienverehrung bei Martin Luther', in *De Cultu Mariano Saeculo XVI – Acta Congressus Mariologici-Mariani Internationalis Caesaroaugustae 1979 celebrati*, Rome 1985, vol. 3, pp. 161–76.

64 G. Winkler, 'Die Regensburger Wallfahrt zur Schönen Maria als reformatorisches Problem', in *Albrecht Altdorfer und seine Zeit*, ed. D. Henrich, Regensburg 1981, pp. 103–21.

65 *Luthers Werke – Tischreden*, vol. 2, p. 207, no. 1755.

66 *Luthers Werke*, vol. 7, pp. 569–70.

67 G. Ebeling, *Luther, Einführung in sein Denken*, Tübingen 1971, p. 223.

68 L. Pinomaa, *Sieg des Glaubens. Grundlinien der Theologie Luthers*, Berlin 1964, p. 83.

69 *Luthers Werke*, vol. 10, I, p. 237.

70 H. von Campenhausen, 'Die Bilderfrage in der Reformation', in H. von Campenhausen, *Tradition und Leben. Kräfte der Kirchengeschichte*, Berlin 1960, p. 405.

71 *Luthers Werke – Tischreden*, vol. 6, p. 350, no. 7036.

72 *Luthers Werke*, vol. 42, pp. 206–7.

73 H. Preuss, *Martin Luther. Der Künstler*, Gütersloh 1931, pp. 89–144; Ch. Wentzel, *Die theologische Bedeutung der Musik im Leben und Denken Martin Luthers*, diss. Münster 1954.

74 R. Wex, 'Oben und unten oder Martin Luthers Predigtkunst angesichts der Torgauer Schlosskapelle', *Kritische Berichte*, 11, no. 3, 1984, pp. 4–25.

75 *Luthers Werke*, vol. 35, p. 479.

2 The iconophobes: Karlstadt, Zwingli and Calvin

1 Ed. H. Lietzmann, Bonn 1911, and – to choose one out of four(!) recent editions of the treatise – in *Flugschriften der frühen Reformationsbewegung (1518–1524)*, ed. A. Laube, Berlin 1983, vol. I, pp. 105–27.

2 *Von Abtuhung*, ed. Lietzmann, p. 4.

3 ibid., p. 5.

4 ibid., p. 8.

5 ibid., p. 19.

6 ibid., p. 13.

7 For a survey of the Protestant attitude to St Christopher, see G. Benker, *Christophorus*, Munich 1977, pp. 154ff.

8 U. Bubenheimer, 'Scandalum et Ius Divinum' (see note 16, Chapter 1), p. 297.

9 G. Rupp, *Patterns of Reformation*, London 1969, p. 109.

10 H. Barge, *Andreas Bodenstein von Karlstadt*, vols 1–2, Leipzig 1905 (repr. Nieuwkoop 1968). Barge's monograph was severely criticized from Lutheran positions in K. Müller, *Luther und Karlstadt. Stücke aus ihrem gegenseitigen Verhältnis*, Tübingen 1907.

11 *Von Abtuhung*, ed. Lietzmann, p. 9.

12 On Karlstadt's Christology, see C. A. Pater, 'Karlstadt's Zürcher Abschiedspredigt über die Menschwerdung Christi', *Zwingliana*, 14, 1974, pp. 1–16.

13 C. Lindberg, 'Carlstadt's Dialogue on the Lord's Last Supper', *Mennonite Quarterly Review*, 53, 1979, pp. 35–77.

14 *Von Abtuhung*, ed. Lietzmann, p. 21.

15 ibid.

16 A new edition of the treatise is in Laube, *Flugschriften* (see note 1), pp. 271–84. See also Ch. Garside, 'Ludwig Hätzer's pamphlet against images: a critical study', *Mennonite Quarterly Review*, 34, 1960, pp. 20–36.

17 *Von Abtuhung*, ed. Lietzmann, p. 16; Laube, *Flugschriften*, p. 280.

18 A good, recent introduction to Zwingli's theology (though underrating somewhat the image question) is W. P. Stephens, *The Theology of Huldrych Zwingli*, Oxford 1986.

19 F. Schmidt-Clausing, *Zwingli als Liturgiker*, Berlin 1952.

20 P. Biel, 'Personal conviction and pastoral care: Zwingli and the cult of saints 1522–1530', *Zwingliana*, 16, no. 1, 1985, pp. 442–69.

21 A good account is Ch. Garside, *Zwingli and the Arts*, New Haven, Conn. 1966, pp. 101–3. See also Chapter 3 below.

22 L. Palmer Wandel, 'Iconoclasts in Zurich', in *Bilder und Bildersturm im Spätmittelalter und in der frühen Neuzeit*, ed. R. W. Scribner and M. Warnke (Wolfenbütteler Forschungen, 46), Wiesbaden 1990, pp. 125–42.

23 For the dispute, see Garside, *Zwingli and the Arts*, pp. 126–46.

24 P. Jezler, 'Etappen des Zürcher Bildersturmes', in *Bilder und Bildersturm* (see note 22), pp. 143–74. See also H. D. Altendorf and P. Jezler, *Bilderstreit. Kulturwandel in Zwinglis Reformation*, Zurich 1984.

25 *Huldreich Zwinglis Sämtliche Werke*, vols 1–14, Berlin 1905–21, (Corpus Reformatorum) vol. 4, p. 103.

26 ibid., p. 102.

27 ibid., p. 105.

28 W. Rordorf, 'Laktanz als Vorbild des jungen Bullinger', in *Bullinger Tagung 1975*, ed. U. Gäbler and E. Zsindely, Zurich 1977, pp. 38, 44.

29 *Zwinglis Werke*, vol. 4, pp. 145–6.

30 ibid., p. 89.

31 B. J. Verkamp, 'The Zwinglians and adiaphorism', *Church History*, 42, 1973, p. 489.

32 *Zwinglis Werke*, vol. 4, p. 119. On Zwingli's Christology, see G. W. Locher, *Die Theologie Huldrych Zwinglis im Lichte seiner Christologie*, Zurich 1952.

33 W. Prynne, *Canterburies Doome, or the First Part of the Commitment, Charge, Tryall, Condemnation, Execution of William Laud*, London 1646, p. 466.

34 *Zwinglis Werke*, vol. 3, p. 906.

35 H. Spoerri, *Zwingli-Studien*, Leipzig 1866, p. 117.

36 A. Rich, *Die Anfänge der Theologie Huldrych Zwinglis*, Zurich 1949, p. 106.
37 *Zwinglis Werke*, vol. 5, pp. 723–4.
38 H. R. Lavater, 'Regnum Christi etiam externum – Huldrych Zwingli Brief vom 4. Mai 1528 an Ambrosius Blarer in Konstanz', *Zwingliana*, 15, no. 5, 1981, pp. 372–3.
39 For Zwingli's stance on adiaphorism and images, see Verkamp, 'Zwinglians and adiaphorism'; Lavater, 'Regnum Christi'. For his critique of Luther's concept of adiaphorism, see *Zwinglis Werke*, vol. 5, p. 821; vol. 8, p. 191.
40 Foremost in his *De Origine Cultus Divorum et Simulachrorum Erronea* (1539) – included in his *De Origine Erroris Libri Duo*, Zurich 1539, and his later *Confessio Helvetica Posterior* (1566) – see E. Koch, *Die Theologie der Confessio Helvetica Posterior*, Neukirchen 1968, pp. 350–7.
41 H. Weber, *Die Theologie Calvins. Ihre innere Systematik im Lichte der strukturpsychologischen Forschungsmethode*, Berlin 1930, p. 59.
42 E. Saxer, *Aberglaube, Heuchelei, Frömmigkeit. Eine Untersuchung zu Calvins reformatorischer Eigenart*, Zurich 1970, p. 26 – one of the best analyses of Calvin.
43 A. Ganoczy, *Le Jeune Calvin*, Wiesbaden 1966, pp. 228–32.
44 *Ioannis Calvini Opera Omnia*, ed. W. Baum, vols 1–58 (Corpus Reformatorum), Braunschweig-Berlin 1863–1900, vol. 26, pp. 150–1.
45 ibid., vol. 49, p. 612.
46 ibid., vol. 3, p. 122.
47 Quoted after Martha Grau, *Calvins Stellung zur Kunst*, diss. Munich 1917, pp. 18–19.
48 *Calvini Opera*, vol. 26, p. 156.
49 B. Garrish, 'Luther and Calvin on the hiddenness of God', *Journal of Religion*, 53, 1973, pp. 263–5.
50 *Calvini Opera*, vol. 26, p. 156.
51 Martin Bucer, ed. R. Stupperich, *Deutsche Schriften*, Gütersloh-Paris 1975, vol. 4, p. 167.
52 *Calvini Opera*, vol. 32, p. 52.
53 Grau, *Calvins Stellung zur Kunst*, p. 18.
54 ibid., p. 19.
55 G. Scavizzi, 'La teologia cattolica e le immagini durante il XVI secolo', *Storia dell'Arte*, 21, 1974, p. 173.
56 For an analysis of this concept in Calvin, see P. Auksi, 'Simplicity and silence: the influence of Scripture on the aesthetic thought of the major reformers', *The Journal of Religious History*, 10, nos 1–4, 1978–9, pp. 352–3.
57 *Calvini Opera*, vol. 3, pp. 134–5.
58 See also R. Bäumer, 'Das zweite Konzil von Nizäa in der theologischen Diskussion des 16. Jh.', *Annuarium Historiae Conciliorum*, 20, no. 1/2, 1988, pp. 414–41, esp. pp. 422–3.
59 See Saxer, *Aberglaube*, p. 87.
60 H. Schützeichel, *Die Glaubenstheologie Calvins*, Munich 1972, pp. 274–5.

NOTES

61 Quoted after P. Romane-Musculus, *La Prière des mains. L'église réformée et l'art*, Paris 1938, p. 80.

62 Saxer, *Aberglaube*, p. 25.

63 The concept of *superstitio* in the Reformation awaits still a comprehensive study on the lines of D. Harmening, *Superstitio Überlieferungs – und theoriegeschichtliche Untersuchung zur kirchlich-theologischen Aberglaubensliteratur des Mittelalters*, Berlin 1979. See also J. Delumeau, 'Les Réformateurs et la superstition', in *Actes du Colloque l'Amiral de Coligny*, Paris 1974, pp. 451–87.

64 H. H. Wolf, *Die Einheit des Bundes. Das Verhältnis vom Alten und Neuen Testament bei Calvin*, Neukirchen 1958, esp. pp. 77–84; B. Buschbeck, *Die Lehre vom Gottesdienst im Werk Johannes Calvins*, Marburg 1968, p. 34.

65 *Calvini Opera*, vol. 41, p. 562; vol. 31, p. 460.

66 L. Wencelius, *L'Esthétique de Calvin*, Paris 1937, p. 158.

67 See his letter to Theodore Beza of 18 February 1562 – *Letters of John Calvin*, ed. J. Bonnet, London 1858, vol. 4, p. 259.

68 J. Hexter, 'Utopia and Geneva', in *Action and Conviction in Early Modern Europe: Essays in Memory of E. H. Harbison*, ed. T. Robb, Princeton, NJ 1969, pp. 77–89.

69 A. Dufour, 'Le Mythe du Genève au XVI siècle', *Revue suisse d'histoire*, 8, 1959, pp. 489–518.

70 *Calvini Opera*, vol. 40, p. 184. On the problem of portraiture in the reformed conception (Calvin and the Swiss were often attacked for a presumed vain, idolatrous attitude toward their own likenesses), see M. G. Winkler, 'A divided heart: idolatry and the portraiture of Hans Asper', *Sixteenth Century Journal*, 17, Summer 1987, pp. 213–30. This question merits further study.

71 A history of the concept of 'histories' in the sixteenth century remains to be written. For the earlier history, see Aidan Nichols, 'The horos of Nicaea II: a theological re-appropriation', *Annuarium Historiae Conciliorum*, 20, no. 1/2, 1988, pp. 175–6.

72 *Calvini Opera*, vol. 26, p. 157; vol. 36, p. 156.

73 ibid., vol. 26, p. 156.

74 ibid., vol. 3, p. 36.

75 H. Bullinger, *De Origine Erroris Libri Duo*, Zurich 1539, p. 127a.

76 So in Wencelius, *L'Esthétique* (to be used with great caution), or M. de Klijn, *De invloed van het Calvinisme op de Noord-Nederlandse Landschapschilderkunst 1570–1630*, Apeldoorn 1982.

77 Waldemar Deonna, *Notes d'histoire et d'art genévois relatives à la Réforme*, Geneva 1943, p. 8.

78 U. Roeder-Bamberger, *Das Begräbniswesen im calvinistischen Genf*, diss. Basle 1975, pp. 28–37.

79 See D. Nugent, *Ecumenism in the Age of Reformation: The Colloquy of Poissy*, Cambridge 1974, pp. 190–1 (with some factual errors); N. Valois, 'Les essais de conciliation religieuse au debut du règne de Charles IX', *Revue d'histoire de l'église de France*, 31, 1945, p. 268.

80 See *Letters of Calvin*, ed. J. Bonnet (see note 67), pp. 205–6.

81 ibid., p. 271.

3 Iconoclasm: rites of destruction

1 *Akta Synodów Róznowierczych 1550–1559*, ed. M. Sipayllo, vol. I, Warsaw 1969, p. 113.
2 A. Gieysztor, 'Lassitude du Gothique? Reflets de l'iconoclasme hussite au XVᵉ siècle', in *Ars Auro Prior! Studia Ioanni Bialostocki Sexagenario Dicata*, Warsaw 1981, p. 225.
3 D. Freedberg, 'The structure of Byzantine and European iconoclasm', in *Iconoclasm*, ed. A. Bryer and J. Herrin, Birmingham 1977, p. 169.
4 M. Warnke, 'Durchbrochene Geschichte? Die Bilderstürme der Wiedertäufer in Münster 1534–35', in *Bildersturm. Die Zerstörung des Kunstwerkes*, ed. M. Warnke, Munich 1973, p. 93.
5 S. Deyon and A. Lottin, *Les 'Casseurs' de l'été 1566. L'iconoclasme dans le nord de la France*, Paris 1981, p. 198.
6 For this iconoclast mode, see C. J. de Bruyn Kops, 'De Zeven Werken van Barmhartigheid van de Meester van Alkmaar gerestaureerd', *Bulletin van het Rijksmuseum*, 23, 1975, pp. 203–36. On the peculiar fascination emanating from a mutilated work of art, see W. Deonna, 'L'image incomplète ou mutilée', *Revue des études anciennes*, 1930, pp. 321–32.
7 M. Netter, 'Zur Restaurierung zweier Holbein-Bilder im Kunstmuseum Basel', *Werkzeitung Geigy*, 18, no. 6/7, 1960.
8 C. C. Christensen, 'Patterns of iconoclasm in the early Reformation: Strasbourg and Basel', in *The Image and the Word*, ed. J. Gutmann, Missoula, Montana 1977, pp. 149–66.
9 Michael Schilling, *Imagines Mundi-Metaphorische Darstellung der Welt in der Emblematik*, Frankfurt 1979, p. 234. M. Aston, 'Iconoclasm in England: rites of destruction by fire', in *Bilder und Bildersturm im Spätmittelalter und in der frühen Neuzeit*, ed. R. W. Scribner and M. Warnke, Wiesbaden 1990, pp. 175–202. See now also M. Flynn, 'Mimesis of the Last Judgment: the Spanish auto da fê,' *Sixteenth Century Journal*, 22, 1991, pp. 281–97.
10 *Basler Chroniken*, ed. W. Fischer and H. Ster, Leipzig 1872, vol. I, p. 447. The first part of this shout appeared also during the iconoclasm of 1527 in Soest – see *Chroniken der deutschen Städte*, 24, 1982, p. 152.
11 R. W. Scribner, 'Volkskultur und Volksreligion: Zur Rezeption evangelischer Ideen', in *Zwingli und Europa*, ed. P. Blickle, Zurich 1985, p. 153.
12 T. Platter, *Lebensbeschreibung*, ed. A. Hartmann, Basle 1944, pp. 61–2.
13 C. C. Christensen, *Art and the Reformation in Germany*, Athens, Ohio 1979, p. 101.
14 I tried to analyse the position of iconoclasm in the process of Reformation in the article 'Die Protestantischen Bilderstürme. Versuch einer Übersicht', in *Bilder und Bildersturm* (see note 9), pp. 72ff.
15 R. W. Scribner, 'Sozialkontrolle und die Möglichkeit einer städtischen Reformation', in *Stadt und Kirche im 16. Jh.*, ed. B. Moeller, Gütersloh 1978, pp. 57–65.

16 J. Schildhauer, 'Der Stralsunder Kirchensturm des Jahres 1525', *Wissenschaftliche Zeitschrift der Ernst-Moritz-Arndt Universität Greifswald, Gesellschaftlich-Sprachwissenschaftliche Reihe*, 8, no. 1/2, 1958/9, pp. 113–20.

17 U. Imhof, 'Niklaus Manuel und die reformatorische Götzenzerstörung', *Zeitschrift für Schweizerische Archäologie und Kunstgeschichte*, 37, 1980, pp. 297–300.

18 Schildhauer, 'Der Stralsunder Kirchensturm', p. 116.

19 See Chapter 4 below.

20 J. Tazbir, *Arianie i Katolicy*, Warsaw 1971, pp. 10–16.

21 See the interesting but very speculative study of L. Rothkrug, 'Religious practices and collective perceptions: hidden homologies in the Renaissance and Reformation', *Historical Reflections*, 7, Spring 1980, p. 78.

22 W. Urban, *Chłopi wobec Reformacji w Malopolsce w drugiej polowie XVI wieku*, Wrocław 1959, pp. 130–5, 151–4.

23 On the few iconoclast acts committed by peasants, see J. Sauer, 'Reformation und Kunst im Bereich des heutigen Baden', *Freiburger Diözesanarchiv*, N.F.19, 1919, pp. 467, 470; F. L. Baumann, *Quellen zur Geschichte des Bauernkrieges in Oberschwaben*, Tübingen 1876, pp. 373, 382–5, 482.

24 This regardless of the fact that the term vandalism, coined by the Abbé Grégoire during the French Revolution, pertained originally to iconoclastic acts.

25 C. C. Christensen, 'Iconoclasm and the preservation of ecclesiastical art in Reformation Nuremberg', *Archiv für Reformationsgeschichte*, 61, 1970, pp. 205–21.

26 J. Phillips, *The Reformation of Images: Destruction of Art in England 1535–1660*, Los Angeles 1973, pp. 90–1.

27 No separate study of the Lutheran–Calvinist iconomachy exists. See the historical local studies of J. Götz, *Die religiösen Wirren in der Oberpfalz von 1576 bis 1620*, Münster 1937; see also H. Schilling, *Konfessionskonflikt und Staatsbildung. Eine Fallstudie über das Verhältnis vom religiösen und sozialen Wandel in der Frühneuzeit am Beispiel der Grafschaft Lippe*, Gütersloh 1981, pp. 212–15.

28 K. Pahncke, 'Abraham Scultetus in Berlin', *Forschungen zur Brandenburgischen und Preussischen Geschichte*, 23, 1910, pp. 35, 44ff.

29 See A. Chroust, 'Aktenstücke zur Brandenburgischen Geschichte unter Kurfürst Johann Sigismund', *Forschungen zur Brandenburgischen und Preussischen Geschichte*, 9, 1897, p. 20; G. C. F. Lisch, 'Über des Herzogs Johann Albrecht II von Güstrow calvinistische Bilderstürmerei', *Jahrbücher des Vereins für Mecklembburgische Geschichte und Altertumskunde*, 1851, pp. 202–3; J. Hemmerle, 'Die calvinische Reformation in Böhmen', *Stifter-Jahrbuch*, 8, 1964, esp. pp. 261–8.

30 M. Aston, *England's Iconoclasts*, vol. 1, Oxford 1988, pp. 310ff.

31 From the vast literature on the events of 1566 in the Netherlands I would like to refer to the recent excellent synthesis of D. Freedberg, 'Art and iconoclasm 1525–1580: the case of the northern Netherlands',

in *Kunst voor de Beeldenstorm*, ed. J. P. Filedt de Kok, Amsterdam 1986, pp. 69–105.
32 No separate study exists here. For Livonia still useful is L. Arbusov, *Die Einführung der Reformation in Liv- Est- und Kurland*, Leipzig 1921, pp. 290–7, 353–7, 382–4, 471–2.
33 The episode is related in Charles Garside, *Zwingli and the Arts*, New Haven, Conn. 1966, pp. 101–3.
34 The letter is quoted after *Huldrych Zwingli – Briefe*, ed. O. Farner, Zurich 1918, vol. 1, p. 160.
35 This against Garside's somewhat narrow view (*Zwingli and the Arts*, p. 103).
36 P. Hofer, *Die Reformation im Ulmer Landgebiet: religiöse, wirtschaftliche und soziale Aspekte*, diss. Tübingen 1977, p. 133.
37 R. Postel, 'Zur Deutung und Bedeutung der Reformation für das religiös-soziale Verhalten des Bürgertums in Hamburg', in *Stadt und Kirche im 16. Jh.*, ed. B. Moeller, Gütersloh 1978, p. 171.
38 R. W. Scribner, 'Incombustible Luther: the image of the Reformer in early modern Germany', *Past and Present*, 110, February 1986, pp. 38–68.
39 Grzegorz z Zarnowca, *Postylla*, Krakow 1582, part 3, sig. L 612r.
40 C. van Mander, *Het Leven der Doorluchtighe Nederlandtsche . . .* , Amsterdam 1617 (see the German edition by H. Floerke, Munich 1906, pp. 55–7).
41 An excellent study – though not concerned with iconoclastic rites – is Wolfgang Brückner, *Bildnis und Brauch. Studien zur Bildfunktion der Effigies*, Berlin 1966.
42 *Luthers Werke*, vol. 54, p. 219.
43 R. W. Scribner, 'Volkskultur und Volksreligion' (see note 11), p. 157.
44 P. Tschackert, *Urkundenbuch zur Reformationsgeschichte des Herzogtums Preussen*, Leipzig 1890, vol. 2, p. 208.
45 S. Deyon, 'La Querelle des images en France', in *La controverse religieuse (XVI–XIX siècles). Actes du Iᵉʳ Colloque Jean Boisset*, Montpellier 1980, p. 43.
46 Freedberg, 'Byzantine and European iconoclasm', p. 75.
47 C. Sachsse, *D. Balthasar Hubmaier als Theologe*, Berlin 1914, p. 150.
48 H. Langerfeld, *Die Verheerungen im Kloster Riddagshausen*, Braunschweig 1887, p. 8.
49 Phillips, *Reformation of Images*, p. 90.
50 S. Deyon and A. Lottin, *Les 'Casseurs' de l'été 1566*, Paris 1981, p. 173.
51 Arbusov, *Einführung der Reformation*, p. 350.
52 O. Pohrt, *Reformationsgeschichte Livlands. Ein Überblick*, Leipzig 1928, pp. 72–3; see the review of Pohrts' book by Leonid Arbusov, in *Baltische Monatsschrift*, 59, 1928, pp. 752–3.
53 M. Aston, 'Iconoclasm in England' (see note 9), p. 187.
54 For this suggestion, see Scribner, 'Volkskultur', p. 152.
55 A. Uckeley, 'Der Werdegang der kirchlichen Reformbewegung im Anfang des 16. Jh. in den Stadtgemeinden Pommerns', *Pommersche Jahrbücher*, 18, 1917, pp. 69–70.

56 R. W. Scribner, 'Reformation, carnival and the world upside-down',
in *Städtische Gesellschaft und Reformation*, ed. I. Batori, Stuttgart
1980, pp. 238–40.
57 *Chronik des Johan Oldecop*, ed. K. Euling, Tübingen 1891, p. 173.
58 H. D. Heimann, ' "Verkehrung" in Volks- und Buchkultur als Argu-
mentationspraxis in der reformatorischen Öffentlichkeit', *Archiv für
Reformationsgeschichte*, 79, 1988, p. 174.
59 According, however, to a very iconodulic Catholic chronicle – see
A. Angele, *Altbiberach um die Jahre der Reformation*, Biberach 1962,
p. 164.
60 J. Schlecht, 'Der Hildesheimer Fasching 1545', *Römische Quartals-
schrift für Christliche Altertumskunde*, 10, 1896, pp. 170–7.
61 H. Zins, 'Poczatki Reformacji na Warmii', *Odrodzenie i Reformacja
w Polsce* 2, 1957, p. 83.
62 M. Wajsblum, in a review of A. Kossowski, *Protestantyzm w Lubli-
nie i w Lubelskiem w XVI–XVII wieku*, Lublin 1933, in *Reformacja
w Polsce* 6, (1934), p. 249.
63 Deyon, 'La Querelle', p. 38.
64 Scribner (see note 56); E. Le Roy Ladurie, *Carnaval de Romans*,
Paris 1979.
65 A. M. Panczenko, 'Szalenstwo Chrystusowe', *Teksty*, 31, 1977, p. 61.
66 Deyon, 'La Querelle', p. 44.
67 B. Moeller, 'Die Basler Reformation in ihrem stadtgeschichtlichen
Zusammenhang' in *Ecclesia Semper Reformanda*, ed. H. Guggisberg,
Basle 1980, p. 21.
68 H. Heimpel, *Der Mensch in seiner Gegenwart*, Göttingen 1954,
p. 134.

4 Icon and pulpit: the Eastern Churches and the Reformation

1 Only one short general overview of the history of the relations exists
– G. Hering, 'Orthodoxie und Protestantismus', *Jahrbuch der Österreichischen Byzantinistik*, 31/2, 1981, pp. 823–74. No study about the
role of the image controversy exists, but there are some short remarks
in N. Thon, *Ikone und Liturgie*, Trier 1979, pp. 129–41.
2 E. Benz, 'Der baltische Russland-Mythos', in E. Benz, *Geist und
Leben der Ostkirche*, Hamburg 1957, p. 180. The fundamental work
about Baltic–Lutheran–Russian relations is still Wilhelm Kahle, *Die
Begegnung des baltischen Protestantismus mit der russisch-orthodoxen
Kirche*, Leiden 1959. See also for Sweden K. Tarkiainen, 'Den svenska
synen pa den grekiska ortodoxa religionen i början av 1600-talet',
Kyrkohistorisk Arsskrift, 71, 1971, pp. 85–115, esp. pp. 109–11.
3 M. Pavlova, 'L'Empire Byzantin et les Tchèques avant la chute de
Constantinople', *Byzantinoslavica*, 14, 1953, p. 222.
4 J. Karmiris, 'Luther und Melanchthon über die orthodoxe Kirche',
Kyrios, 6, 1966, pp. 77–104, 150–75.
5 *Luthers Werke*, vol. 50, pp. 577–8.
6 *Calvini Opera*, vol. 2, p. 78.
7 H. von Campenhausen, 'Die Bilderfrage in der Reformation', in *H.

von Campenhausen, Tradition und Leben. Kräfte der Kirchengeschichte, Tübingen 1960, p. 382.

8 See E. Benz, *Wittenberg und Byzanz*, Marburg 1949, pp. 34–58 (very apologetic); H. Petri, 'Jakobus Heraklides Basilikus, Fürst der Moldau', *Zeitschrift für Kirchengeschichte*, 9, 1928, pp. 105–43. The main contemporary account of the despot's life has been written by the Italian Catholic Antonio Maria Gratiani, *De Ioanne Heraclide Despota Vallachorum Principe Libri Tres* . . . , Warsaw 1759. See also E. Legrand, *Deux vies de Jacob Basilicos*, Paris 1889.

9 Gratiani, *De Ioanne Heraclide* p. 32; Legrand, *Deux vies*, p. 177.

10 H. Barycz, *Jan Lasicki*, Warsaw 1973, pp. 151–3.

11 Only the later Calvinist rulers of Transylvania seem to have drawn certain conclusions regarding iconomachy – see E. Ch. Suttner, 'Die rumänische Orthodoxie des 16. Jh. und 17. Jh. in Auseinandersetzung mit der Reformation', *Kirche im Osten*, 25, 1982, pp. 64–101, esp. p. 82.

12 W. J. Jorgenson, 'The Augustana Graeca and the Correspondence between the Tübingen Lutherans and Patriarch Jeremias', Ph. D. diss. Boston, Mass. 1979, pp. 7–56.

13 On the negotiations of 1574–81 see the most recent publications – G. Mastrantonis, *Augsburg and Constantinople: The Correspondence between the Tübingen Theologians and Patriarch Jeremiah II of Constantinople on the Augsburg Confession*, Brookline, Mass. 1982; Jorgenson, *The Augustana*; D. Wendebourg, *Reformation und Orthodoxie. Der ökumenische Briefwechsel zwischen der Leitung der Württembergischen Kirche und Patriarch Jeremias II von Konstantinopel in den Jahren 1573–1581*, Göttingen 1986; G. Podskalsky, *Griechische Theologie in der Zeit der Türkenherrschaft (1453–1821)*, Munich 1988, pp. 102–15.

14 D. Chytraeus, *Oratio de statu Ecclesiarum hoc tempore in Graecia, Asia, Boemia, [etc.]*, Frankfurt 1569 (quoted after Rostock edn 1580) p. 89.

15 Chytraeus, *Oratio*, pp. 17–18.

16 J. Irmscher, 'Das Lutherbild der griechischen Orthodoxie', in *Martin Luther. Kolloquium anlässlich der 500. Wiederkehr seines Geburtstages*, Berlin 1983, p. 77.

17 *Stephan Gerlach des Älteren Tagebuch*, Frankfurt 1674.

18 ibid., p. 468.

19 ibid., p. 473.

20 ibid., p. 451.

21 Salomon Schweigger, *Ein newe Reyssebeschreibung auss Teutschland nach Constantinopel und Jerusalem*, Nuremberg 1608 (repr. Graz 1964), pp. 212–13.

22 ibid., p. 119.

23 L. E. Berry and R. D. Crummey, *Rude and Barbarous Kingdom: Russia in the Accounts of Sixteenth-Century English Voyagers*, Madison, Wis. 1968, pp. 35, 66, 76, 97; K. H. Ruffmann, *Das Russlandbild im England Shakespeares*, Göttingen 1952, pp. 134–5.

24 Adam Olearius, *Vermehrte, Newe Beschreibung der Moscowitischen*

NOTES

und Persianischen Reise, Schleswig 1656 – for an abridged English translation, see S. H. Baron, *The Travels of Olearius in Seventeenth-Century Russia*, Stanford, Calif., 1967. See also U. Mende, *Westeuropäische Bildzeugnisse zu Russland und Polen bis 1700*, diss. Cologne 1968, pp. 60–4; B. Uspenski, *The Semiotics of the Russian Icon* Lisse 1976, pp. 22–9.

25 Olearius, *Vermehrte*, pp. 294–8; Baron, *Travels of Olearius*, pp. 253–7.

26 Olearius, *Vermehrte*, p. 298. On Neronov, see L. Ruscynskii, *Religiosnyi byt Russkich po swiedeniam inostrannych pisatelei XVI i XVII wieka*, Moscow 1877, pp. 79–80.

27 See note 13. The original edition of the correspondence is in *Acta et Scripta Theologorum Wirtembergiensum et Patriarchae Constantinopolitani D. Hieremiae . . .*, Wittenberg 1584; English translation in Mastrantonis (my quotations are somewhat changed).

28 Mastrantonis, *Augsburg*, p. 140.

29 ibid., pp. 190–203, esp. p. 198.

30 ibid., p. 201.

31 ibid.

32 For the relevant passages, see ibid., pp. 273–81.

33 ibid., pp. 305–6.

34 ibid., p. 312.

35 On these negotiations, see G. Williams, *The Orthodox Church of the East being the Correspondence between the Eastern Patriarchs and the Nonjuring Bishops*, London 1868; J. H. Overton, *The Non-jurors*, London 1902, pp. 451–66; H. W. Longford, 'The Nonjurors and the Eastern Orthodox', *Eastern Church Review*, 2, 1966/7, pp. 118–32.

36 Williams, *Orthodox Church*, p. 100.

37 ibid., pp. 137–8.

38 ibid., p. 99.

39 ibid., p. 61.

40 C. R. A. Georgi, *Die Confessio Dosithei (Jerusalem 1672)*, Munich 1940, pp. 50–1. For the anti-Protestant background, see Podskalsky, *Griechische Theologie*, pp. 285–6.

41 For the political aspects, see G. Hering, *Ökumenisches Patriarchat und europäische Politik 1620–1638*, Wiesbaden 1968.

42 The literature on Lucaris is very extensive but often biased – see R. Schlier, *Der Patriarch Kyrillos Lukaris von Konstantinopel*, Marburg 1927; G. Hadjiantoniou. *Protestant Patriarch: The Life of Cyril Lucaris (1572–1672)*, London 1961.

43 J. Michalcescu, *Die Bekenntnisse und die wichtigsten Glaubenszeugnisse der griechisch-orientalischen Kirche*, Leipzig 1904, pp. 262–76.

44 ibid., p. 276.

45 E. Legrand, *Bibliographie Hellénique au 17ᵉ siècle*, Paris 1903, vol. IV, pp. 329–40, esp. pp. 336–8.

46 See Podskalsky, *Griechische Theologie*, pp. 180–1 for the consequences of Lucaris' stance. See also G. P. Michaelides, 'The Greek Orthodox position on the confession of Cyril Lucaris', *Church History*, 12, June 1943, pp. 118–29. For the Anglican iconophobic legend of Lucaris,

see Th. Smith, 'An account of the Greek Church under Cyrillus Lucaris', in Th. Smith, *An Account of the Eastern Church*, London 1680, esp. pp. 211–13.

47 For general works on Russia's pre-Reformation heretics, see A. I. Klibanov, *Reformatsionnyje dvizheniia v Rossii v XIV-pervoi polovine XVI vv*, Moscow 1960 (fundamental, but one has to peel off the Marxist layer); N. A. Kazakova and Ia. S. Lure, *Antifeodalnye ereticheskie dvizheniia na Rusi, XIV-nachala XVI wieka*, Moscow–Leningrad 1955; E. Hösch, *Orthodoxie und Häresie im Alten Russland*, Wiesbaden 1975. See also, for iconophobia in particular, K. Onasch, *Die Ikonenmalerei*, Leipzig 1967, pp. 146–50.

48 N. A. Kazakova, 'Idieologia strigolnicestva', *Trudy Otdiela Drewnerusskoj Literatury*, 11, 1955, p. 116, and Onasch, *Die Ikonenmalerei*, p. 147 espouse the iconophobic hypothesis; Klibanov, *Reformatsionnyje dvizheniia*, p. 165 is sceptical.

49 Klibanov, *Reformatsionnyje dvizhenniia*, pp. 164–5.

50 The literature on the Judaizers is vast and very polemical: C. Vernadsky, 'The heresy of the Judaizers and the policies of Ivan III of Moscow', *Speculum*, 8, 1933, pp. 436–54; D. Oljancyn, 'Was ist die Häresie der Judaisierenden?', *Kyrios*, 1, no. 1, 1936, pp. 176–89; J. L. Wieczynski, 'Hermetism and cabalism in the heresy of the Judaizers', *Renaissance Quarterly*, 27, no. 1, 1975, pp. 17–28; F. von Lilienfeld, 'Das Problem der Ikonographie, der Ikonentheologie und der Ikonenverehrung bei Erzbischof Gennadij von Nowgorod . . .', *Forschungen zur Osteuropäischen Geschichte*, 38, 1986, pp. 110ff.; J. R. Howlett, 'The heresy of the Judaizers and the problem of the Russian Reformation', diss. Oxford 1976.

51 This in spite of the attempts of S. Wollgast, 'Eine Entwicklungslinie in der europäischen Frühaufklärung (Verbindungen häretischer Bewegungen in Mittel- und Westeuropa zur Nowgoroder–Moskauer Häresie)', diss. Berlin (East), 1964, pp. 112–13 to compare these phenomena.

52 Von Lilienfeld, 'Das Problem', pp. 114–15.

53 See Klibanov, *Reformatsionnyje dvizhenniia*, pp. 264–301; Hösch, *Orthodoxie und Häresie*, pp. 138–41. Kosoi's views are known foremost through the – not very objective – treatise of his antagonist Zinovij Otenskii – see R. M. Mainka, *Zinovij von Oten*, Rome 1961, pp. 56–8, 100–12, 214–19. Interestingly enough, Zinovii's treatise was published as late as 1642 as a pamphlet against Protestant iconophobia – D. Tsvetayev, *Literaturnaja Borba s protestanstvom v Moskovskom gosudarstve*, Moscow 1887, pp. 102–3.

54 Mainka, *Zinovij von Oten*, p. 217.

55 Kahle, *Die Begegnung*, p. 21.

56 B. Rüssow, *Chronica der Provinz Lyfflandt, 1584*, p. 45 (repr. Hanover 1967).

57 E. W. Fechner, *Chronik der evangelischen Gemeinden in Moskau*, Moscow 1876, vol. 1, pp. 56–7.

58 L. Müller, *Die Kritik des Protestantismus in der russischen Theologie vom 16. bis zum 18. Jh.*, Wiesbaden 1951, pp. 8ff.

59 The only information about this episode is the *Slavonia Reformata* of Andrzej Węgierski (1609) – see *Andreae Wengierscii Libri Quattuor Slavoniae Reformatae*, ed. Ianussius Tazbir, Warsaw 1973, pp. 68–9.

60 See the polemic of the Monk Artemii (not to be confused with the Artemii of the Vitebsk episode) against Reformation iconophobia in *Russkaja Istoricheskaja Biblioteka*, 4, 1978, col. 1243. See also R. Mainka, 'Des Starzen Artemii Polemik gegen die Zehn Gebote. Aus der Auseinandersetzung der russischen Orthodoxen mit den Lutheranern Litauens im 16. Jh.', *Ostkirchliche Studien*, 13, 1964, p. 125. (These were not Lutherans, however.)

61 See the edition in V. A. Tumins, *Tsar Ivan IV's Reply to Jan Rokyta*, The Hague 1971; and J. Lasicius, *De Russorum, Moscovitarum et Tratarorum Religione . . .* , Speyer 1582, pp. 125–32.

62 Müller, *Die Kritik*, pp. 28–9, was the first to prove it, but Tumins, *Tsar Ivan IV's Reply*, p. 30 (some factual errors) still thinks that Iurodivyi is a pseudonym of Ivan the Terrible.

63 Lasicius, *De Russorum Religione*; the chapter called 'Lasitius contra Imagines' is on pp. 133–47.

64 *Altrussische Dichtung aus dem 11.–18. Jh.*, ed. H. Graßhoff, Leipzig 1977, p. 108.

65 Fechner, *Chronik*, vol. 1, p. 84.

66 The introductory remarks of the tsar and the exposé of Rokita were edited in Paul Oderborn's *Wunderbare, erschreckliche und unerhörte Geschichte . . . Nemlich des nechst gewesenen Grossfürsten in der Moschkaw Joann Basilidis*, Görlitz 1588 (translated into German by Heinrich von Räteln), without pagination. All quotations are from this edition. See also N. S. Ionescu, *Ivan IV il Terribile – Jan Rokyta. Dispute sul Protestantismo, una confronta tra Ortodossia e Riforma nel 1570*, ed. L. Ronchi de Michelis, Turin 1979.

67 K. H. Bernhardt, *Gott und Bild. Ein Beitrag zur Begründung und Darstellung des Bilderverbotes im Alten Testament*, Berlin 1956, pp. 17–20.

68 A. Jobert, 'Aux origines de l'Union de Brest. Le Protestantisme en Ruthénie', in *Ksiega Pamiatkowa 150 – lecia AGAD*, Warsaw 1958, pp. 371–8; A. Lewicki, 'Socynianie na Rusi', *Reformacja w Polsce*, 3, 1922, pp. 205–6.

69 S. Kot, 'Szymon Budny, der grösste Häretiker Litauens im 16. Jh.', *Wiener Archiv für Geschichte des Slawentums und Osteuropas*, 2, 1956, pp. 67–8.

70 Lewicki, 'Socynianie', pp. 205–8; the whole text is edited by Tazbir, *Andreae Wengierscii*, pp. 409–503.

71 Lewicki, 'Socynianie', p. 210.

72 The whole treatise was edited in *Russkaja Istoricheskaja Biblioteka*, 7, 1882, pp. 600–938, the chapter on images on pp. 900–38.

73 ibid., p. 929.

74 Quoted after D. M. Tsvetayev, *Protestanstvo i Protestanty w Rossii do epochi preobrazenii*, Moscow 1890, p. 604.

75 D. Oljancyn, 'Zur Frage der Generalkonföderation zwischen Protestanten und Orthodoxen in Wilna', *Kyrios*, 1, 1936, pp. 29–46.

76 J. Łukaszewicz, *Dzieje Kosciolów wyznania helweckiego na Litwie*, vol. 1, Poznań 1853, p. 122.

77 M. Kosman, *Reformacja i Kontrreformacja w Wielkim Ksiestwie Litewskim*, Warsaw 1973, p. 181.

78 N. Andreyev, 'Nikon and Avvakum on icon-painting', *Revue des études slaves*, 37, 1961, pp. 43–4.

79 A. S. Jeleonskaja, *Russkaja publicistika vtoroj poloviny XVII wieka*, Moscow 1978, p. 211.

80 F. Kämpfer, 'Verhöre über das Entfernen von Ikonen aus der Kirche. Ein Vorgang aus dem Moskau des Jahres 1654', in *Unser ganzes Leben Christus unserem Gott überantworten. Festschrift F. von Lilienfeld*, Göttingen 1982, pp. 295–303.

81 Tsvetayev, *Protestanstvo*, pp. 625–6.

82 An excellent analysis is in H. P. Niess, *Kirche in Russland zwischen Tradition und Glaube. Eine Untersuchung der Kirillova Kniga und der Kniga o Vere aus der ersten Hälfte des 17. Jh.*, Göttingen 1977, esp. pp. 130–6.

83 R. Wittram, 'Peters des Grossen Verhältnis zur Religion und den Kirchen', *Historische Zeitschrift*, 173, 1952, pp. 270ff.; J. Cracraft, *The Church Reform of Peter the Great*, London 1971.

84 See Müller, *Die Kritik*, p. 56.

85 A. Carjevski, *Pososhkov i evo sochinenia*, Moscow 1883, pp. 164–5.

86 I. Morjev, *Kamen very Mitropolita Stiefana Iavorskovo* . . . , St Petersburg 1904, pp. 59–67, Müller, *Die Kritik*, p. 74. On Iavorsky see J. Serech, 'Stefan Iavorsky and the conflict of ideologies in the age of Peter the Great', *The East European and Slavonic Review*, 30, 1951, pp. 57–8.

87 Foremost Johannes Franciscus Buddeus, *Epistola Apologetica pro Ecclesia Lutherana contra Calumnias et Obtrectationes Stephani Javorskii* . . . , Jena 1729. See also B. Dąb-Kalinowska, *Miedzy Bizancjum i Zachodem. Ikony Rosyjskie XVII–XIX wieku*, Warsaw 1990, p. 63.

88 N. S. Tichonrawow, 'Moskovskije volnodumcy nachala 18 veka i Stefan Iavorskii', in N. S. Tichonrawow, *Sochinenia*, Moscow 1898, vol. 2, pp. 156–304; D. Cyzewskij, 'Zwei Ketzer in Moskau', *Kyrios*, 6, 1942/3, pp. 46–60.

89 J. Kämmerer, *Russland und die Hugenotten im 18. Jh. (1689–1789)*, Wiesbaden 1978, p. 42.

90 Tichonrawow, 'Moskovskije volnodumcy', pp. 227–9; H. H. Nolte, *Religiöse Toleranz in Russland 1600–1725*, Göttingen 1969, p. 178, errs, however, in assuming here an uninterrupted link with the old iconophobic currents.

91 Prokopovich's intentions are still debated, some scholars considering him a committed iconophobe. I join H. J. Härtel, *Byzantinisches Erbe und Orthodoxie bei Feofan Prokopovich*, Würzburg 1970, pp. 186–98, who considers Feofan to be moderately in favour of religious art.

92 P. Oderborn, 'De Russorum Religione', in Ioannes Lasicius, *De Russorum, Moscovitorum* . . . (see note 61), p. 217.

NOTES

93 Berry and Crummey, *Rude and Barbarous Kingdom*, p. 76.
94 See G. Lenhoff, 'Christian and pagan strata in the east Slavic cult of St Nicholas: polemical notes on Boris Uspenski', *Slavic and East European Journal*, 28, no. 2, Summer 1984, p. 147, with further references.
95 Michael Siricius, *Dissertatio de Religione Moscovitorum*, Giessen 1661.
96 M. Chemnitius, *Examen das ist Erörterung des Tridentinischen Concilii*, Frankfurt 1576, part IV, pp. 29–30.
97 I. Gentillet, *Examen Concilii Tridentini*, Gorinchen 1678, p. 277.
98 Quoted from the treatise 'Shield of Faith' after Müller, *Die Kritik*, p. 49.
99 See I. Kretzenbacher, *Das verletzte Kultbild*, Munich 1977, p. 103.
100 Tsvetayev, *Protestanstvo*, p. 780.
101 F. H. Philipp, *Tolstoj und der Protestantismus*, Giessen 1959, p. 136.
102 A. Blane, 'Protestant sects in late Imperial Russia', in *The Religious World of Russian Culture: Essays in Honour of G. Florovsky*, The Hague 1973, pp. 267–305, esp. pp. 276–7; W. Gutsche, *Westliche Quellen des russischen Stundismus*, Kassel 1956, p. 74.
103 These two cases are related in Wilhelm Kahle, *Evangelische Christen in der Sowjetunion*, Wuppertal 1978, pp. 518–19.
104 P. Florenskii, 'Ikonostas', *Bogoslowskije Trudy*, 9, 1972, p. 118.
105 V. Shklovsky, *Eisenstein*, Moscow 1976, p. 238.
106 Clara Zetkin, 'Erinnerungen an Lenin', in Clara Zetkin, *Ausgewählte Reden und Schriften*, Berlin 1960, vol. 3, p. 96.
107 H. Sedlmayr, *Die Revolution der modernen Kunst*, Hamburg 1955, p. 100.

5 Symbols and commonplaces, or the conceptual background of the dispute on images

1 A. Peters, *Realpräsenz. Luthers Zeugnis von Christi Gegenwart im Abendmahl*, Berlin 1960; H. Sasse, *This is my Body. Luthers Contention for the Real Presence in the Sacrament of the Altar*, Minneapolis, Minn. 1959; T. G. A. Hardt, *Venerabilis et adorabilis Eucharistia. Eine Studie über die lutherische Abendmahlslehre im 16 Jh.*, Göttingen 1988.
2 J. Rogge, *Virtus und Res. Um die Abendmahlswirklichkeit bei Calvin*, Berlin 1965; A. Barclay, *The Protestant Doctrine of the Lord's Supper: A Study in the Eucharistic Teachings of Luther, Zwingli and Calvin*, Glasgow 1927.
3 W. Neuser, *Die Abendmahlslehre Melanchthons in ihrer geschichtlichen Entwicklung*, Neukirchen 1968, pp. 70–8, 224–32.
4 The most important study – to which I owe much – is S. Gerö, 'The Eucharistic doctrine of the Byzantine iconoclasts and its sources', *Byzantinische Zeitschrift*, 68, 1975, pp. 4–23.
5 G. Martelet, *Zmartwychwstanie, Eucharystia, Czlowiek*, Warsaw 1976, pp. 163–4.
6 J. P. Migne, *Patrologia Graeca*, vol. 99, col. 498A.

7 J. P. Migne, *Patrologia Latina*, vol. 120, cols 1278 B–C. See also A. Gerken, *Theologie der Eucharistie*, Munich 1973, p. 106.

8 G. A. Benrath, *Wyclifs Bibelkommentar*, Berlin 1966, pp. 24–37; M. Aston, *England's Iconoclasts*, Oxford 1988, vol. 1, pp. 98–103.

9 L. Kaczmarek, 'Nauka Jana Wiklefa o tropicznej obecnosci Chrystusa Pana w Eucharystii', *Studia Theologica Varsoviensia*, 7, no. 1, 1969, pp. 55–89.

10 ibid., p. 69.

11 *Tracts and Treatises of John de Wycliffe D.D.*, ed. R. Vaughan, London 1845, p. 281.

12 W. R. Cook, 'The Eucharist in Hussite theology', *Church History*, 42, 1973, pp. 338–40.

13 P. de Vooght, *Jacobellus de Stribro. Premier théologien du hussitisme*, Louvain 1972, p. 144.

14 M. Aston, *Lollards and Reformers: Images and Literacy in Late Medieval Religion*, London 1984, p. 192.

15 Quoted after H. Merczyng, *Szymon Budny jako krytyk tekstów Biblijnych*, Kraków 1913, p. 113.

16 J. Knox, *Works*, ed. D. Laing, vol. 6 Edinburgh 1846, pp. 172–3.

17 Quoted after Rogge, *Virtus*, p. 42.

18 K. Kuypers, *Der Zeichen- und Wortbegriff im Denken Augustins*, Amsterdam 1934; U. G. Leinsle, *Res et Signum. Das Verständnis zeichenhafter Wirklichkeit in der Theologie Bonaventuras*, Munich 1976; H. Brinkmann, *Mittelalterliche Hermeneutik*, Tübingen 1980, pp. 45–51.

19 Neuser, *Abendmahlslehre*, pp. 70–7.

20 G. Vogler, *Nürnberg: 1524/25. Studien zur Geschichte der reformatorischen und sozialen Bewegungen in der Reichsstadt*, Berlin 1982, p. 190.

21 W. Kaliner, *Katechese und Vermittlungstheologie im Reformationszeitalter: Johann VIII, Bischof von Meissen und seine Christliche Lehre*, Leipzig 1981, p. 141.

22 Peters, *Realpräsenz*, p. 89–90; M. Lienhard, *Martin Luthers christologisches Zeugnis*, Berlin 1980, pp. 149, 166.

23 E. Iserloh, *Der Kampf um die Messe in den ersten Jahren der Auseinandersetzung mit Luther*, Münster 1952, p. 42.

24 *Zwinglis Werke*, vol. 6/2, p. 200; see also vol. 2, p. 757.

25 M. Kunzler, *Die Eucharistietheologie des Hadamarer Pfarrers und Humanisten Gerhard Lorich. Eine Untersuchung der Frage nach einer erasmianischen Meß- und Eucharistietheologie des 16. Jh.*, Münster 1981, pp. 28–32.

26 A. Schilsohn, *Theologie als Sakramentaltheologie. Die Mysterientheologie Odo Casels*, Mainz 1982, pp. 279–80.

27 H. G. Gadamer, *Wahrheit und Methode*, Tübingen 1965, pp. 131–2.

28 J. Lotman, 'Zeichen und Zeichensystem in Bezug auf die Typologie der russischen Kultur (11. bis 19. Jahrhundert)', in J. Lotman, *Kunst als Sprache*, Leipzig 1981, p. 155, 159. See also J. Bolte, 'Der zerstückte Spiegel', *Euphorion*, 16, 1909, pp. 785–7.

29 For Wyclif, see n. 11 above; St Thomas Aquinas, *Summa Theologiae*,

NOTES

III, g. lxxvii, a. iii; *Luthers Werke*, vol. 26, p. 338. See also H. Grabes, *Speculum, Mirror and Looking Glass: Kontinuität und Originalität der Spiegelmetapher in den Buchtiteln des Mittelalters und der englischen Literatur des 13. bis 17. Jh.*, Tübingen 1973, p. 118.

30 E. Auerbach, 'Figura', *Archivium Romanicum*, 22, 1939, pp. 436–89.

31 I. Morjev, *Kamen very Mitropolita Stiefana Iavorskovo*, St Petersburg 1904, p. 59.

32 B. Uspenski. 'O semiotyce ikony', *Znak*, 28, no. 12, 1976, p. 1607.

33 P. Henry, 'What was the iconoclastic controversy about?', *Church History*, 45, no. 1, 1976, p. 31.

34 A. Ferenc,, 'Herezja Stefanitów w Etiopii w XV–XVI wieku', *Euhemer*, 1–2, 1969, pp. 71–2.

35 *Luthers Werke*, vol. 10, I, p. 55.

36 Quoted after K. Rebe, *Studien zur Geschichtsbibel Sebastian Francks*, Basle 1952, p. 65.

37 On the Neoplatonic conception of internal images, see W. Raith, *Die Macht des Bildes. Ein humanistisches Problem bei Gianfrancesco Pico della Mirandola*, Basle 1952, p. 65.

38 F. Yates, *The Art of Memory*, Chicago 1972, pp. 27, 277–9.

39 William Perkins, *Works*, Cambridge 1603, pp. 833, 716.

40 ibid., p. 830.

41 ibid., p. 841.

42 A. Ch. Gorfunkel, *Gumanism i naturfilosofia italianskavo Vosrozdenija*, Moscow 1977, pp. 311–12.

43 *Flugschriften der frühen Reformationsbewegung, 1518–1524*, ed. A. Laube, Berlin 1983, vol. 1, p. 280. See also *Zwinglis Werke*, vol. 2, p. 657.

44 Quoted after E. Koch, *Die Theologie der Confessio Helvetica Posterior*, Neukirchen 1968, p. 351.

45 W. Rordorf, 'Laktanz als Vorbild des jungen Bullinger', in *Bullinger-Tagung 1975*, ed. U. Gäbler and E. Zsindely, Zurich 1977, pp. 37–42.

46 M. Paton Ramsay, *Calvin and Art considered in Relation to Scotland*, Edinburgh 1938, pp. 68–70.

47 Martin Bucer, *Deutsche Schriften*, ed. R. Stupperich, Gütersloh–Paris 1960, vol. 1, p. 270.

48 W. Gewehr, 'Der Topos "Augen des Herzen". Versuch einer Deutung durch die scholastische Erkenntnistheorie', *Deutsche Vierteljahrsschrift für Literaturwissenschaft und Geistesgeschichte*, 46, 1972, pp. 626–49.

49 K. Kolbuszewski, *Postyllografia Polska XVI i XVII wieku*, Kraków 1921, p. 268.

50 P. Auksi, 'Wyclif's sermons and the plain style', *Archiv für Reformationsgeschichte*, 66, 1975, p. 11.

51 O. K. Olson, *The Missa Illyrica and the Liturgical Thought of Flacius Illyricus*, Hamburg 1967, p. 93.

52 See the *Letter of the Polovtsian Smera*, cited in Chapter 4 above.

53 The famous Polish Catholic preacher, Fabian Birkowski stated in 1629: 'their churches are like pig-sties or barns' – W. Tomkiewicz, *Pisarze Polskiego Odrodzenia o Sztuce*, Wrocław 1955, p. 251.

54 *Bogowie Falszywi. Nieznany traktat antykatolicki z XVI wieku*, ed. A. Kawecka-Gryczowa, Warsaw 1983, p. 226.
55 W. Wischmeyer, 'Die Entstehung der christlichen Archäologie', *Zeitschrift für Kirchengeschichte*, 89, no. 1, 1978, p. 138.
56 H. Davies, *Worship and Theology in England 1603–1690*, Cambridge 1975, p. 343.
57 O. Farner, *Huldrych Zwingli*, Zurich 1954, vol. 3, p. 488.
58 H. Berger, *Calvins Geschichtsauffassung*, Zurich 1955, pp. 48, 166–8 (on the chronological delimitations between corrupted and uncorrupted Church). For the radical Reformation, see F. Heyer, *Der Kirchenbegriff der Schwärmer*, Leipzig 1939, p. 22.
59 Quoted after an anonymous Polish treatise (1592) – M. Korolko, *Klejnot Swobodnego Sumienia*, Warsaw 1974, p. 241.
60 Kolbuszewski, *Postyllografia*, p. 219.
61 E. Rietschel, *Das Problem der unsichtbar-sichtbaren Kirche bei Luther*, Leipzig 1932.
62 See M. Loos, 'Einige strittige Fragen der ikonoklastischen Ideologie', in *Studien zum 8. und 9. Jahrhundert in Byzanz*, ed. F. Winkelmann, Berlin 1983, p. 149.
63 In his *Liber de Felici Liberalitate* (1532–4) – see *Paracelsus. Das Licht der Natur. Philosophische Schriften*, Leipzig 1973, pp. 115ff. Paracelsus was not iconophobic.
64 A. Blarer (1534) – see H. Oberman, *Werden und Wertung der Reformation*, Tübingen 1979, p. 328.
65 T. Carlyle, *On Heroes, Hero-Worship and the Heroic in History*, London 1898, p. 148.
66 L. Hätzer, *Ein Urteil Gottes* (1523) – see Laube, *Flugschriften*, vol. 1, p. 275.
67 Bucer, *Deutsche Schriften*, pp. 269–70.
68 S. Deyon, 'La Querelle des images' (see note 45, Chapter 3), p. 41.
69 A. Karlstadt, *Ob man gemach soll fahren* (1524) – see E. Hertzsch, *Karlstadts Schriften aus den Jahren 1523–25*, Halle 1956, vol. 1, p. 88.
70 J. Schmadin (1530) – see P. Schwarz and H. D. Schmid, *Reutlingen. Aus der Geschichte einer Stadt*, Reutlingen 1973, p. 108.
71 *Quellen zur Geschichte der Täufer*, ed. M. Krebs and H. G. Rott, vol. 7, *Elsaß*, Part I, Gütersloh 1959, no. 241, p. 316.
72 H. Rupprich, *Albrecht Dürer. Der schriftliche Nachlass*, Berlin 1956, vol. 1, p. 215.
73 F. Kalb, *Die Lehre vom Kultus der lutherischen Kirche zur Zeit der Orthodoxie*, Berlin 1959, pp. 80–1.
74 Sir William Mure, *True Crucifixe* (1629) – see Ramsay, *Calvin and Art*, p. 64.
75 S. Willard (1689, 1701) – J. W. McCoubrey, *American Art 1700–1960*, Englewood Cliffs, NJ 1965, pp. 3–4.
76 This was proposed in 1569, in his treatise on the question of images, by the bishop of Bergen (Norway), Jens Skielderup – see R. Bugge, 'Holdninger til Bilder i kirkene i Norge i Reformasjonärhundred', in *Fra Sankt Olav til Martin Luther*, Oslo 1975, pp. 195–206.

NOTES

77 P. Leyser, *Christianismus, Papismus und Calvinismus*, Dresden 1602, pp. 19, 21.
78 F. Kluge, *Etymologisches Wörterbuch*, Berlin 1975, p. 266; H. Winkler, *Der Wortbestand von Flugschriften aus den Jahren der Reformation und des Bauernkrieges*, Berlin 1975, p. 207.
79 See Kaliner, p. 81 (Bishop of Meissen, 1540).
80 M. van Beek, *An Inquiry into Puritan vocabulary*, Groningen 1969, pp. 41–2.
81 See also B. J. Verkamp, *The Indifferent Mean: Adiaphorism in the English Reformation to 1554*, Athens, Ohio 1977.
82 H. Voit, 'Nikolaus Gallus und das Interim. Eine anonyme Druckschrift aus dem Jahre 1548', *Archiv für Reformationsgeschichte*, 65, 1974, p. 279.
83 H. Greiffenberger (1523) in Laube, *Flugschriften*, p. 267.
84 G. Stuhlfauth, 'Künstlerstimmen und Künstlernot aus der Reformationsbewegung', *Zeitschrift für Kirchengeschichte*, 3, 1937, pp. 510–11; A. Rüstow, 'Lutherana tragoedia artis', *Schweizerische Monatshefte*, 39, 1959, pp. 891–906 (not wholly objective).
85 Th. Klein, *Der Kampf um die zweite Reformation in Kursachsen 1586–1591*, Cologne 1962, p. 174.
86 E. Peschke, *Die böhmischen Brüder im Urteil ihrer Zeit*, Berlin 1964, pp. 51–3.
87 G. Wiederanders, *Albrecht Dürers theologische Anschauungen*, Berlin 1975, p. 92.
88 D. J. Kuspit, 'Melanchthon und Dürer: the search for a simple style', *The Journal of Medieval and Renaissance Studies*, 3, 1973, pp. 177–202.
89 H. Emser, *Das man der heyligen Bilder yn den Kirchen nit abthon noch unehren soll*, Dresden 1522, folio Hiij.

Appendix

1 *Stephan Gerlach des Älteren Tagebuch*, Frankfurt 1674, p. 89.
2 G. Reginald, *Calvinoturcismus . . .*, Antwerp 1597, pp. 345–50.
3 Manuscript from 1587, quoted in J. Menzhausen, *Dresdner Kunstkammer und Grünes Gewölbe*, Dresden 1977, p. 24.
4 S. Geddicus, *Von Bildern und Altarn . . .*, Magdeburg 1597, sig. Tiii.
5 P. Rycaut, *The Present State of the Greek and Armenian Church*, London 1678, p. 330.
6 A. Pichler, *Geschichte der kirchlichen Trennung zwischen Orient und Okzident*, Munich 1884/5, p. 507.
7 Voltaire, *Dictionnaire philosophique*, ed. R. Naves and J. Benda, Paris 1967, p. 250, n. 204. Let us note here a modern continuation of this comparative practice in M. Hodgson's 'Islam and image', *History of Religion*, 3, 1964, pp. 220ff. Hodgson compares Calvinist and Muslim aniconism by introducing the category of 'factualism' – a less than felicitous choice.

Guide to further reading

The short bibliography presented here does not follow exactly the scheme of the chapters, additional subdivisions being established. Generally speaking, I have tried to chose more recent, and preferably English-language, studies (but there are obvious limits to such an attempt). Histories of the Reformation, great monographs or literature concerned with the Byzantine image controversy have been, with few exceptions, omitted. A very good list of literature up to 1984 is in the bibliographical guide of L. B. Parshall and P. W. Parshall, *Art and the Reformation: An Annotated Bibliography*, Boston, Mass., 1986.

THE QUESTION OF IMAGES BEFORE THE REFORMATION

Aston, M. *Lollards and Reformers: Images and Literacy in Late Medieval Religion*, London 1984.

Baynes, N. H. 'Idolatry and the early Church', in N. H. Baynes, *Byzantine Studies and other Essays*, London 1955, pp. 116–44.

Bernhardt, K. H. *Gott und Bild. Ein Beitrag zur Begründung und Deutung des Bilderverbotes im Alten Testament*, Berlin 1956.

Boespflug, F. and Lossky, N., eds *Nicée II. Douze siècles d'images religieuses*, Paris 1987.

Bredekamp, H. *Kunst als Medium sozialer Konflikte. Bilderkämpfe von der Antike bis zur Hussitenrevolution*, Frankfurt 1975 (subjective but stimulating).

Bryer, A. and Herrin, J. *Iconoclasm*, Birmingham 1977 (a fairly recent good collection of articles on the 'over-explained' Byzantine image controversy).

Cook, W. R. 'The question of images and the Hussite movement in Prague', *Cristianesimo nella Storia*, 3, 1982, pp. 329–42.

Dohmen, Ch. *Das Bilderverbot. Seine Entstehung und Entwicklung im Alten Testament*, Königstein 1985.

GUIDE TO FURTHER READING

Elliger, W. *Die Stellung der Alten Christen zu den Bildern in den ersten vier Jahrhunderten*, Leipzig 1930.

Fazzo, V. *La Giustificazione delle Immagini Religiose dalla Tarda Antichità al Cristianesimo*, vol. 1, *La Tarda Antichità*, Naples 1977 (pinpointing an important transition period).

Gutmann, J., ed. *The Image and the Word: Confrontations in Judaism, Christianity and Islam*, Missoula, Montana 1977 (good collection of articles).

Kollwitz, J. 'Bild und Bildertheologie im Mittelalter', in *Das Gottesbild im Abendland*, ed. W. Schöne, Witten-Berlin 1959, pp. 77–109.

Link, Ch. 'Das Bilderverbot als Kriterium theologischen Redens von Gott', *Zeitschrift für Theologie und Kirche*, 74, 1977. pp. 58–65.

Thümmel, H. G. *Bilderlehre und Bilderstreit. Arbeiten zur Auseinandersetzung zur Ikone und ihre Begründung vornehmlich im 8. und 9. Jahrhundert*, Würzburg 1991.

POPULAR PIETY AND RELIGIOUS ART BEFORE THE REFORMATION

Belting, H. *Bild und Kul. Eine Geschichte des Bildes vor dem Zeitalter der Kunst*, Munich 1990 (it will become a classic in its own right).

Camille, M. *The Gothic Idol: Ideology and Image-Making in Medieval Art*, Cambridge 1989.

Clemen, O. *Die Volksfrömmigkeit des ausgehenden Mittelalters* (Studien zur Religiösen Volkskunde, 3), Munich, 1937.

Scribner, R. W. 'Popular piety and modes of visual perception in late-medieval and Reformation Germany', *Journal of Religious History*, 15, no. 4, December 1989, pp. 448–69.

Wirth, J. 'Théorie et pratique de l'image sainte à la veille de la Réforme', *Bibliotheque d'humanisme et Renaissance*, 48, 1986, pp. 319–58.

GENERAL STUDIES: ART AND THE REFORMATION

Christensen, Carl C. *Art and the Reformation in Germany*, Athens, Ohio, 1979 (good but somewhat conventional).

—— 'Reformation and art', in *Reformation Europe: A Guide to Research*, ed. S. Ozment, St Louis, Miss. 1982, pp. 249–70.

Hofmann, W., ed. *Luther und die Folgen für die Kunst* (exhibition cat.), Hamburg 1983 (stimulating and brilliant).

Ullmann, E., ed. *Von der Macht der Bilder. Beiträge des C.I.H.A. – Kolloquiums 'Kunst und Reformation'*, Leipzig 1983 (very uneven collection of articles, also pertaining to the image question).

THE PROTESTANTS AND POPULAR PIETY

Clemen, O. *Luther und die Volksfrömmigkeit seiner Zeit*, Dresden–Leipzig 1938.

Davis, N. Z. 'From "popular religion" to religious culture', in *Reformation*

Europe: A Guide to Research, ed. S. Ozment, St Louis, Miss. 1982, pp. 321–42.

Jezler, P. 'Die Desakralisierung der Zürcher Stadtheiligen Felix, Regula und Exuperantius in der Reformation', in *Heiligenverehrung in Geschichte und Gegenwart*, Ostfildern 1990, pp. 296–319.

Scribner, R. W. *Popular Culture and Popular Movements in Reformation Germany*, London 1987.

Whiting, R. *The Blind Devotion of the People: Popular Religion and the English Reformation*, Cambridge 1989.

THE PROTESTANT IMAGE CONTROVERSY – GENERAL WORKS

Arvidsson, B. *Bildstrid-Bildbruk-Bildlära. En idéhistorisk undersökning av bildfragen inom den begynnande lutherska traditionen under 1500-talet*, Lund 1987.

Auksi, P. 'Simplicity and silence: the influence of Scripture on the aesthetic thought of the major reformers, *Journal of Religious History*, 10, 1979, pp. 343–61.

Bauer, W. 'Das Bilderverbot im Heidelberger Katechismus', *Beihefte zur Zeitschrift für alttestamentarische Wissenschaft*, 35, 1918, pp. 17–27.

Cieslak, K. 'Die "Zweite Reformation" in Danzig und die Kirchenkunst', *Zeitschrift für Historische Forschung*, Beiheft 12 'Historische Bildkunde' (ed. B. Tolkemitt, R. Wohlfeil), Berlin 1991, pp. 165–77.

Ehmer, H. 'Das Uracher Bildergespräch 1537, *Blätter für Württembergische Kirchengeschichte*, 90, 1990, pp. 65–91.

Eire, C. M. N. 'The Reformation critique of the image', in *Bilder und Bildersturm im Spätmittelalter und in der frühen Neuzeit*, ed. R. W. Scribner and M. Warnke, Wiesbaden 1990, pp. 51–69.

Ch. Göttler, 'Die Disziplinierung des Heiligenbildes durch altgläubige Theologen nach der Reformation, in *Bilder und Bildersturm im Spätmittelalter und in der frühen Neuzeit*, ed. R. W. Scribner and M. Warnke, Wiesbaden 1990, pp. 265–98.

Kibbey, Ann *The Interpretation of Material Shapes in Protestantism: A Study of Rhetoric, Prejudice and Violence*, Cambridge 1986.

Moxey, K. P. F. 'Image criticism in the Netherlands before the iconoclasm of 1566', *Nederlands Archief voor Kerksgeschiedenis*, 57, 1977, pp. 148–62.

—— *Pieter Aertsen Joachim Beuckelaer and the Rise of Secular Painting in the Context of the Reformation*, New York 1977.

Rohls, J. ' "... unser Knie beugen wir doch nicht mehr", Bilderverbot und bildende Kunst im Zeitalter der Reformation', *Zeitschrift für Theologie und Kirche*, 81, 1984, pp. 322–51.

Scavizzi, G. *Arte e Architettura Sacra. Croniche e documenti sulla controversia tra riformati e Cattolici (1500–1550)*, Reggio Calabria 1981.

—— 'La teologia cattolica et le immagini durante il XVI secolo', *Storia dell'Arte*, 21, 1974, pp. 171–213.

Stirm, M. *Die Bilderfrage in der Reformation*, Gütersloh 1977 (important work, but sees the Reformation more as a static process).

von Campenhausen, H. 'Die Bilderfrage in der Reformation', in H. von Campenhausen, *Tradition und Leben. Kräfte der Kirchengeschichte*, Tübingen 1960, pp. 361–407.

von Loewenich, W. 'Bilder, VI. Reformatorische und nachreformatorische Zeit', in *Theologische Realenzyklopädie*, vol. 6, Berlin 1980, pp. 557–68 (excellent summary).

Woodfield, R. 'On the emergence of aesthetics', *British Journal of Aesthetics*, 18, 1978, pp. 217–27.

LUTHER AND THE QUESTION OF IMAGES

Bergmann, R. 'A "tröstlich pictura": Luther's attitude in the question of images', *Renaissance and Reformation*, 5, 1981, pp. 15–25.

Christensen, C. C. 'Luther's theology and the uses of religious art', *The Lutheran Quarterly*, 22, 1970, pp. 147–65.

Kantzenbach, F. 'Bild und Wort bei Luther und in der Sprache der Frömmigkeit', *Neue Zeitschrift für Systematische Theologie und Religionsphilosophie*, 16, 1974, pp. 57–74.

Knolle, Th. *Luther und die Bilderstürmer in seinen und seiner Zeitgenossen Aussagen*, Wittenberg 1922.

Lehfeldt, P. *Luthers Verhältnis zu Kunst und Künstlern*, Berlin 1892.

Preuss, H. *Martin Luther, der Künstler*, Gütersloh 1931 (apologetic, but rich information).

Rogge, Ch. *Luther und die Kirchenbilder seiner Zeit*, Leipzig 1912.

Spelman, L. P. 'Luther and the arts', *Journal of Aesthetics*, 10, 1951, pp. 166–75.

Starke, E. 'Luthers Beziehungen zu Kunst und Künstlern', in *Leben und Werk Martin Luthers von 1526 bis 1546. Festgabe zu seinem 500. Geburtstag*, ed. H. Junghans Göttingen 1983, vol. 1, pp. 531–48; vol. 2, pp. 905–16.

KARLSTADT

Barge, H. *Andreas Bodenstein von Karlstadt*, vols 1–2, Leipzig 1905 (repr. Nieuwkoop 1968) (though of course dated and very partial, still a classic of Reformation historiography).

Bubenheimer, U. *Consonantia Theologiae et Iurisprudentiae. Andreas Bodenstein von Karlstadt als Theologe und Jurist*. Tübingen 1977.

—— 'Scandalum et ius divinum. Theologische und rechtstheologische Probleme der ersten reformatorischen Innovationen in Wittenberg 1521/22', *Zeitschrift der Savigny-Stiftung für Rechtsgeschichte. Kanonistisch-Germanistische Abteilung*, 59, 1973, pp. 263–342 (excellent analysis).

Pater, C. A. *Karlstadt as the Father of the Baptist Movements: the Emergence of Lay Protestantism*, Toronto 1984 (somewhat speculative).

Preus, J. S. *Carlstadt's 'Ordinaciones' and Luther's Liberty: A Study of the Wittenberg Movement 1521–22*, Cambridge, Mass. 1974.

Sider, R. J. *Andreas Bodenstein von Karlstadt: The Development of his Thought 1517–1525*, Leiden 1974 (good study).

THE REFORMATION AND THE VISUAL ARTS

—— *Karlstadt's Battle with Luther: Documents in a Liberal-Radical Debate*, Philadelphia 1978.

ZWINGLI

Altendorf, H. D. and Jezler, P., eds *Bilderstreit. Kulturwandel in Zwinglis Reformation*, Zurich 1984.

Biel, P. 'Personal conviction and personal care: Zwingli and the cult of saints 1522–1530', *Zwingliana*, 16, I, 1985, pp. 442–69.

Garside, Ch. *Zwingli and the Arts*, New Haven, Conn. 1966.

Lehmann, H. 'Zwingli und die zürcherische Kunst im Zeitalter der Reformation', in *Ulrich Zwingli. Zum Gedächtnis der Zürcher Reformation 1519–1919*. Zurich 1919, cols 213–58.

Senn, M. 'Die Zürcher Reformatoren zur Bilderfrage', in *Zürcher Kunst nach der Reformation. Hans Asper und seine Zeit*. (exhibition cat.) Zurich 1981, pp. 33–8.

Winkler, M. G. *Art, Patronage and Civic Life in a Reformed City: 16th century Zurich (Switzerland)*. Ann Arbor, Mich. 1983.

CALVIN

Grau, M. *Calvins Stellung zur Kunst*, diss. Munich 1917.

Pollmann, J. *Calvins Aesthetica*. 's-Hertogenbosch 1939.

Saxer, E. *Aberglaube, Heuchelei, Frömmigkeit. Eine Untersuchung zu Calvins reformatorischer Eigenart*, Zurich 1970.

Sommer, E. 'Of idols and images: Calvin and Luther on religious art', *Essays in History*, 29, 1985, pp. 67–82.

Spelman, L. P. 'Calvin and the arts', *Journal of Aesthetics and Art Criticism*, 1948, 3, pp. 246–53.

Wencelius, L. *L'Esthétique de Calvin*, Paris 1937 (very apologetic about Calvin).

PROTESTANT ICONOCLASM

Aston, M. *England's Iconoclasts*, vol. 1: *Laws against images*, Oxford 1988 (a work of great promise).

Christensen, C. C. 'Patterns of iconoclasm in the early Reformation: Strasbourg and Basel', in *The Image and the Word*, ed. by J. Gutmann, Missoula, Minn. 1977, pp. 149–64.

Christin, O. *Une révolution symbolique: L'iconoclasme huguenot et la reconstruction catholique*, Paris 1991.

Collinson, P. *From Iconoclasm to Iconophobia: The Cultural Impact of the Second English Reformation*, Reading 1986.

Crew, Ph. Mack *Calvinist Preaching and Iconoclasm in the Netherlands 1544–1569*, Cambridge 1978 (more for the socio-religious background than for the events themselves).

Davidson, C. and Nichols, A. and E. *Iconoclasm vs. Art and Drama*, Kalamazoo, Mich. 1989 (collection of articles on England).

Davis, N. Z. 'The rites of violence: religious riot in sixteenth-century

France', in N. Z. Davis, *Society and Culture in Early Modern France*, Stanford, Calif. 1975, pp. 152–88 (excellent analysis).

Deyon, S. and Lottin, A. *Les 'Casseurs' de l'été 1566: L'iconoclasme dans le nord de la France*, Paris 1981.

Eire, C. M. N. *War against the Idols: The Reformation of Worship from Erasmus to Calvin*, Cambridge 1986.

Feld, H. *Der Ikonoklasmus des Westens*, Leiden 1990.

Freedberg, D. *Iconoclasm and Painting in the Revolt of the Netherlands 1566–1609*, New York 1987.

—— 'The structure of Byzantine and European iconoclasm', in *Iconoclasm*, ed. A. Bryer and J. Herrin, Birmingham 1977, pp. 165–78 (short but very incisive analysis).

McRoberts, D. 'Material destruction caused by the Scottish Reformation', *Innes Review*, 10, 1959, pp. 126–72.

Ozment, S. *The Reformation in the Cities*, New Haven, Conn. 1975, pp. 42–6.

Phillips, J. *The Reformation of Images: Destruction of Art in England 1535–1660*, Berkeley, Calif. 1973.

Rasmussen, J. *'Bildersturm* and *Restauratio'*, in *Welt im Umbruch. Augsburg zwischen Renaissance und Barock*, vol. 3, Augsburg 1981, pp. 95–111 (very good local analysis).

Réau, L. *Les monuments détruits de l'art français: Histoire du vandalisme*, Paris 1959, vol. 1, pp. 65–106 (*Le vandalisme Huguenot*) (written by France's great conservative scholar with an utterly ahistoric anger).

Regnault, J. and Vermader, P. 'Las crise iconoclaste dans la region de Armentieres: Essai de description et de interpretation', *Revue du nord*, 59, 1977, pp. 222–31.

Scheerder, J. *De Beeldenstorm*, Bussum 1974.

Scribner, R. W. 'Reformation, carnival and the world turned upside-down', in *Städtische Gesellschaft und Reformation*, ed. I. Batori, Tübingen 1980, pp. 234–65.

Scribner, R. W. and Warnke, M., eds *Bilder und Bildersturm im Spätmittelalter und der frühen Neuzeit* (Wolfenbütteler Forschungen 46), Wiesbaden 1990 (the most recent collection of articles).

Warnke, M. 'Durchbrochene Geschichte? Die Bilderstürme der Wiedetäufer in Münster 1534–35', in M. Warnke, *Bildersturm. Die Zerstörung des Kunstwerks*, Munich 1973 (1977, 1989), pp. 65–98.

THEOLOGY OF THE ORTHODOX ICON

Evdokimov, P. *L'Art de l'icone: Théologie de la beauté*, Paris 1970.

Ouspenski, L. *Theology of the Icon*, Crestwood, NY 1978.

Thon, N. *Ikone und Liturgie*, Trier 1979.

Uspenski, B. *The Semiotics of the Russian Icon*, Lisse 1976.

THE PROTESTANTS AND THE EASTERN ORTHODOX CHURCHES

Benz, E. *Wittenberg und Byzanz*, Marburg 1949 (repr. 1971) (a pioneering, but not always objective book).

Calian, C. S. *Icon and Pulpit: The Protestant–Orthodox Encounter*, Philadelphia 1968 (a sympathetic small book).

Cooper, D. J. 'The Eastern Churches and the Reformation in the sixteenth and seventeenth centuries', *Scottish Journal of Theology*, 31, 1978, pp. 417–33.

—— 'The theology of images in Eastern Orthodoxy and John Calvin', *Scottish Journal of Theology*, 35, 1982, pp. 219–41.

Davey, C. 'The Orthodox and the Reformation 1450–1600', *Eastern Church Review*, 2, no. 1, 1968, pp. 8–16, no. 2, pp. 138–60.

Hering, G. 'Orthodoxie und Protestantismus', *Jahrbuch der Österreichischen Byzantinistik*, 31/2, 1981, pp. 823–74 (a very good review with documentary references).

Kahle, W. *Die Begegnung des baltischen Protestantismus mit der russischorthodoxen Kirche*, Leiden 1959.

Müller, L. *Die Kritik des Protestantismus in der russischen Theologie vom 16. bis zum 18. Jh.*, Wiesbaden 1951 (though in many aspects superseded, still a classic work on the subject).

Podskalsky, G. 'Die Kritik der lutherischen Theologie in der griechischen Orthodoxie vom 16. Jh. bis in unsere Zeit', *Catholica*, 22, 1968, pp. 193–206 (a more modest undertaking, complementing the book of Müller).

—— *Griechische Theologie in der Zeit der Türkenherrschaft (1453–1821). Die Orthodoxie im Spannungsfeld der nachreformatorischen Konfessionen des Westens*, Munich 1988 (a very important synthesis, showing new possibilities of research, also as regards the image question).

Runciman, S. *The Great Church in Captivity*, Cambridge 1968 (popular but stimulating).

THE CONCEPT OF IMAGE

Auerbach, E. 'Figura', *Archivium Romanicum*, 22, 1939, pp. 436–89.

Bauch, K. 'Imago', in *Beiträge zur Philosophie und Wissenschaft. Wilhelm Szilasi zum 70. Geburtstag*, Munich 1960, pp. 9–28.

Eltester, F. W. *Eikon im Neuen Testament*, Berlin 1958.

Gerö, S. 'The Eucharistic doctrine of the Byzantine iconoclasts and its sources', *Byzantinische Zeitschrift*, 68, 1975, pp. 4–22.

Ladner, G. 'The concept of image in the Greek Fathers and the Byzantine iconoclastic controversy', *Dumbarton Oaks Papers*, 7, 1953, pp. 3–34.

Michalski, S. 'Bild, Spiegelbild, Figura, Repraesentatio. Ikonitätsbegriffe im Spannungsfeld zwischen Bilderfrage und Abendmahlskontroverse' *Annuarium Historiae Conciliorum*, 20, 1/2, 1988, pp. 458–88.

Volp, R. 'Das Bild als Grundkategorie der Theologie', in *Theologische Realenzyklopädie*, 6, 1980, pp. 557–68.

Warncke, C. P. *Sprechende Bilder – sichtbare Worte. Das Bildverständnis der frühen Neuzeit*, Wiesbaden 1987.

PROTESTANT ICONOGRAPHY

Andersson, C. 'Religiöse Bilder Cranachs im Dienste der Reformation', in *Humanismus und Reformation als kulturelle Kräfte in der deutschen Geschichte*, ed. L. W. Spitz, Berlin–New York 1981, pp. 43–79.

Christie, S. *Den lutherske Ikonografi i Norge inntill 1800*, vols 1–2, Oslo, 1973 (extensive English summary).

Harasimowicz, J. ' "Scriptura sui ipsius interpres". Protestantische Bild-Wort Sprache des 16. und 17. Jh.', in *Wort und Bild, Bild und Text*, ed. W. Harms, Stuttgart 1990, pp. 262–81.

—— Lutherische Bildepitaphien als Ausdruck des 'Allgemeinen Priestertums der Gläubigen' am Beispiel Schlesiens', *Zeitschrift für Historische Forschung, Beiheft* 12: 'Historische Bildkunde', ed. B. Tolkemitt, R. Wohlfeil, Berlin 1991, pp. 135–64.

Harbison, C. H. *The Last Judgement in Sixteenth Century Northern Europe: A Study of the Relation between Art and Reformation*, New York 1975.

Hoffmann, K. 'Die reformatorische Bewegung im Bilderkampf', in *Martin Luther und die Reformation in Deutschland* (exhibition cat., Germanisches Nationalmuseum Nürnberg), Nuremberg 1983, pp. 219–54.

Koepplin, D. 'Reformation der Glaubensbilder. Das Erlösungswerk Christi auf Bildern des Spätmittelalters und der Reformationszeit', in *Martin Luther und die Reformation in Deutschland*, (exhibition cat., Germanisches Nationalmuseum Nürnberg), Nuremberg 1983, pp. 333–78.

Krücke, A. 'Der Protestantismus und die bildliche Darstellung Gottes', *Zeitschrift für Kunstwissenschaft*, 13, 1959, pp. 59–90.

Mai, H. 'Der Einfluss der Reformation auf Kirchenbau und kirchliche Kunst', in *Das Jahrhundert der Reformation in Sachsen*, ed. H. Junghans, Berlin 1989, pp. 153–77.

Ohly, F. *Gesetz und Evangelium. Zur Typologie bei Luther und Lucas Cranach. Zum Blutstrahl der Gnade in der Kunst*, Münster 1985.

Scharfe, M. *Evangelische Andachtsbilder. Studien zur Intention und Funktion der Bilder vornehmlich des schwäbischen Raumes*, Stuttgart 1968.

Scribner, R. W. *For the Sake of Simple Folk: Popular Propaganda for the German Reformation*, Cambridge 1981.

von Haebler, H. C. *Das Bild in der evangelischen Kirche*, Berlin 1957.

Warnke, M. *Cranachs Luther. Entwürfe für ein Image*, Frankfurt 1984.

Wirth, J. 'Le dogme en image: Luther et l'iconographie', *Revue de l'art*, 52, 1981, pp. 9–24.

Wohlfeil, R. 'Lutherische Bildtheologie', in *Martin Luther: Probleme seiner Zeit*, ed. V. Press and D. Stievermann, Stuttgart 1986, pp. 282–93.

Index

INDEX

Kopistenski, Zachary 148, 155
Kosoi, Feodosii 130–1, 134, 168
Kurbskii, Andrei 135, 138

Lactantius 55, 183–4
Łasicki, Jan 108, 137, 152
Łaski, Jan 106
Last Supper, iconography of 33, 41
latreia (latria) 66, 116, 120, 155
Laventie 77
Law and Grace 34
Leipzig debate 104
Lenhoff Gail 161
Lenin, Vladimir 167
Le Roy Ladurie, E. 95
Lewicki, O. 144
Libri Carolini 66–7, 120
Linck, Wenzeslaus 11
Lippstadt 94
Livonia 86–7, 102, 132–3
London 86
Lord of Suffering, theme 33–4, 94
Lovejoy, Arthur 185
Lower Saxony 92
Lübeck 31
Lublin province 95
Lucaris, Cyril 121–4, 169
Lucerne 52, 90
Lüneburg 35
Luther, Martin 1–44, 46, 57–8,
  60–1, 74, 90, 97, 104–5, 131,
  133, 136, 139, 141, 150, 169, 173,
  176–8, 180–1, 188, 190–1, 193;
  Lenten Sermons 13–21; Against
  the Heavenly Prophets 25–9
Lutheranism 1, 4, 22, 28, 33–6, 48,
  69, 83–5, 89, 102, 105, 109–11,
  117–18, 120, 123, 131–2, 134,
  135–6, 152, 154, 157–9, 162–3,
  177, 179, 184, 189, 191, 195–6
Lüti, Heinrich 53
Lvov 143
Lyon 74

Malevich, Kazimir 168
Mallerbach 23, 88
Malmö 132
Mander, Carel van 89
Manuel Deutsch, Niklaus 80

Marburg 30, 85
Marcian 126
Marian images 26, 34–6, 77, 89,
  92–3, 95–6, 110, 112, 143,
  161–2, 164
Martelet, Gustave 171
Maximilian I 131
Melanchthon, Philipp 10, 34, 105,
  108, 111, 169, 176, 193
Moeller, Bernd 97
Mohyla, Peter 121
Moldavia 102, 106, 152
Monophysitism 170, 180
Moscow 127–9, 133, 136, 139, 153,
  158–9
Mount Athos 111
Münster 29, 77, 84
Müntzer, Thomas 22–4, 29, 77, 83,
  130
Mure, Sir William 184, 189
music 39–40
Muslims 119–20; muslin aniconism
  103, 195–6
Myconius, Oswald 87

Narva 115
Nasedka, Ivan 154, 162
Nebra 90
Neeffs, Pieter 154
neoplatonism 49, 172, 180
Neronov, Ivan 115
Nestorianism 56, 170, 180
Netherlands 72, 77, 80–1, 84, 86,
  89, 154, 155, 167
Neuser, Adam 195
Neuser, Wilhelm 176
Niceanum II, resolutions of 65–7,
  118, 120, 123, 162
Nicene Creed 101
Nicholas St, images of 114, 130,
  158, 161
Nieświez 143
Night of St Bartholomew 93
Nikon 153, 156
Nil Sorskii 129, 133–4, 148
Nilovites (Non-Possessors) 129,
  135, 160
nominalism 4, 180
Nonjurors 115, 119–21

229